American-Arab Relations from Wilson to Nixon

by Faiz S. Abu-Jaber
State University of New York
Oswego, New York

University Press
of America™

Library of Congress Catalog Card Number: 78-65853

Dedication:

To Tarik Ibn Ziad

For I must speak what wisdom would conceal,
And truths, invidious to the great reveal.
Bold is the task, when subjects, grown too wise,
Instruct a monarch where his error lies.

Homer, <u>Iliad</u> (tr. Pope)

Contents

Introduction

"That which is unjust" wrote Henry
George, "can profit no one; that
which is just can really harm no one."[1]

The loss of Palestine to world Zionism is at the center of Arab
grievances against the Western nations generally and the United
States in particular. It violated the principles of Arab nationalism, unity and territorial integrity. By its very actions favoring
and backing the Zionist penetration of Palestine and the eastern
Meditteranean area, the United States became the major perpetrator
of Arab losses and grievances. Naturally American-Arab relations
suffered accordingly. For by the middle 1960s Israel was viewed
by most Arabs as the beachhead of American imperialism in the
Middle East and the West's cat's paw against Arab nationalism.
America's policies after the Israeli occupation of all Palestine
after June 1967 as well as good parts of Egypt and Syria proper,
confirmed to many Arabs either total American commitment to expan-
sionist Zionism or a total Zionist domination of American foreign
policy in the Middle East. Either way, the Arabs began to view the
United States as a confrontation state just as much as Israel.

The 1973 war led many Arabs to hope that the usual one-sided
American policies always favouring Israel would be abandoned. Yet
by the end of the Nixon and Kissinger era, there was only verbal
commitment to American impartiality in the Middle East dispute.
Yet Israel was again armed to the teeth by the United States after
1973, while the Arabs were getting more promises of peace with
relative justice in Palestine. Israel's intransigence, naturally
while heavily armed by the United States, might yet force the Arabs
to rely again on the Soviet Union for military aid and comfort. It
might yet force the Arabs again to use their oil weapon against the
United States again to extract a measure of simple justice in the
focal question of Palestine. In a sorry state of another confrontation, naturally the major loser would be the United States just as
it was the loser after the Arab oil embargo of 1973. The hope,
though, is for peace with justice.

---

[1] The Land Question

Chapter I

American-Arab Relations, 1917-1948

American diplomatic involvement in the affairs of the Arab world began indirectly through American involvement and sympathy to the Zionist cause in Palestine. It began with the Balfour Declaration of 1917 which promised a national home for the Jews in Palestine. Between the two world wars and after, the United States was further committed to the Zionist point of view on Palestine. This commitment was to prove a major stumbling block in the way of creating a profitable American-Arab relationship in general, and American-Egyptian relationship in particular.

Egypt had emerged after the Second World War from its isolationism vis-a-vis the rest of the Arab states surrounding it, aspiring for the leadership of Arab nationalism. The United States had emerged from the Second World War as one of the two leading world powers. It, too, was forced from its isolationism due to the powerful Soviet military and political challenge after the war. And while the Arabs, led by Egypt, tended to be pre-occupied with their regional problems--such as erasing the last vestiges of colonialism, and coping with the Zionist challenge in Palestine--the United States was more prone to see the Middle East in terms of possible communist aggression. The Arab expectations of ridding themselves of British and French presence were played down by America, in the Arab view, in favor of the common Western front against the challenge of the Soviet Union.

This was manifested to the Arabs in American insistence after the Second World War on the creation of military pacts in the area to forestall any possible Soviet attack. The Arabs naturally resented what they felt was American relegation of their regional problems in favor of Western defense schemes. The American assumption was that the Arabs should have been as concerned as the Western World with the Soviet threat to the Middle East and its significance to the West in strategy and oil. The Arabs, led by Egypt, proved to be more concerned with their regional problems. Thus a new obstacle to profitable American-Arab dialogue was created. This dialogue became more futile due to the American persistence, in the Arab view, in seeing one side of the question in the grave problem of Palestine. In the vacuum of confidence that was created between the United States leading the Western World, and Egypt leading the Arab world, the Soviet Union was bound to operate and eventually succeed in temporarily neutralizing the area.

1

The following discussion is therefore concerned with exploring American-Arab relations before and during the inter-war period. This background sheds light on the later difficult American relations with the Arabs after the Second World War.

American active diplomatic involvement in the affairs of the Arab world in general dates back less than thirty years. This late involvement is due to the fact that before the Second World War the United States generally followed a policy of isolation outside the Western hemisphere. Moreover, much of the Arab world was controlled by the imperial powers, and any American-Arab contact was made through their capitals. All official business concerning this region, whether it was of a political, cultural, or economic nature, was transacted either in Constantinople until 1918, or in London and Paris until the end of the Second World War, or even later.(1) Nevertheless, American cultural and educational contacts before and after the American Civil War and their impact on the Arab national movement are of considerable significance. According to George Antonius they rank in importance with the impact of the French educational efforts in Egypt in the wake of Napoleon's conquest of Egypt in 1797.(2) American missionaries, also, before and after the American Civil War, were rapidly opening schools in various parts of Syria and Egypt.(3)

Except for these cultural contacts between the American missionary groups and the Arabs, American political interests in the Arab world were extremely nebulous up to and until the end of the First World War. This was altered after the war due mainly to President Wilson's sympathy for the Zionist cause in Palestine.

With its involvement in the First World War the United States was also to become entangled in Arab and Jewish nationalisms, and the conflicting promises to both Arabs and Jews by her major allies—Britain and France. There were also promises by Britain and France to each other on how to divide the spoils of victory in the Ottoman empire after its anticipated defeat. Hence came the British promises to Sherif Hussain of Mecca, inciting the

---

[1]Georgiana G. Stevens, ed., The United States and the Middle East (Englewood Cliffs, N.Y.: Prentice Hall, Inc., 1964,)p. 1.
[2]The Arab Awakening (London: Hamish Hamilton, 1961), pp. 42-43.
[3]Ibid; Other Arab historians like Antonius agree on the magnitude of the early American educational influence on the revival of Arab language and nationalism. See Philip K. Hitti, History of the Arabs (New York: The Macmillan Co., 1951), pp. 745-747.

Arabs to rebellion against Turkey, and implying complete independence for all Syria and Arabia under the leadership of Hussain. These promises were incorporated in what is known as the Hussain-McMahon Correspondence during late 1915 and early 1916, bringing about the Arab revolt on June 5, 1916.

Between April and May of 1916, America's later allies secretly agreed to divide the Ottoman empire between themselves after the war. This was done through the Sykes-Picot Agreement and the Anglo-Franco-Russian Agreement of April-May, 1916. Russia, according to the note of April 26, 1916, was allotted rights in the Turkish Straits' areas plus five provinces on the Russian-Turkish border. France was granted the coastal area of Syria and its hinterland up to roughly the present boundaries of Iraq, while Britain was promised what later became known as Palestine, Jordan and Iraq.

Then on November 2, 1917, came the well-known Balfour Declaration, promising the world Zionists a national homeland for the Jews in Palestine. This, incidentally, was the first occasion on which the United States--already involved in the war since April 6, 1917--became involved in the political affairs of the Arabs. The above-mentioned declaration was approved by President Woodrow Wilson before it was issued.

According to William Yale,(4) President Wilson's agreement to the declaration came during Lord Balfour's visit of one month to the United States starting April 22, 1917. Lord Balfour at that time met Justice Louis Brandeis who was then a leading figure in the American Zionist movement and a trusted advisor to President Wilson. Brandeis had already won the sympathy of President Wilson to the Zionist cause, and assured Lord Balfour that the President was actively sympathetic to a Jewish home in Palestine.(5) Therefore, when the Balfour Declaration was issued in the form of a note from Lord Balfour to Lord Rothschild--a leading English Zionist--on November 2, 1917, it had the approval of the British cabinet as well as the approval of the President of the United

---

[4]The Near East (Ann Arbor: The University of Michigan Press, 1958), p. 269. Captain Yale was a member of the American King-Crane Commission sent by President Wilson in 1919 to investigate the wishes of the Syrian people as to the final political settlement in Syria.
[5]Ibid.

3

States. Yet Mr. Wilson insisted upon adding the modifying clauses to the declaration before he accepted it.(6) The President later publicly acknowledged the Balfour Declaration on October 29, 1918 in a letter addressed to Rabbi Stephen S. Wise.(7)

In 1918, Mr. Wilson showed his interest in the future of the Arabs in the form of the famous Fourteen Points. Point Twelve indirectly refers to the Arabs, as well as to other minorities in the Ottoman empire. It states:

> The Turkish portions of the
> present Ottoman empire should be
> assured a secure sovereignty, but
> other nationalities which are now
> under Turkish rule should be assured
> an undoubted security of life and an
> absolutely unmolested opportunity of
> autonomous development.(8)

President Wilson's idealism, as illustrated in this point, and his self-determination policy expounded in Point Five, seem to be consistent with his acceptance of the Balfour Declaration as modified. To Arab leaders like Prince Faisal, the son of Sherif Hussain and the Chief spokesman for the Arab cause in the Versailles Peace Conference, Wilson's twelfth point was interpreted later in the Versailles Peace Conference to foreshadow and nullify the Balfour Declaration and all the Allied secret agreements during the war. For a policy of self-determination would at once block the Zionist aims in Palestine, as well as the imperial powers' ambitions in the area. The Jews in Palestine then constituted at best not more

---

6 Sydney N. Fisher, The Middle East (New York: Alfred A. Knopf, 1960), p. 371. The text of the declaration is as follows:
His Majesty's Government views with favor the establishment in Palestine of a national home for the Jewish people and will use their best endeavors to facilitate the achievement of this object it being clearly understood that nothing shall be done which may prejudice the civil and religious rights of existing non-Jewish communities in Palestine or the rights and political status enjoyed by Jews in any other country.
7 George Lenczowski, The Middle East in World Affairs (Ithaca, N.Y.: Cornell University Press, 1958), p. 81. See also Nadav Safran, The United States and Israel (Cambridge: Harvard University Press, 1963), pp. 36-37.
8 Ray A. Billington, Bert J. Loewenberg, Samuel H. Brockunier, ed., The Making of American Democracy, Readings and Documents (New York: Rinehart & Company, 1950), p. 410.

than 10 per cent of the population and a policy of counting heads
would favor Palestine's inclusion in an Arab state as pledged to
Sherif Hussain of Mecca by the High Commissioner of Egypt, Henry
McMahon, in 1916. Therefore, neither the Zionists nor the representative of Great Britain or France were later happy with the expressions of Wilson's idealism. And, "Had it been pushed to its
logical conclusion," according to Lenczowski, "the President's
program would have conflicted with practically every one of the
secret agreements, with the exception, perhaps, of the British-
Arab accord."(9) Nor did Wilson's comments during the discussions
at the Versailles Peace Conference, in which he warned against the
parcelling of the Middle East among the great powers, gain a favorable reception among the allies.(10)

At the Versailles Peace Conference, Prince Faisal met with
three major forces at work in opposition to Arab aspirations: The
British, the French, and the world Zionists. Only in President
Wilson did he find a sympathetic listener. On January 29, 1919,
Prince Faisal proposed that an impartial commission of inquiry be
appointed by the Conference to visit Syria and Palestine, and as-
certain the wishes of the population through an investigation on
the spot. President Wilson was the only leader of the three great
powers at Versailles that responded favorably to this proposal.(11)
In fact, Wilson insisted on such a commission, and despite intense
Zionist objections voiced by Professor Felix Frankfurter, and
British and French refusal to participate in such a commission,
President Wilson appointed a purely American commission.(12) This
commission was led by Dr. Henry C. King, President of Oberlin College, and Charles Crane, a prominent American businessman. Between
May and July, 1919, the King-Crane Commission made a six weeks
tour of Syria and Palestine, held hearings, and on August 28, 1919,
presented their report to the President.(13)

The King-Crane report testified to the high regard the Arabs
of Syria and Palestine had for President Wilson and the United
States. According to the report, the Commission found the inhabi-
tants of Syria and Palestine insistent on an independent and united

---

9
Lenczowski, p. 88.
10Foreign Relations: The Paris Peace Conference, 1919, Vol. III
(Washington: U.S. Government Printing Office, 1943), pp. 213-214.
11Antonius, p. 287.
12Lenczowski.
13Full text of the recommendations of the King-Crane Commission is
found in Antonius, Appendix H., pp. 443-458. Other members of the
Commission were Professor Albert H. Lybyer, Dr. George R. Mont-
gomery, Captain William Yale and Captain Donald M. Brodie. Antonius,
p. 295.

Arab state, and recommended that Prince Faisal be made head of such a united Syrian state. Failing to achieve complete independence, the great majority of the Syrians were found to favor the United States coming in as a mandatory power rather than any other power.

The recommendation of the Commission's report were not followed, and in fact were not even discussed by the Paris Peace Conference. "It was simply buried in the archives of the American delegation, and ignored by the conferees. It was not published until 1922, long after the peace settlement."(14) This neglect of the Commission's report is attributed to President Wilson's departure in the midsummer of 1919 from Versailles, later to fight strong domestic opposition to the League of Nations as well as the whole proposed Treaty of Versailles. President Wilson's failure to convince the American Senate of the soundness of the Versailles Treaty as is well known, affected the whole general question of America's involvement in world affairs between the two World Wars. And in Wilson's absence from Versailles, the Commission's report was simply not pressed by the rest of the American delegation and was ignored by the major powers, who proceeded later in the San Remo Conference of April 24, 1920 to divide greater Syria into French and British mandates. As these mandates were allocated, the United States on August 24, 1921, made clear in an "Open Door Policy" statement that she expected her interests and the "fair and equal opportunities which it is believed the United States should enjoy in common with the other powers" to be safe-guarded!(15)

Egypt had been occupied by Britain since 1882. On December 18, 1914, Britain declared Egypt a protectorate. This British act was vehemently opposed by the Egyptian nationalists who, under the leadership of Sa'ad Zughlul after the First World War, insisted on the right to send a delegation to the Paris Peace Conference to state Egypt's case for independence. America's reaction to the violent Egyptian nationalist demands was contained in a cautious communique from the American Consul in Cairo to the British High Commissioner in Egypt on April 22, 1919:

> In this connection, I am desired
> to say that the President and the American
> people have every sympathy with the legiti-
> mate aspirations of the Egyptian people for

14
  Lenczowski.
15Mandate for Palestine (Washington: U.S. Government Printing
  Office, 1927), pp. 49-50.

a measure of self government, but
that they view with regret any effort
to obtain the realization thereof by
a resort to violence.(16)

Other than such general statements of sympathy—in effect to
both sides, Great Britain and Egypt—the United States was rightly
careful between the two World Wars not to involve herself in what
were then considered the internal affairs of Great Britian.
America's general policy of isolationism between the two World Wars
also curtailed any meaningful political contacts with the people
of that whole general area.

Only in the Arabian peninsula did there emerge after the First
World War two completely independent Arab states, those of Hijaz
and Yemen. Hijaz and northern Arabia, from October 1918 until
January 1926, became the scene of a struggle for power between the
Hashemite family, under the leadership of Sherif Hussain of Mecca,
and the Saudi family under the leadership of Abdel Aziz Ibn Saud.
The struggle was decided in favor of Ibn Saud, who on January 8,
1926, proclaimed himself king of what today constitutes Saudi Arabia.
In its mood of isolationism, the United States did not extend
Ibn Saud recognition until May 1931, and diplomatic relations were
not established until February 5, 1940.(17) By that time, most of
the major European powers had already extended recognition to the
new Saudi regime. The tune was set by the Soviet Union, who hoped
to use independent Saudi Arabia and Yemen as a base for Soviet
anti-imperalist propaganda in the Arab world.(18)

On May 29, 1933, the first concession in Saudi Arabia was
given to the Standard Oil Company of California, (known as ARAMCO
since 1944) thus beginning a new era of heavy American economic
investment in the Arab world. This, of course, was bound to generate more American political and military interest in the affairs
of the Arab East. Oil was first discovered in the vicinity of
Dhahran in March 1938, and by 1971 Saudi Arabia had become the largest producer of oil in the Middle East.

16
Foreign Relations of the United States, 1919, Vol. 2 (Washington:
17 U.S. Government Printing Office, 1934), p. 204.
Foreign Relations of the United States, Vol. IV (Washington: U.S.
18 Government Printing Office, 1955), p. 831.
See H. St. John Philby, Saudi Arabia (New York: Frederick A.
Praeger, 1955), p. 299.

During the Second World War, Saudi Arabia remained officially neutral until March 1, 1945, when it declared war on Germany. Yet there was no mistaking King Saud's sympathy with the Allied cause. For in 1942, he sent one of his sons, Mansoor, to address the British Indian troops in Egypt on the eve of the decisive battle of El-Alamain. Moreover, in 1943, the United States secretly secured a three-year lease from King Saud to build an air base at Dhahran. The construction began in 1944 and the base was completed in 1946. "The acquisition of this base," according to Lenczowski, "emphasizes the long way the United States has covered from its initially isolationist position, and the extend of the cordial relations already developed between the United States and Saudi Arabia."(19)

The situation in Palestine throughout the period between the two World Wars was very much on the minds of Arab leaders inside and outside Palestine. By 1939, many Arab notables and organizations, sensing that the official American attitude was more favorable to the Zionist point of view than to theirs, had already sent protests to the American government in this regard.(20) Among these was a letter from King Ibn Saud to President Roosevelt dated November 29, 1938.(21) This, incidentally, is the first letter concerning Palestine from an Arab chief of state to the United States government.(22) The United States had already issued a policy statement for Palestine on October 14, 1938,(23) and Mr. Roosevelt, answering King Ibn Saud in a letter on February 15, 1939, referred the letter to that policy statement.(24) American policy toward Palestine will be discussed later in more detail, but suffice it to mention here that United States-Saudi relations became so cordial by the end of the Second World War, due to oil and air-base concessions, that it was deemed appropriate to arrange for a meeting between President Roosevelt and King Ibn Saud.(25) Therefore, while on his way back from the Yalta Confer-

---

19 Lenczowski, p. 442.
20 For correspondence regarding this American attitude, see Foreign Relations of the United States, 1938, Vol. 2 (Washington: U.S. Government Printing Office, 1954), pp. 888-889.
21 For the full text of this letter see ibid., pp. 994-998.
22 Foreign Relations..., 1939, Vol. IV (Washington: U.S. Government Printing Office, 1955), p. 695.
23 Foreign Relations..., 1938, p. 889.
24 Foreign Relations..., 1939, p. 696.
25 This was due largely also to the efforts of two well-trained, Arabic speaking American Foreign Service officers, James S. Moose and Colonel William A. Eddy. Richard H. Sanger, The Arabian Peninsula (Ithaca, N.Y.: Cornell University Press, 1954), pp. 4-5.

ence in February, 1945, President Roosevelt met King Ibn Saud. This meeting, which took place on board the United States destroyer "Quincy" at Great Bitter Lake in the Suez Canal, marked the high point in American-Arab friendship, according to Richard Sanger.(26)

South of Saudi Arabia lies the Kingdom (Imamate) of Yemen, (a republic since 1962), which, like Hijaz to the north of it, became independent after the First World War. Here too, the United States accumulated a measure of goodwill between the two World Wars, thanks to the efforts of two Americans, Mr. Charles R. Crane (later a member of the King-Crane Commission to Palestine in 1919) and Mr. Karl S. Twitchell. Mr. Crane had lived much of his youth in Egypt, where he had developed an interest in Arab affairs. During 1926-1927, he went to Yemen and there developed a friendship with Imam Yahya of Yemen. The Imam a few years earlier had opened the doors of Yemen to the American mining engineer and oil prospector R.A. McGovern, who by 1926 had already abandoned his explorations. Mr. Crane, after meeting Imam Yahya offered to send at his own expense a mining engineer to Yemen to examine and report on the mineral resources of the country. The offer was accepted, and Mr. Crane hired the engineer Karl S. Twitchell to help develop Yemen's resources. "Thus did Twitchell, the father of economic development in the peninsula, enter the Arabian scene."(27) Yet diplomatic relations between Yemen and the United States were not established until May, 1946.(28)

THE UNITED STATES AND THE PALESTINE QUESTION, 1917-1947

Nowhere else in the Middle East after the First World War was the United States, and in particular American Jews, more concerned than in Palestine. It was partially due to the efforts of Justice Louis Brandeis as mentioned above, and to his influence on President Wilson, that the latter recognized, accepted, and encouraged the

---

26 Ibid.
27 Sanger, op. cit., pp. 243-244. At the request of King Ibn Saud, Twitchell in 1942 headed an American agricultural mission to Saudi Arabia to advise on irrigation and related problems. See Lenczowski, p. 442.
28 Lenczowski, p. 459.

issuance of the Balfour Declaration in 1917. After 1917, American policy statements and involvement in the political question of Palestine—which helped bring about the establishment of the state of Israel—played no small part in shaping Arab-American relations. Therefore to understand fully the events of the 1950's and the obstacles that met American diplomacy in the Arab World during this period, it is imperative that we understand the undercurrents of Arab resentment of America's Palestine policy. This policy explains in part the motivations behind Arab neutralism and non-alignment after the Second World War, which in turn helped facilitate the entry of Soviet influence into the area.

As mentioned earlier, the first sally of American political involvement in the Middle East came with the Balfour Declaration of 1917. The policy announced in the Balfour Declaration was in part implemented with the establishment of the mandate system under the terms of the San Remo Agreement of April 24, 1920. For a rider was added to the San Remo Agreement to the effect that the mandate for Palestine would carry with it an obligation to apply the Balfour Declaration.(29) In correlation with this, and to serve as an American reminder to Britain to fulfill this obligation, a Congressional resolution on Palestine was passed unanimously on June 30, 1922. This declared "that the United States of America favors the establishment in Palestine of a national home for the Jewish people."(30) The resolution goes on to repeat almost entirely the wording of the Balfour Declaration: "it being clearly understood that nothing shall be done which may prejudice the civil and religious rights of Christian and all other non-Jewish communities in Palestine. . . ."(31)

It is either indicative of the ignorance or the bias or both of the British government's attitude as well as this Congressional resolution, that in none of these statements—Balfour Declaration, the text of the Mandate, or the above-mentioned Congressional resolution—was the word "Arab" used. The Arabs who formed over 90 per cent of the population of Palestine at that time were referred to as the "all other non-Jewish communities in Palestine."

---

[29] See text of the "Mandate for Palestine," in J.C. Hurewitz, Diplomacy in the Middle East, A Documentary Record: 1914-1956, Vol. 2 (Princeton, N.J.: D. Van Nostrand Company, 1956), pp. 106-111.

[30] William A. Williams, ed., America and the Middle East (New York: Rinehart and Company, 1958), p. 41.

[31] Ibid.

Jewish immigration to Palestine proceeded under the British mandate throughout the 1920's and 1930's, and by the time the Palestine Partition resolution was adopted by the United Nations on November 29, 1947, the Jewish population in Palestine had risen, mainly through immigration--legal and otherwise--from about 56,000 in 1918 to over 540,000 in 1947.(32)   Arab opposition to this immigration was manifested by major uprisings in 1922, 1926, and 1933; and in a major rebellion in 1936 that lasted until 1939. These Arab uprisings were usually followed by the issuance of a British policy statement in which the British government reaffirmed the promise made to the Zionists in the Balfour Declaration. Of these, the Churchill Memorandum of July 1, 1922(33) established the major lines of British policy in Palestine until the issuance of the Palestine White Paper of May 17, 1939. In this memorandum, Mr. Churchill cautioned the Zionists not to hope for the acquisition of all of Palestine. This was supposed to allay the fears of the Arabs of Palestine and mollify their opposition to Zionism. Yet the memorandum went on to reaffirm the promise of Balfour, and to state that Jewish immigration to Palestine would be "as of right and not on sufferance." It further stated that Jewish immigration should be encouraged, and that the Jewish National Home should be internationally guaranteed. These, of course, were the points which the Arabs of Palestine particularly opposed. The United States Congressional resolution, mentioned above, was issued one day before the Churchill Memorandum,(34) and emphasized the same points.

American sympathy toward the establishment of a Jewish homeland in Palestine was further manifested by a joint resolution of Congress signed by the President on September 21, 1922.(35) It recorded the favorable attitude of the United States toward such a homeland. "It is in the light of this interest that the American Government and people have watched with the keenest sympathy the development in Palestine of the National Home, a project in which American intellect and capital have played a leading role."(36)

---

[32]For a year by year record of this immigration, see Fawzi Abu-Diab, Immigration to Israel (New York: Arab Information Center, 1960), p. 6. See also Yale, op. cit., p. 389. For a partial list (1937-1946) see The Political History of Palestine Under British Administration (New York: British Information Services, 1947), p. 32.
[33]Full text of this memorandum is in Hurewitz, pp. 103-106.
[34]The American resolution was passed on June 30, 1922. Williams, p. 41.
[35]Congressional Record, Vol. LXII, 9799.
[36]Foreign Relations. . . , 1938, p. 954.

11

One might add here immediately, that it was in the light of this American sympathy that later Arab-American relations were heavily influenced, and impaired.

The American government, constantly reminded by American Zionist interest groups, carefully watched every major development in Palestine. Thus, when the British Peel Commission submitted its report on July 7, 1937, for the first time recommending the partition of Palestine between Arabs and Jews,(37) the United States government in numerous communiques reserved its right, in due time, to comment on the partition proposal.(38) This was to give time to the two parties concerned--Arabs and Jews--to study and react to the proposal. The Arab response was uncompromisingly negative.(39) Instead, the Arab High Committee of Palestine sent a memorandum to the League of Nations and the British Colonial Secretary demanding the end of the British mandate. It also demanded the immediate cessation of a Jewish Homeland in Palestine; and immediate independence for Palestine.(40)

The Zionist attitude was defined in the resolutions of the Twentieth Zionist Congress which assembled at Zurich on August 3, 1937, to study the British proposal. In this Congress the American Zionists opposed the partition, "being afraid of the effect which the existence of a Jewish state might ultimately have on their own status in America."(41) The final resolutions were a compromise between those who opposed and those who favored partition. While declaring that the scheme of partition put forward by the Peel Commission was unacceptable, the Zionist Congress empowered the Zionist Executive Committee, chaired by David Ben Gurion, "to enter into negotiations with a view to ascertaining the precise terms of His Majesty's Government for the proposed establishment of a Jewish state."(42) Even then, the American Zionist delegation abstained from voting on this compromise, which was carried.(43)

After rejecting the partition scheme, the Arab High Committee

---

[37] For a summary and discussion of this report see, The Political History of Palestine Under British Administration, pp. 21-24.
[38] Foreign Relations. . . , 1938, p. 954.
[39] Survey of International Relations (London: Royal Institute of International Affairs, 1937), Vol. I, p. 549.
[40] Ibid., pp. 550-551.
[41] Ibid., p. 543.
[42] Ibid., p. 546.
[43] Ibid., p. 547.

sent letters to neighboring Arab heads of states asking them to intervene with Britain, and put moral pressure on the United States to stop Jewish immigration to Palestine and to stop the partition of that country. In response, numerous letters from Arab leaders were sent to President Franklin Roosevelt between 1937 and 1939. Among these was the letter of November 29, 1938, cited above, from King Ibn Saud. Simultaneously, Zionist pressure was being applied on Roosevelt to keep alive the American commitment to the Jewish National Home scheme. These diverse pressures brought about the State Department policy statement of October 14, 1938, (44) which was in effect a further American commitment to the Zionist cause in Palestine. It reviewed the whole history of America's interest in the development of the Jewish National Home in Palestine up to 1938. The statement then voiced the hope that Britain would keep the United States government fully informed of any proposals which might alter or modify the Palestine Mandate.

Zionist pressures were then due to their fear that Britain might take a new course in Palestine more agreeable to the Arabs. For, in August and September of 1938, Britain was subjected to a wave of Moslem protests and demonstrations throughout the Moslem world from Tunis to India.(45) A Pan-Arab Conference also met at Bludan, Syria on September 8-10, 1938, and proclaimed Palestine to be part of the Arab fatherland. The Bludan conference also warned Britain that if its policy regarding Palestine remained unchanged, the Arabs would be forced to seek a new alliance to protect their rights.(46) This hint did not go unnoticed by Britain especially when developments in Europe were creating the conditions for a second World War. Britain, therefore, sent a new High Commissioner, Sir Harold MacMichael, to Palestine in October, 1938. His past service in Trans-Jordan made him suspect in Zionist circles as pro-Arab.(47) Sir MacMichael extended an invitation from the British

---

[44] Foreign Relations. . . , 1938, pp. 953-955.

[45] Survey of International Affairs, p. 553. Even Jawaherial Nehru, a Hindu, addressed a pro-Arab demonstration in Allahabad on September 3, 1938. This day was observed then as Palestine Day.

[46] Ibid.

[46] Ibid., p. 552.

[47] Suspected as pro-Arab in Zionist circles, he was the object of a Zionist assassination plot on August 8, 1944. This was part of a general campaign by the extremist Zionist groups, the Irgun and Stern, of assassinating British officials in the Middle East during the Second World War. On November 6, 1944, Lord Moyne, the British Commissioner in Egypt, was shot dead by two young Jews of the Stern Gang. John G. Glubb, Britain and the Arabs (London: Hodder and Stoughton, 1959), p. 281.

Colonial Office to both Arab and Jews to meet at a round table conference in London. The Arab states of Eygpt, Iraq, Trans-Jordan, Saudi Arabia, and Yemen were also invited to send delegates to that conference, as were Zionist groups from outside Palestine. Zionist delegates from Britain, the United States, France, Germany, Belgium, Poland and South Africa attended the conference.(48) This conference, which opened on February 7, 1939, marked the point at which the Palestine question officially became the concern not only of Palestinian Arabs, but of Arab nationalism in general.

At the London Conference, which lasted from February 7, until March 15, 1939, the British government proposed the reduction of Jewish immigration to Palestine, and the establishment of a united independent Palestine after ten years. Neither Arab nor Jews accepted these proposals, and Britain proceeded on her own to issue, on May 17, 1939, a White Paper which laid down principles concerning Palestine.(49) In effect, the White Paper was an effort to mollify Arab public opinion throughout the area of the east Mediterranean at that critical moment of history.(50) In it, Britain basically repeated the proposals extended in the London Conference, but now as official policy. Zionist circles vehemently opposed it, for then was their neediest hour for immigration due to the desperate situation of the Jews in Germany. Both American Zionist and American government efforts failed to forestall such a policy.(51) Mr. Roosevelt' reaction to the British White Paper is quoted in part below from a memorandum he sent to the Secretary of State the same day the White Paper was issued:

> I have read with interest and a
> good deal of dismay the decisions of
> the British Government regarding its
> Palestine policy... Frankly, I do
> not believe that the British are wholly
> correct in saying that the framers of
> the Palestine Mandate could not have
> intended that Palestine should be con-
> verted into a Jewish state against the

---

48 Fisher, p. 442.
49 Full text in Hurewitz, pp. 218-226.
50 Lenczowski, p. 324.
51 In this regard, see various letters of Mr. Weizman, the President of the Jewish Agency for Palestine, to Mr. Louis Brandeis, and Brandeis' correspondence with the State Department, Mr. Roosevelt and other correspondences in Foreign Relations. . . , 1939, Vol. IV, pp. 744-757.

will of the Arab population of the
country. . . . My off-hand thought
is that while there are some good
ideas in regard to actual administration of government in this new White
Paper, it is something that we cannot
give approval to by the United States.

My snap judgment is that. . .
that during the next five years the
75,000 additional Jews should be
allowed to go to Palestine and settle;
and at the end of the five years the
whole problem could be surveyed. . . .
I believe that the Arabs could be
brought to accept this because it
seems clear that 75,000 additional
immigrants can be successfully settled
on the land and because also the Arab
immigration into Palestine since 1921
has vastly exceeded the total Jewish
immigration during this whole period.(52)

On May 22, 1939, five days after Roosevelt's memorandum was
issued, over fifty American Congressmen and Senators called on the
Secretary of State and expressed their disapproval of the British
White Paper and requested that the British parliament disavow it.(53)

The American official attitude here regarding the Palestine
question is self-explanatory. What is curious in his memorandum
though is Roosevelt's notion that there was "Arab immigration into
Palestine since 1921 which vastly exceeded the total Jewish immigration during this whole period." Needless to say, no such thing
existed. Nevertheless, it was indicative of the misconceptions
which many American statesmen believed regarding the Arab case in
Palestine. Whether this was prompted by a profound sympathy for the
Jewish predicament in general, or profound respect for the articu-
late Jewish leadership within the United States, or by simply being
misled by Zionist propaganda regarding Palestine, does not alter the
fact that later United States-Arab relations were adversely affected
by these misconceptions.

On May 11, 1942, the American Zionist Organization, meeting in

---

[52]Foreign Relations. . . , 1939, Vol. IV, pp. 757-758.
[53]For a list of their names see Ibid., pp. 763-765.

New York City, adopted the so-called Biltmore Program. In this they called for the establishment of a Jewish state which would embrace the whole of Palestine.(54) This program became the official policy of world Zionism when the General Council of the Zionist Organization in Jerusalem accepted it on November 10, 1942.(55) Along with the adoption of the Biltmore Program, this Zionist Council called for the exertion of further pressure on American politicians and statesmen. Yielding to Zionist pleas, many state legislatures passed pro-Zionist resolutions.(56) Then in February 1944, a pro-Zionist resolution was introduced before both houses of Congress. This resolution called for the opening of Palestine to unrestricted Jewish immigration "so that the Jewish people may ultimately reconstitute Palestine as a free and democratic Jewish Commonwealth."(57) The vote on this resolution was postponed at the last moment, according to Lenczowski, because of the objections of General Marshall, then Chief of Staff, who on the basis of reports from the Middle East believed that such a resolution would harm the Allied war effort.(58) Nevertheless, numerous Arab protests to this proposed resolution were sent to the State Department.(59)

It was in this atmosphere of Arab anxiety over the political future of Palestine that Roosevelt met with King Ibn Saud on his way back from the Yalta Conference in February, 1945. In this meeting, and in a later letter to Ibn Saud dated April 5, 1945,

---

[54] Full text of this program in Hurewitz, pp. 234-235.
[55] Lenczowski, p. 327.
[56] Ibid.
[57] Full text of this resolution in Williams, p. 41.
[58] Lenczowski, Op. cit. See also comments by the then Secretary of War, Henry L. Stimson, on the undesirability of passing such a resolution due to numerous Arab protests, quoted in Williams, pp. 41-42.
[59] "Almost all the Arab states protested to the Department of State in March 1944. . . . The Department repeated on 13 March the earlier assurances given to King Ibn Saud in identical notes to the Egyptian government and Yemen. These read in part that "it is the view of . . . the United States that no decision altering the basic situation of Palestine should be taken until an appropriate time is reached. . . and in full consultation with both Arabs and Jews." Hurewitz, Middle East Dilemmas (New York: Harper and Brothers, 1953), p. 131.

16

Roosevelt assure the King that:

> I would take no action in my capacity
> as Chief of the Executive Branch of
> this Government, which might prove
> hostile to the Arab people. It gives
> me pleasure to renew to your Majesty
> the assurances you have previously
> received regarding the attitude of my
> Government and your own, as Chief
> Executive, with regard to the question
> of Palestine and to inform you that the
> policy of this Government in this re-
> spect is unchanged. . . .(60)

It is clear here that there is an obvious contradiction in
the President's policies.(61) This contradiction, according to
Yale, "goes back to the contradiction between President Wilson's
Fourteen Points and his endorsement of the Balfour Declaration.
This contradiction was one of the underlying causes of the Arab-
Zionist war of 1948-1949,"(62) since both Arabs and Jews simulta-
neously felt encouraged by these American actions.

Roosevelt died the same month in which he wrote the above
letter to King Ibn Saud, and with his death died his "assurances"
to the Arabs. His successor, Harry Truman, responding to heavy
Zionist pressures and demands,(63) began to exert, in turn, pressure
on the physically exhausted Britain to give in to Zionist demands
regarding Palestine. This American pressure, according to Nadav
Safran, "was crucial in compelling Britain to bring the whole
Palestine question before the United Nations in 1947, and American
support was decisive in winning the decision of this organization

---

60
  Department of State Bulletin, October 21, 1945, p. 623.
61"Duplicity" is the word used by Mr. Bartley C. Crum in character-
  izing Mr. Roosevelt's policies regarding Palestine. Mr. Crum was
  a member of the Anglo-American Committee of inquiry that was sent
  to Palestine in 1945, and later wrote Behind the Silken Curtain
  (New York: Simon and Schuster, 1947), p. 75; Yale, pp. 402-408.
62Yale, p. 402.
63In his memoirs, Mr. Truman wrote, "I do not think I ever had as
  much pressure and propaganda aimed at the White House as I had in
  this instance. The persistence of a few of the extreme Zionist
  leaders. . . disturbed and annoyed me. Some were even suggesting
  that we pressure sovereign nations into favorable votes in the
  General Assembly." Quoted in Michael Ionides, Divide and Lose:
  The Arab Revolt 1955-1958 (London: Geoffrey Bles, 1960), p. 78.

in favor of partitioning Palestine between a Jewish and an Arab
state."(64)

On August 31, 1945, President Truman addressed an appeal to
British Prime Minister Clement Attlee asking for the immediate
admission of 100,000 Jewish refugees to Palestine. The British
government then suggested, and Mr. Truman accepted, the creation of
an Anglo-American commission of inquiry to go and study the situation
in Palestine. After holding meetings in Washington, London, and
displaced persons' camps in Germany, Austria and Palestine, this
commission submitted its report to the two governments concerned on
April 20, 1946.(65) The most important recommendation in this report, aside from endorsing Truman's appeal for the immediate admission of 100,000 Jews into Palestine and the abrogation of the
British White Paper of 1939, was that a United Nations trusteeship
be set up in Palestine until Arab and Jewish hostility disappeared.(66)

No action was taken on these recommendations. Then the
Morrison-Grady Commission, originally formed to study the above
report, suggested in July, 1946, the formation of an Arab-Jewish
federation in Palestine.(67) This suggestion, too, was neglected.
Meanwhile the British position inside and outside Palestine was
slowly becoming untenable. "Subjected to official American pressure,
at odds with the Zionists and with the Arabs, and facing growing
disorder in its mandated territory, the British government decided
to take the question of Palestine before the United Nations."(68)

Britain submitted the question of Palestine before the

---

64 Nadav Safran, The United States and Israel (Cambridge, Mass.:
Harvard University Press, 1963),pp. 3-4.
65 Text of this report is in A Decade of American Foreign Policy,
Basic Documents 1941-1949 (Washington: U.S. Government Printing
Office, 1950), pp. 811-815.
66 Ibid., p. 813.
67 The Political History of Palestine Under British Administration,
p. 36.
68 Lenczowski, op. cit., p. 332. American pressure was particularly
heavy in the autumn of 1946, around Congressional election time.
Zionist pressure on prospective Congressmen was felt in the State
Department and in turn in London. Mr. Ernest Bevin, British Secretary of State for Foreign Affairs, subsequently deplored the
fact that the Palestine question had been the subject of local
elections in the United States. New York Times, February 26, 1947,
p. 1. See also Glubb, op. cit., pp. 281-283.

United Nations in a letter to the Secretary General dated April 2, 1947. The General Assembly, in a special session between April 28 and May 15, 1947, created a United Nations Special Committee on Palestine (U.N.S.C.O.P.) to study the problem again.(69) This committee submitted its report to the General Assembly on September 3, 1947, in which the majority recommended the partition of Palestine into an Arab and a Jewish state.(70) The Arab delegates strongly opposed the partition plan. "The United States not only stood on the side of partition," according to Safran, "but in the crucial moments before the decision threw her full weight into the effort to mobilize the votes that were still needed. Without this effort, it is very doubtful whether the partition resolution would have obtained the statutory two-thirds majority of the General Assembly."(71)

The vote on the partition resolution took place on November 29, 1947. Thirty-three states voted for partition, including the United States and the Soviet Union. Ten states abstained, including the United Kingdom. Thirteen states opposed partition. These were the then six Arab member-states: Egypt, Iraq, Lebanon, Saudi Arabia, Syria and Yemen--plus Afghanistan, Pakistan, Iran, India, Turkey, Cuba and Greece.

In view of the fact that the Arabs failed to convince the great powers of voting against the partition of Palestine in the General Assembly, the Arab High Committee of Palestine declared on February 6, 1948 that the Arabs would use force to oppose the establishment of a Zionist state. Violence followed in that country. Great Britain had already declared on January 1, 1948, that as long as both Arabs and Jews could not agree on a solution, she would terminate her mandate in Palestine by May 15, 1948, come what may.

---

[69] Eleven states were represented on this committee: Australia, Canada, Czechoslovakia, Guatemala, India, Iran, Netherland, Peru, Sweden, Uruguay and Yugoslavia. L. Larry Leonard, The United Nations and Palestine (International Conciliation), October 1949, p. 630.

[70] For the recommendations in this report see Department of State Bulletin, September 21, 1947, p. 546.

[71] Safran, p. 35. For a full discussion of Zionist and official American pressure on other United Nation members, especially Latin American states, to vote favorably on the partition plan, see Kermit Roosevelt, "The Partition of Palestine: A Lesson in Pressure Politics," Middle East Journal, January,1948, pp. 1-16.

The first American political action in favor of the new state of Israel came the day Britain terminated its mandate. It happened as follows: during the debate in the General Assembly on proposals for an international regime for Jerusalem on May 14, 1948, a representative of the Jewish Agency informed the delegates of the United Nations that 10:00 a.m. (Eastern Standard Time) a Jewish state had been proclaimed. The mandate was to expire at 6:00 p.m. on that same day. Word spread on the floor of the General Assembly that the United States had granted de facto recognition to Israel.(72) This the United States delegation could not confirm immediately, but a little later the United States delegate read the following statement from the President of the United States:

> This government has been informed
> that a Jewish state has been proclaimed
> in Palestine, and recognition has been
> requested by the Provisional Government
> thereof. The United States recognizes
> the Provisional Government as the de
> facto authority of the new state of
> Israel.(73)

The immediate recognition of the state of Israel by the United States(74) climaxed a crisis of confidence between the Arabs and the United States. Subsequent Arab military defeat in the Palestine war created a crisis of confidence between Arab nationalists and their leaders,(75) as well as with Britain,who was bound by treaty obligations to have trained the Arab armies of Egypt, Iraq, and Jordan. Nevertheless, these armies were found to be inadequate in the Palestine war. Later American sympathy and aid to Israel in the political, cultural and economic fields were to keep this crisis of confidence alive, and were to contribute in large measure to Arab neutralism in the cold war.

72Leonard, p. 667.
73Official Records of the Second Special Session of the General Assembly, Vol. 1, April 16-May, 1948, p. 42.
74According to Sidney N. Fisher, Mr. Truman announced de facto recognition of Israel sixteen minutes after Mr. Ben Gurion's proclamation of the establishment of that state in Tel Aviv, op. cit., p. 585. See New York Times, May 11, 1964, p. 1, concerning the role played by Cardinal Spellman of New York on the admission of Israel to the United Nations in 1949.
75See the section entitled "The Impact of the Palestine Defeat," in Chapter IV of Peter Calvocoressi, Survey of International Affairs, 1952 (New York: Oxford University Press, 1955), pp. 191-203

This neutralism paved the way for an extension of Soviet influence in the Arab world by the middle 1950s in the form of economic and military aid, and further alienation between much of the Arab World and the United States.

Chapter II

Israel and American-Egyptian Relations, 1952-1955: Establishing the Pattern

The years 1952-1955 were selected here because in the opinion of the author,those were key years in which American relations with the revolutionary leaders of Egypt leading the Arab national-ist movement were shaped for many years to come.

July 23, 1952 brought a revolution in Egypt against the defunct rule of King Farouk. The Free Officers who came to power were seemingly intent not only to liberate Egypt from foreign domination, but also to liberate the wider Arab homeland from the same heritage. They took it upon themselves to speak in the name of the Arab nationalist movement. And since the Palestine question had become the focal point of the Arab nationalist movement since the Second World War, the new revolutionary leaders in Egypt assumed the leadership in espousing the Arab cause in Palestine.

The year 1952 also brought about the election of Dwight D. Eisenhower to the presidency of the United States. His campaign on the slogan of "peace with justice" in the world, and his promise of American "impartiality" in dealing with the Middle East gave rise to Arab expectations, chief among them the new Egyptian leaders, that the Truman-style one-sided American view of the Middle East, always favoring the Zionists, might now be changed. Nevertheless, these Arab hopes were largely buried by 1955, and America's moral stature in the Arab world was vastly diminished-- thanks in large measure to the Israeli and American Zionists' role in obstructing any friendly and profitable dialogue between the Arab nationalists and the United States. The result was a further-ing of the crisis of confidence between the Arabs and the West generally which began with the Truman administration, whereby only Israel and the Soviet Union were bound to profit.

American foreign policy decisions invariably reflect domestic considerations and various groups' sentiments. American policy in regard to Palestine affords an extreme example of this. It is particularly true in this question because it involves a highly influential American pressure group--the Zionists--committed since 1917 to the creation of a Jewish state in Palestine. In contrast, there is no comparable American Arab pressure group to influence American foreign policy in favor of the Arab position on Palestine.

23

Now, as long as the United States was isolationist, and this American sympathy to the Zionists was largely confined to statements and Congressional resolution, it could do little to harm either the American national interests in the Arab world or the Arabs. But World War II changed all that. The United States emerged from it as the leading power in the Western world, and her new position of leadership in the Middle East as elsewhere demanded new decisions and new statemanship from her.

One look at the map would suggest that American economic and strategic interests lay mostly in the Arab world and not Israel. Nevertheless, American political and economic leaders were so committed to the idea of creating a new Israel by the end of the Second World War, that the American position vis-a-vis Palestine was extremely difficult to alter--that is, unless great statesmanship and firm leadership was to be exercised by the new President of the United States, Mr. Eisenhower. Therefore when Eisenhower began his first administration by promising impartiality in the Arab-Israeli dispute, he was soon to find out how difficult this promise was to effect, and how strong was the American Zionist resistance to the implementation of that promise.

The Arab world for its part emerged from the Second World War with new hopes and aspirations for the future. It looked toward the United States and the United Nations for a fair deal in its struggle for complete emancipation from colonial rule, and its struggle with Zionism. In their anxiety to secure this, the Arabs were soon to resent the American reluctance to pressure her Western allies, Britain and France, to satisfy Arab nationalist demands. In the Palestine case in particular, the Arabs were soon to realize that the country might have been better off under British rule than with what the Arabs discovered was the further one-sided pro-Zionist American view of that issue.

As mentioned above (and regardless of the Republican Platform of 1952 which points to the contrary), the Eisenhower administration began with a promise of impartiality between Arabs and Zionists in the Palestine question. This promise was later put in concrete form in the Dulles report on the Middle East after the American Secretary of State visited the area in May, 1953. It could be assumed that the new Republican administration had recognized that along with the problem of the British occupation of the Suez Canal bases, the unsolved problems of Palestine lay at the root of Egyptian opposition to any Arab cooperation in the American-sponsored Middle East defence scheme proposed since October, 1951. The promise of impartiality, therefore, was designed to satisfy

24

the Arabs, and if implemented, was to help bring them into the fold of Western defences. This impartiality never came. A case in point is the Eisenhower Administration's role in trying to implement the Jordan Valley Authority Scheme, discussed later. Nevertheless, Arab spokesmen then became cautiously optimistic and the Egyptian press also reflected that optimism. Israel on the other hand was in a somber mood. On March 13, 1953 Ben Gurion made a statement to the press in which he voiced Israel's extreme concern over the reports of what he called "the new United States Middle East policy." His concern was also voiced by influential friends and Israeli sympathizers in the United States, before and after his statement. The list includes Senator Robert Taft, Henry Morgenthau and Rabbi Silver.

It was due to the Israeli fear of such an eventuality whereby the United States would be truly impartial in the Palestine issues, that ever since 1948, Israel felt that any and every profitable dialogue between the United States leading the Western powers, and Egypt, leading the Arab states, might adversely effect its vital interests. On such occasion when American-Egyptian relations were going well, or threatening to go well, Israel and her powerful Zionist backers would act alarmed and effectively register their apprehension in the American Congress, the White House and the mass-media. This "fear" was viewed by the Egyptians as nothing but a ruse, since the new Egyptian leaders had specifically made various statements at various occasions to the effect that they had no intention whatsoever to attack Israel. The Naguib pledge of August 9, 1952 is a case to verify the point. Any talk of Israeli fear or apprehension was therefore artificial, from the Egyptian view, and aimed at obstructing friendly American relations with the Arabs. Israel, in fact, was ready to go the full length to obstruct such an eventuality, and even act "in a reckless manner," in the words of one of her Zionist sympathizers.(1) Perhaps the best and the most dramatic example of this Israeli reckless action was the infamous "Lavon Affair."

The Lavon Affair was an Israeli reaction to the general atmosphere of friendship and hopeful-waiting that developed between the United States and the new leadership in Egypt from 1952 and until 1954. This was reflected in the favorable American press coverage of the Free Officers revolution, and the development of early friendly contacts between the then-American Ambassador, Jefferson Caffery, and the Free Officers. Thus, an Israeli espionage ring was sent to Egypt to bomb American offices

---

1
Nadav Safran, The United States and Israel (1963), p. 235.

and institutions in Egypt to appear as if done by Egyptians. British properties were also subject to this scheme. This Zionist ring was successful in burning the American consulates and libraries in Cairo and Alexandria among many other European establishments. Finally, it was uncovered by the Egyptian police in Alexandria on July 23, 1954.

Another example of the Israeli adverse reaction to good relations between the Arabs and the West was in the case of the Anglo-Egyptian agreement over Sudan in 1953.

The Anglo-Egyptian agreement over the future of Sudan came about in February, 1953. It represented a major compromise on the part of the Free Officers since they accepted the principle of self-government for Sudan. The United States had a powerful hand in bringing about final agreement. The United States was then hopeful that an early solution to the Sudan question might induce the new Egyptian leaders to join the then proposed American defence system for the Middle East. On the same line of thinking both Britain and the United States made in August, 1952, statements to the effect that they would supply Egypt with requested arms for defence. These mere statements, though, alerted Israel and her Zionist friends. That is why the apparent leader of the Free Officers then, Mohammad Naguib, made the above-mentioned promise of August 10, 1952, that any American or British arms given to Egypt would not be used to attack Israel. In fact Naguib stood on record as opposing any such action by other Arab states--a position uncomfortable for any Arab leader to take.

Western arms to Egypt never came. For even though Egypt signed an agreement with Britain over Sudan, she remained embroiled with the latter in a bitter dispute until 1954 over the issue of British evacuation of Egypt itself. Meanwhile, British arms to Egypt would be out of the question. American arms were not given either, due in part to the Zionist clamour against it. Neither would they have been accepted, according to the Egyptian Al-Ahram (July 6, 1953) "because the conditions which the United States attaches to this military aid are incompatible with the policies which the new Egyptian leadership wants to pursue." Chief among these conditions was the Egyptian adherence to the American Middle East defence scheme. This scheme was still unacceptable to the new nationalist leaders in Cairo--not while there were still outstanding regional and colonial problems with the West to be solved to the satisfaction of the Arabs.

But to repeat, and regardless of the fact that there was no

prospect of Western arms delivery to Egypt, Israel remained vigilant in obstructing such a possibility. For instance, on December 29, 1952 the New York Times reported that Israel had stated her alarm to Britain over the "proposed arms sale" to Egypt. A day later the same paper reported that Britain was "justifying the arms sale" to Egypt on the basis of the Three Power Tripartite Declaration of 1950. This declaration by France, Britain and the United States promised to keep an arms balance between Israel and her Arab neighbors. This ludicrous proposition of having Israel alone as strong as all the Arab states surrounding her was never enforced, anyhow. Rather, Israel somehow became better armed than the Arabs, regardless. On January 1, 1953 Israel was reported in the American press as "demanding" that Western arms should not go to Egypt. Five days later the then-Israeli Ambassador to Washington, Ebba Eban, conferred with the American Secretary of State, Dean Acheson, over the same issue.

In correlation with official Israeli clamour and pressure on both Britain and the United States, powerful Zionist and pro-Zionist voices in both countries were also vociferous. The theme of these voices was almost identical. It opposed any arms aid to the Arabs since such action would endanger the security of Israel. And since Israel was the "only democratic outpost" in the Middle East, any Western aid to the Arabs would but help their "undemocratic regimes" to destroy the Israeli "democracy." Thus on January 1, 1953 the American Zionist Council sent a letter in that regard to the American Secretary of State.

On February 2, 1953 British Labor leader and Member of Parliament Hugh Gaitskill raised his voice in defence of Israel. On February 6, Rabbi Silver registered his protests to the American State Department. On February 12, Supreme Court Justice William Douglas raised his voice. Observing this phenomenon, the Egyptians saw it as no coincidence that on February 9, 1953 a bomb exploded on the premises of the Soviet legation in Tel Aviv. This was seen by the Egyptian press as designed by Israel to cause a break between her and the Soviet Union, thus being able to portray herself in the United States far more effectively and convincingly as the sole "outpost of democracy" in the Middle East, endangered from all sides by totalitarian regimes. The Soviet break would have the Soviet Union woo the Arabs on behalf of Israel, and mainly in words. Meanwhile, American and Western military and economic aid would be channeled still further to Israel and to the exclusion of the Arab states. In effect, if that Israeli strategy worked, and it did, the Arabs would be punished by the Western powers for something they had nothing to do with, nor solicited in any way.

27

What happened after the bomb explosion in Tel Aviv helped confirm Egyptian suspicions. For, three days later the Soviet Union did break diplomatic relations with Israel. The Soviet Union also did use the incident to woo the Arabs, (2) followed by the statements of Eban and Douglas and Senator Gillette, etc., mentioned above.

For this reason and in an attempt to thwart the Israeli objectives of pressuring the State Department, and due to Arab fears that the Soviet-Israeli rift might play into the hands of Israel in Washington, at a time when the Arabs were hoping for a "new deal" from Eisenhower, seven Arab ambassadors visited the State Department on February 17, 1953. They met with Under-Secretary of State, Walter Bedell Smith, and directed his attention to the "tendency in America" for the Zionists to exploit the Israeli-Soviet rift, and that any further aid to Israel would only play into the hands of the Soviet Union.

Egyptian and other Arab diplomats residing in the United States must have been aware of the interest-group politics and demands inside the United States. But when these demands, in their estimation, became excessive and intolerable as it concerned Arab interests, then any acquiescence of the United States to such demands could not be tolerated by the Arabs, and in turn was bound to reflect itself adversely on Arab-American relations. In the Arab view, American-Zionist demands often far exceeded the limit of Arab toleration.

DULLES TRIP TO THE MIDDLE EAST AND HIS REPORT ON PALESTINE

Eisenhower's keen interest in solving impartially the problems besetting the Middle East was manifested by sending his Secretary of State, John Foster Dulles, on a fact-finding mission to the area in May of 1953.

The Dulles trip to the area aroused hope in Egypt as well as the rest of the Arab states that finally an important Western statesman was interested in just solutions of the major problems

---

[2]See for example, The Literaturnaya Gazeta, February 17, 1953; The Current Digest of the Soviet Press, Vol. No. 5, p. 13. It bitterly attacked Israel as "the arm of the American and British imperialists in Arab lands."

of the region. Foremost among them, of course, were the problems
related to the Palestine question. Anticipating this, General
Naguib made a statement a day before Dulles' arrival on May 12, in
which he chided the "unwise" Palestine policy of Mr. Truman and
hoped for an impartial American policy in Palestine from then on.
Al-Ahram, which reported the Naguib statement, was more specific.
It quoted the Washington Post as saying that since the creation
of the state of Israel, United States diplomacy in the Middle East
had been without any direction. Al-Ahram wrote that America wanted
peace between the Arabs and Israel, but no peace would ever occur
until the Palestine refugees and other problems connected with
Palestine were impartially solved. Then all the Middle East
states might join the defense system which the United States was
proposing. Al-Ahram then added that this would happen only if
Britain also agreed to the evacuation of the Suez.

Dulles arrived the next day in Cairo and from there went to
Tel Aviv and to other Arab capitals. He later dealt at length
with the Arab-Israeli problems in his report. In it he verbally
infused life into the then defunct 1950 Tripartite Declaration on
arms balance in the area, by promising that the United States
would stand fully behind it, especially in opposition to any violation of the frontiers between Israel and the Arab states. He
repeated the words of the Declaration:

> The three governments, should
> they find that any of these states
> was preparing to violate frontiers
> of armistice lines, would, consistently
> with their obligations as members of the
> United Nations, immediately take action,
> both within and outside the United Nations,
> to prevent such violation.

On May 21, 1953 and while Dulles was still in the Middle
East, Israel attacked five Jordanian villages. This had already
been a pattern of behaviour on the part of Israel since its
creation, supposedly in response to alleged Arab infiltrators
from the neighboring Arab states. But according to Commander
Elmo H. Hutchison, an American who served from 1951 to 1955 on
the United Nations military observers Truce Commission in
Palestine, "many students of the Israeli-Arab problems have long
suspected that Israel views a 'tense border' as the most effective
way of assuring that outside interests remain alert to their
obligations, to Israel."(3) And since Dulles was still there, the

---

[3] Violent Truce (1958), p. 120.

Israeli attacks on Jordan were nothing but a reminder to him and President Eisenhower of what Israel thinks of American impartiality in the Middle East. To the Arabs, the Israeli attacks seemed another proof of the little respect Israel had for Dulles, Eisenhower and the Three Power Declaration of 1950.

Again on May 29, 1953 another Israeli attack occurred in the Gaza strip whereby three Egyptians were killed. A day later, Al-Ahram headlined what it called the gravest attack on Jordan by Israel since the end of the Palestine war. Jordan, according to the report, contacted both Britain and the United States and reminded them of their obligation under their Tripartite Declaration of 1950. Both powers advised Jordan to negotiate directly with Israel. It must be remembered of course that the Arab states have been in unanimous agreement since 1948 that no Arab state should negotiate either directly or individually with Israel. Any Western call therefore on any Arab state to negotiate individually with Israel is extremely suspect to the Arabs, and is viewed as an attempt at coercing the Arab states to make a piece-meal peace with Israel. Alluding to this long-standing Arab position on negotiations with Israel, Al-Ahram just added that "of course Jordan repeated the well-known Arab policy in this regard to both Britain and the United States."

The above American position was highly unsatisfactory to the Arabs who, of course, expected Mr. Eisenhower, then still talking "impartiality," at least to enforce the 1950 Tripartite Declaration. It was such a situation that rendered the above-mentioned Declaration meaningless and an object of derision to the Arabs by this time. Dulles' repetition of the wording of that Declaration a day later in his report to the American nation served only to bring further derision and frustration in Cairo and other Arab capitals. This feeling was reinforced a day later by another Israeli armed aggression. For practically while Dulles was reading his report to the American people on June 2, 1953, the Israeli armed forces attacked and demolished the Jordanian village of Qilqilya. Other Israeli attacks followed the Dulles report, and each was more violent than the other. And inasmuch as "all of the sensational raids executed by Israel against Jordanian, Egyptian, and Syrian territory and the Huleh dispute occurred while the Republicans were in office," one must agree with George Lenczowski that there must have been a correlation between the Republican promise and attempt at impartiality in the Palestine question, and the Israeli resentment that American impartiality might be truly implemented.(4)

---

[4]George Lenczowski, The Middle East in World Affairs (1958), p. 365.

Wary that its primary goal of eventually enlisting the Arab states, primarily Egypt, in Western defence schemes, would be frustrated by these Israeli actions (that is to assume that these actions were not designed to do just that), the Republican administration solicited the help of Republican Representative Jacob Javits of New York. On June 12, 1953 Javits made a plea in the New York Times for the support of American Jews of the Administration's efforts to strengthen regional cooperation and defenses in the Middle East. The non-committal response to Javits' plea came on the same page of the New York Times. Dr. Emmanuel Neumann, President of the Zionist Organization of America, somehow speaking for Israel, stated that Israel "backs the United States but opposes concessions to its hostile neighbors."

Another case in point whereby Israel acted regardless of strong American opposition to her action was in the case of moving the Israeli Foreign Ministry from Tel Aviv to Jerusalem in July, 1953 as a prelude to making Jerusalem the Israeli political capital. Since 1949 a number of Israeli ministries were moved to Jerusalem and in December, 1949 the Knesset met there. Those actions were definitely opposed by the American State Department, the United Nations as well as the Arabs. Egypt protested this Israeli unilateral action to the United Nations on July 16, 1953. American opposition to such an action was reaffirmed only four weeks before by Dulles in his report to the American people about his trip to the Middle East. In his report, he recalled the United Nations General Assembly resolution of December 9, 1949 affirming the international status of Jerusalem. He then added that the "world religious community has claims in Jerusalem which takes precedence over the political claims of any particular nation." Nevertheless, Israel proceeded to do just that on July 12, 1953. Al-Ahram's headlines in Cairo read, "Israel Challenges the United States Again." This challenge came at a time when Israel and her Zionist friends in the United States were presumably in one of their "apprehensive" moods. That was due to a State Department announcement on June 22, 1953 that the United States was allegedly ready to allow the sale of some of her arms to the Arab states. These periodic announcements of "arming" the Arabs on the part of the American State Department, and actual arms delivery somehow never materializing, was seen by some observers(5) as perhaps one method of putting American pressure on Israel to cooperate. Nevertheless, the United States never really had the will to contain Israel, either by arming the Arabs to be able to defend themselves, or by curtailing American military and economic aid to Israel.

---

[5] See the London Times, May 11, 1953, on this point.

On October 15, 1953 Israel made its attack on the Jordanian village of Qibya, killing 53 civilians. This Israeli attack was carried out one day after the announcement in Washington on October 14 that President Eisenhower was sending Eric Johnston to the Middle East as his personal envoy with the rank of ambassador. Johnston was to "explore with the governments of the countries of that region certain steps which might be expected to contribute to an improvement of the general situation in the region."[6]   The major step which Eisenhower had in mind was to bring about an Arab-Israeli agreement over the joint development and exploitation of the Jordan River waters.   This mission was also in part an answer to Syrian complaints to the Western powers, culminating in a complaint to the Security Council on October 16, 1953 that Israel had been engaged in unilateral diversion of the Jordan River waters since 1952.

The fact that the Israeli attack on Qibya occurred right after the announcement in Washington of the Johnston mission, and only three days after the start of the Anglo-Egyptian negotiations over the future of the Suez bases, October 12, 1953 brought about the charge by Al-Ahram on October 19, that the Israeli attack was specifically timed and designed to torpedoe both of these Western efforts before they started.   The fact is that Israel did succeed in doing just that.   For when Johnston arrived in the Middle East right after the Qibya massacre, the Arabs were in an extremely bitter mood against the United States, and in no mood either to discuss any joint plans with Israel over the Jordan waters.   In effect therefore Israel extremely weakened his mission before he even submitted his proposals.   His mission was further doomed to failure as it was soon discovered by the three riparian Arab states concerned (Syria, Jordan and Lebanon) that Johnston was proposing to allot to Israel approximately half of the amount of water allotted to the three Arab states combined.   In view of the fact that the three major tributaries of the Jordan River spring entirely from Arab territories, and, in view of the fact that the announced principal purpose of the whole project was to help alleviate the destitute conditions of the Palestine Arab refugees, the large share of water allotted to Israel by Johnston could not but bring about Arab rejection of his proposals.   Johnston finally made four trips to the area between 1953 and 1955, and all failed to bring about Arab agreement.   The failure of his mission was essentially another failure in Arab minds of the Eisenhower prom- ised impartiality in Middle Eastern affairs.   And as the Arabs

---

[6]Department of State Bulletin, October 26, 1953, p. 553.

rejected the Johnston proposals, Israel could well afford to let
it be known that "it was keeping an open mind on the project."(7)
Meanwhile, it proceeded unilaterally to divert the waters of the
River Jordan. (See Chapter 3).

The Egyptians also saw the United States government and its
press as partial to Israel in regard to the Israeli demand for
freedom of navigation through the Suez Canal. Ever since the armistice agreement was signed in 1949 between Egypt and Israel, the
Egyptian government refused to allow Israeli ships or Israeli-
bound ships to go through the canal. In September, 1951, the
Security Council recommended, over Egyptian protests, that Egypt
"terminate the restrictions on the passage of international com-
mercial shipping and goods through the Suez Canal wherever
bound. . . ."(8) The United States then voted in favor of Israel.
Egypt held then and since that her blockade of Israel was admiss-
able under the terms of the Constantinople Convention of 1888
regulating Suez navigation, being her right of self-defense against
a belligerent power prescribed in Article X. Israel, on the other
hand, has made periodical test cases since 1951 of what she claimed
was her right of free navigation through the canal. One test case
came on January 24, 1954. Israel timed this when the Qibya attack
and the Israeli diversion of the Jordan River had brought her adverse world public opinion and American condemnation.

On January 24, 1954, the Italian ship Franca Maria entered the
Suez Canal with a cargo destined for Israel. The Egyptian author-
ities stopped the ship and confiscated the cargo. On January 28,
Israel lodged a complaint to the Security Council against Egypt.
The Israeli complaint was also echoed very strongly by the usual
Zionist and pro-Zionist voices in the United States. Their outcry
was to have the United States force Egypt and the rest of the Arab
states to lift their blockade of Israel.

Al-Ahram, on January 25, 1954 pointed out that the whole
episode of the Franca Maria and the fracas that followed was nothing
but an Israeli maneuver to switch world and American public opinion
in her favor at a time when Israel was being condemned for a variety of aggressive actions against the Arabs. A few days later
(January 31) Al-Ahram charged that Britain was also in on these
Israeli maneuvers. It based its charge on a statement made by the
British Minister of State, Selwyn Lloyd, to the House of Commons

---

[7]Peter Calvocoressi, Survey of International Affairs, 1953 (1956),
p. 145.
[8]Yearbook of the United Nations, 1951, p. 299.

immediately after the arrival of the Franca Maria to Seuz. In it
Lloyd stated that "we deem any Egyptian interference in the Suez
shipping a very dangerous matter and we are studying international
measures necessary to stop any such interference." The British
reasons for instigating the Israeli maneuver, Al-Ahram wrote, was
to use the Egyptian stoppage and seizure of the Franca Maria as
an excuse to delay the Anglo-Egyptian negotiations over the British evacuation of the Suez Canal and its bases. Thus Britain,
like Israel, would succeed in diverting world public opinion then
from her forced occupation of Egyptian territory. Even the London
Times of January 26, 1954 suspected the same.

American statements in the Security Council were sympathetic
to Israel. This prompted the Egyptian Foreign Minister, Mahmoud
Fawzi, to see the American Ambassador to Egypt, Jefferson Caffrey,
on January 31 and warn him that an American final vote in favor
of Israel on the navigation issue would further worsen Egyptian-
American relations and further estrange the Arab world from the
United States.

The Egyptian position in regard to Suez navigation was summed
up by Al-Ahram on February 16, 1954. This article also articulated
Egyptian frustration over what seemed to Egypt the Western ina-
bility to be fair and impartial when dealing with matters that
involved Arab-Israeli questions.

> Israel is back again raising
> the issue of navigation through Suez.
> This comes at a time when she just
> finished wiping out another Jordanian
> village. She of course wants to di-
> vert adverse world public opinion
> away from her and switch it to Egypt.
> As usual she uses the pro-Zionist
> press in the West in these efforts.
> It is sad indeed that respectable
> Western newspapers like the Manchester
> Guardian falls for Israel intrigues
> and portrays Israel in the role of
> victim in the Middle East when the
> Israeli record in the United Nations
> speaks for itself. . . . Does Egypt
> need to remind a British newspaper,
> for example, that Britain closed the
> Suez Canal in two world wars to inter-
> national shipping except to what was
> compatible with her military purposes?

Egyptian efforts to have the West, especially the United
States, see her point of view in regard to the navigation issue,
did not succeed. Perhaps as a last resort the Egyptians tried
shock tactics to frighten the United States out of her persistent
backing of the Israeli navigation demand. On February 16, 1954
the Egyptian chief delegate to the Security Council debate,
Dr. Mahmoud Azmi, held a press conference in New York in which he
dropped what was described by both major Egyptian newspapers,
Al-Ahram and Al-Gumhuriyah, as a "bomb not expected by the United
States." He warned that if the United States kept insisting on
enforcing the 1951 Security Council recommendation over Suez
navigation, Egypt might convene a conference of those powers
signatory to the Constantinople Convention of 1888. This, he
stated, was prescribed by the Convention itself, whereby any
signatory to the Convention could call for such a meeting. Egypt,
he reminded the newsmen, was one of these powers. To make his
warning clear, he added that Russia also was a signatory to that
Convention but not the United States.

These Egyptian warnings notwithstanding, the United States
voted in favor of Israel when the vote was finally taken on
March 29, 1954. By that time the United States was being openly
attacked daily in the Egyptian press, not only for that, but also
for attempting to divide the Arabs among themselves by enlisting
Iraq into the American Middle East defence schemes. These American actions, along with the Israeli policy of "retaliation"--that
seemed to the Arabs if not encouraged by the United States, at
least unchecked--helped bring about the ascendency to power of
Gamal Abdel Nasser in Egypt. Nasser was far more militant than
the mild General Naguib. Naguib was forced to resign on February 25,
1954. And even though he was brought back to office some three
days later and remained in the Presidential post until November
1954, it was clear that Nasser was the real power in Egypt from
then on.

Nasser, of course, had no physical power to follow a tough
policy either with the United States, Britain, or Israel. Western
arms had been effectively curtailed from reaching Egypt due to the
various circumstances discussed above. The only power Egypt had
until she bought Eastern bloc arms was the power of the word, and
the Voice of the Arabs radio proved to be a potent Egyptian weapon
for Arab nationalism against French rule in North Africa as well
as British interests and rule in the Arabian peninsula, Jordan,
Iraq and Egypt itself. The United States also fell under heavy
and bitter Egyptian polemics from then on.

The worsening relations between the Western powers and Egypt were of benefit to two parties: the Soviet Union and Israel. It gave Israel a freer hand to persist in her tough policy with the Arabs in general and Egypt particularly, the policy which culminated in her invasion of Egypt in October, 1956. Throughout the period between early 1954 and October, 1956, and judging from the events that happened in the process of enlisting Iraq into the Western defence pact and the bloodshed along the Israeli borders, it could be safely stated that American-Egyptian relations were invariably on the brink of diplomatic breakdown. This was true of American-Arab relations in general. On April 8, 1954, for example, five Arab Ambassadors walked out of an official dinner prepared by the State Department. The walk-out resulted from a speech by the Chief of the Rabbinical Council of America, referring to Israel as the "only democratic state in the Middle East." There followed in Cairo talk of diplomatic rupture with the United States. And any further American talk of "impartiality" or mediation in the Arab-Israeli conflict was only met with derision in Cairo.(9) Thus Israel succeeded in establishing a pattern of bad American-Egyptian relations ever since.

The Soviet Union was the other major beneficiary of the worsening relations between Egypt and the United States and other Western powers. The Soviet took full advantage of this by backing more and more Arab nationalist demands inside and outside the United Nations. This backing began to reap results by March, 1954 when the first significant trade agreement between Egypt and the Soviet Union was ratified. This happened to be also the first important Soviet trade agreement with any Arab country. This agreement was signed on March 28. One day later a vote was taken in the Security Council on the Western-sponsored New Zealand resolution over freedom of navigation in the Suez Canal. This resolution was favorable to Israel but strongly opposed by Egypt. The Soviet delegate, Andrei Vyshinsky, vetoed the resolution. He announced as part of the reason for his veto (and quoted with obvious exaltation by both Al-Ahram and Al-Gumhuriyah) that the navigation issue was part and parcel of the whole Palestine question, and that Israel herself should obey earlier United Nations resolutions on Palestine if she hoped to have the Arabs obey also United Nations resolutions.

In effect, the Soviet delegate was spouting exactly the Arab position on the Arab-Israeli conflict. From then on the Soviet Union found this line extremely profitable in undermining Western

---

9
See, for example, an article by Kamal Abdel Hamid in Al-Ahram, July 17, 1954.

influence in the area. They also discovered in the increasingly popular voice of Gamal Abdel Nasser in the Arab world a very potent and most welcome coincidental ally in fighting the creation of the Western-initiated Middle East defence system and Western military encirclement of the Soviet Union.

Chapter III

Eisenhower and the Jordan Valley Authority Scheme

One of the major components of the Arab-Israeli struggle
in Palestine, and a case in point from the Arab view of Israel's
insistence in the last two decades on solving these questions on
her own terms, is the question of the division and the diversion
of the waters of the River Jordan. Western public opinion has
been led to view Arab opposition to the Israeli irrigation schemes
and Western proposals for the division of the Jordan waters as
another case of Arab obstructionism and negativism. This is not
the case. According to Edward Rizk:

> "Israel's diversion of the waters
> of the River Jordan is not a simple
> water project 'within its own borders'
> to irrigate land legally owned by Jews,
> which the Arab states are attempting
> to obstruct by what some misinformed
> writers have described as a 'dog-in-
> the-manger' attitude. Much more is
> at stake.... The Arab States' re-
> fusal . . . is basic and stems from
> the fact that the River Jordan pro-
> ject is an integral part of the
> Palestine problem as a whole and
> must be treated within an overall
> solution of that problem, not nibbled
> at to serve the interests of Israel
> alone."(1)

Beyond the fact that the Arabs would, and have insisted for over
two decades on the solution of the whole of the Palestine question
before cooperating with Israel in any development schemes, they
also viewed the proposed American diversion schemes after 1953 as
heavily partial to Israel. And even if the Arabs would have been
agreeable to cooperate with Israel at least on this project alone,
they would have opposed it solely on the basis of what they deemed
as American heavy partiality to Israel in the suggested division
of the waters of the river.

1
 The River Jordan (New York: The Arab Information Center, 1964),
 p. 1.

Regardless of the Republican Platform of 1952 which points to the contrary, the first Eisenhower Administration began its relations in the Middle East with an attempt and a promise of impartiality between Arabs and Israelis in the Palestine question. For it may have been recognized by the new Republican Administration that the unsolved Palestine question lay at the root of much of Arab neutralism after the Second World War. And since the United States has been attempting to enlist the Arab states, mainly Egypt, into a Middle East defence scheme akin to the North Atlantic Treaty Organization since 1951, and to no avail, President Eisenhower was of the hope that by attempting to solve some of the Palestine problems through genuine American impartiality, that that might be a way of having the Arab states join the Western-sponsored defence projects for the area.

Needless to say, the mere talk in the United States in early 1953 of American impartiality in Palestine, was revolutionary in the Arab view, and was greatly welcomed in the Arab world. For a while, therefore, there was an atmosphere of great expectations and wishful thinking in Arab capitals. For instance, the influential Al-Ahram of Cairo made much of two statements made on March 3, 1953, one by the Egyptian Ambassador in Washington, Ahmad Hussain, and the other by Dr. Charles Malik, the Lebanese Ambassador. Both Arab Ambassadors commended highly the New Eisenhower Administration in Washington for what seemed to be genuine interest on its part for finding just and impartial solutions in Palestine.

Israel, as mentioned earlier (chapter 2) fell in a somber mood, and her actions against her Arab neighbors were designed to torpedoe President Eisenhower's persuit of impartiality. Soon that impartiality proved illusive anyhow. A case in point was the Jordan Valley scheme.

THE JORDAN VALLEY AUTHORITY

The Israeli attack on the Jordanian village of Qibya (53 dead) was carried out one day after the announcement in Washington on October 14, 1953 that President Eisenhower was sending Eric Johnston, President of the Motion Picture Association, to the Middle East as his personal representative with the rank of Ambassador. Johnston's mission, according to the announcement, was "to explore with the governments of the countries of that region certain steps which might be expected to contribute to an improvement of the general situation in the region."(2) The "coincidence" in timing between the above announcement and the Israeli attack on the Jordanian village brought the comment from Al-Ahram that the Israeli attack was again designed to put pressure on the Arabs to accept peace on Israel's terms, and to put pressure on the Eisenhower administration to force the Arabs to accept such a peace. It was also designed, according to Al-Ahram, to disrupt the Anglo-Egyptian negotiations over the evacuation of the Suez bases which had started on October 13, 1953.(3)

Johnston's mission, therefore, was presaged by the above "misfortune" while still enroute to the Middle East. The prime purpose of his mission was to bring about Arab-Israeli agreement over the joint development and exploitation of the Jordan River waters. For, according to the announcement of the Johnston trip, Eisenhower stated:

> It is my conviction that
> acceptance of a comprehensive
> plan for the development of the
> Jordan Valley would contribute
> greatly to stability in the Near
> East and to general economic pro-
> gress of the region. I have asked
> Mr. Johnston to explain this position
> to the states concerned, seek their
> cooperation . . .

His mission was also in answer to Syrian complaints to the Western powers, culminating in a complaint to the Security Council on October 16, 1953(4) that Israel had been engaged in unilateral diversion of the waters of the Jordan River since 1952. The Israeli diversion work was first revealed in a report to the New York Times by Dana Adams Schmidt on December 22, 1952.

Now that Johnston had arrived right after the Qibya attack, the Arabs were in no mood to discuss any joint plans with Israel for the diversion of the river.(5) In effect, Israel weakened his mission before it started which understandably angered Washington. It prompted the State Department to send a strong note to Israel on October 19 that if her diversion work on the

---

[2] Department of State Bulletin, October 26, 1953, p. 553.
[3] Al-Ahram, October 19, 1953.
[4] United Nations Document S/3108/Rev. 1
[5] Georgiana G. Stevens, "The Jordan River Valley, International Conciliation, No. 506, p. 262.

41

river was not stopped forthwith,the United States would immediately stop economic aid to Israel.(6) A day later economic aid was suspended.(7)

Arab satisfaction was echoed by Al-Ahram of October 23, when it wrote:

> Of course it is natural that
> Arabs should feel heartened for
> this positive action on the part
> of Washington. It is a step in
> the right direction, and should
> be coupled with American economic
> and military aid to the Arabs.
> Our only hope is that the United
> States will sustain an honest and
> just policy in the Palestine case,
> for this is the only way for
> Washington to restore Arab confi-
> dence.

Arab satisfaction, though, was short-lived, for only eight days later, on October 28, American aid to Israel was resumed in a statement by Dulles.(8) This resumption came only one day after Israel announced her agreement to suspend temporarily her diversion of the river. Al-Ahram of October 30, made a bitter note of this timing, and that part of the Dulles statement which threatened both Arabs and Israel that the United States would suspend aid to both if these acts of violence did not stop. And even though Israel promised, according to the Dulles statement on the resumption of aid, "in the future to cooperate with the Council's efforts to reach a solution" of the Jordan Valley project, she proceeded to divert unilaterally the Jordan River after the Arabs rejected the Johnston proposals. And by 1964 the Israeli diversion works were completed without ever reaching an agreement with the Arabs. Meanwhile, Israel took what she felt was her due from the Jordan River waters.(9) Arab complaints to the three Western powers since have failed to stop Israel from diverting the river or to convince the Western Powers to

---

6
7Lenczowski, p. 361.
7Ibid.
8Department of State Bulletin, November 16, 1953, pp. 674-675.
9Kathryn B. Doherty, "Jordan Waters Conflict," International Conciliation, No. 553, 1965, p. 16.

force Israel to do so.(10)

The Arab states directly concerned with the Johnston mission were completely dissatisfied with the original plan Johnston proposed for dividing the river waters. His proposals were based on a study and report prepared by Gordon Clapp of the Tennessee River Valley Authority and accepted by the State Department.(11) According to these proposals, Israel's share of the river waters would be approximately 394 million cubic meters (mcm), Jordan was allotted 774 mcm, and Syria 45 mcm. The announced principal purpose of the whole river scheme was to make possible a start toward a permanent settlement of the Palestine Arab refugees.(12) The plan called for the building of a dam across the Yarmuk River, the Jordan River's main tributary and a reservoir to store 500 mcm of water.

In the Arab view, the fact that the three major tributaries of the Jordan River spring entirely from Arab territories,(13) the largest being the Yarmuk River in Jordan, and in view of the fact that the announced principal purpose of the whole project was to help alleviate the destitute conditions of the Palestine Arab refugees, the largest percentage of water given to Israel could not help but bring Arab refusal of this proposal. Arab dissatisfaction becomes more obvious when one notes the disparity in population between Israel and the three Arab states concerned. The three Arab states involved--Syria, Lebanon and Jordan--had then approximately 7 million people and Israel had about one million. Therefore, one Arab state after the other refused Johnston's proposals. This rejection was repeated three times in the course of the next two years, until his mission was finally given up for failure.(14) Jordan first rejected it on November 14, 1953 and Syria and Lebanon rejected it on November 17.(15)

Johnston eventually made four trips to the Middle East in

---

[10] The government of Jordan, for example, summoned the Ambassadors of Britain, France and the United States on November 2, 1954, and asked them to call on Israel to put an end to her unilateral diversion of the river. Current History, XXVII (1954), p. 328.
[11] Middle East Journal, VIII (1954), p. 75.
[12] Ibid.
[13] Don Peretz, "Development of the Jordan Valley Waters," Middle East Journal, IX (August, 1955), p. 400.
[14] Stevens, "The Jordan River Valley," p. 272.
[15] See New York Times, November 15 and 18, 1953 respectively.

pursuit of gaining Arab-Israeli agreement on a unified Jordan
Valley Authority, and failed. His last trip came in August,
1955(16) His original plan was modified by 1955 but still remained a far cry from the Arab Plan prepared in 1954 by the Arab
League Technical Committee, which allotted Israel approximately
20 percent of the Jordan waters.(17) The following chart shows
the final three plans proposed: one proposed by Johnston called
the Main Plan, the Cotton Plan proposed by Israel, and the Arab
Plan.(18) The Israeli Cotton Plan proposed to draw on two wholly
Arab rivers in Syria and Lebanon, not figured by either the Main
Plan of Johnston or the Arab Plan.

Amount of million cubic meters (mcm) of water allotted to
each state:

	Main Plan	Arab Plan	Cotton Plan (Israel)
Lebanon	---	35	450.7
Israel	394	182	1,290
Jordan	774	698	575
Syria	45	132	30

The political and economic reasons for the rejection of
the Johnston plan were summed up in an article by Al-Ahram on
February 10, 1954. It began by calling the plan "a basically
Zionist one; based on the Zionist Dr. W.C. Lowdermilk plan of
1944."(19) This "impartial" proposal, wrote Al-Ahram, was mainly
designed to irrigate the Israeli Negev desert and not the valley
of Jordan as it professed to do. The Arabs, therefore rejected

---

16 Stevens, p. 272.
17 Doherty, pp. 22-26.
18 Taken from Peretz, p. 407.
19 Michael G. Ionides, British Director of Development in the
government of Jordan from 1937 to 1939, in a well-documented
article, agrees with the relationship between the Lowdermilk and
Johnston plans. "The Disputed Waters of Jordan," Middle East
Journal, VII (1953), pp. 153-165; Lowdermilk's plan was elabora-
ted upon in his book, Palestine, Land of Promise (New York:
Harper Brothers, 1944); Johnston himself, therefore, was charged
by the Iraqi government as being a Zionist and was refused an
Iraqi visa to enter the country in October, 1953. He was
finally allowed to enter in an unofficial capacity on November 1,
1953, "in response to a special request from Dulles," according
to Al-Ahram, November 2, 1953.

it for the following reasons:

1. It gave a lion's share of water to Israel even though Israel had no tributary adding to the Jordan waters.

2. It aimed at settling more Zionist refugees in the Negev desert, hence adding to the military aggressiveness of Israel.

3. It was not designed to alleviate the plight of the Arab refugees as it presumed to do.

4. Diversion of the Jordan River would lower the level of the Dead Sea. This would adversely affect the mining projects of the state of Jordan located on that sea. (Salt and Potash mining, ed.)

5. It would also adversely affect the sites of a number of Christian Holy Places in the state of Jordan. Such a site, for example, is the Baptisimal Place on the River Jordan, the object of pilgrimage for thousands of Christians every year.

6. It would add to the salinity of the river and would eventually ruin Jordanian farms on the course of the river.

7. It would also mean implicit recognition of the state of Israel.

8. The Arabs insisted that the Jordan Valley Authority should be supervised by an international body, and Israel refused such a proposal.(20)

Again, while Johnston was practically on his way for the

---

[20]See also a statement by the Lebanese Delegate to the United Nations, Dr. Charles Malik, published in Al-Ahram, January 23, 1954, following the same lines as this article; see Peretz, pp. 407-408 on this last point—No. 8.

second trip in June, 1954, Egyptian newspapers(21) attacked the Johnston proposals. Al-Ahram anticipated his arrival by charging in a lead article on May 18, 1954 that the whole Jordan Valley scheme was becoming a major method of the United States of putting pressure on the Arabs to recognize Israel at any cost.(22) It quoted at length from an interview with Hussain Khalidy, Foreign Minister of Jordan at the time of the first Johnston trip to Jordan, October, 1953. According to Al-Ahram, Khalidy said:

> As I met with the American Special Envoy, Mr. Johnston, he told me that Jordan as well as the rest of the Arab states should be practical and recognize how powerful Israel is militarily. He added that Israel is very powerful in the outside world, and that great powers back her, and that she is in the Middle East to stay regardless of what the Arabs think of her.
> Needless to say, I thought then, as I do now, that that private statement of Johnston was a very strong form of open pressure. And as I submitted my resignation later to the King, I submitted a note to my government advising it not to allow Johnston again to Jordan.(23)

With the Arabs in this frame of mind and suspicious of the very nature of the Johnston mission as well as the very character of Johnston himself, it was easy to see why his mission ended in failure. The failure of his mission was essentially a failure in the Arab mind of the Eisenhower-promised "impartiality"; and while the Arabs rejected the original Johnston proposals, Israel "let it be known that it was keeping an open mind on the project."(24) This seeming agreeableness on the part of Israel gave her supporters in the United States further ammunition to portray the Arab states as uncooperative, while portraying Israel

---

21 Al-Gumhuriyah, June 13, 1954; Al-Ahram, May 18, 1954.
22 Al-Ahram, May 18, 1954.
23 Ibid.
24 Calvocoressi, p. 145.

in a favorable, peaceloving role in the American press and communication media. Arab spokesmen and diplomats felt this situation was very unfair. It prompted such charges as that made by
Abdel Khalik Hassouna, Secretary General of the Arab League, in
a speech to the Overseas Press Club in Washington on November 3,
1953 that the American Press and other media of communications
were openly biased in favor of Israel, and colored the facts of
the Middle East accordingly.(25) The American Press, he charged,
deliberately misinformed the American people on the Palestine
question, and American reporters in the Arab world were subject
to "the censureship of the friends of Zionism" in the United
States. This, he stated, made it impossible for the American
people to see all sides of the coin in the Middle East. Hassouna
also stated that American diplomats and observers in the Arab
world "who of course know better than what is being reported in
the United States," complained that even though they furnished
their home presses with the real facts, they either refused to
publish reports that were unfavorable to Israel, or they edited
these facts to justify the Israeli position first and foremost.(26)
Arab frustrations over this situation, says a thoughtful Arab
intellectual, Dr. Boutros B. Ghali, and Arab resentment of the
"perpetual betrayal" by the West of their cause, finally convinced the Arabs that "no dialogue with the West was possible."(27)

Meanwhile, and to repeat again, neither Arab complaints nor
lack of Arab agreement due to what they felt was an unjust American proposal to divide the Jordan River waters, stopped Israel
from unilaterally diverting the Jordan River. And by 1964 the
Israeli diversion works were completed--another case of Israeli
politics of fait accompli since 1948. Nevertheless, all this
went on somehow unpublicized in the United States.

---

[25] Al-Ahram, November 15, 1953. The New York Times, for example,
saw fit to ignore reporting this important speech from the
spokesman of the Arab League. See Chapters VI and VII entitled "The New York Times, et al," and "Magazines, Radio and
TV, Too," of Alfred M. Lilienthal, The Other Side of the Coin:
An American Perspective of the Arab-Israeli Conflict (New York:
The Devin-Adair Company, 1965), pp. 112-163, verifying Hassouna's
point.
[26] Al-Ahram, November 15, 1953.
[27] "Foreign Policy of Egypt," Foreign Policies in a World of Change.
Edited by J.E. Black and K.W. Thompson. (New York: Harper and
Row, 1963), p. 342.

Chapter IV

America, Egypt and the Defence of the Middle East: 1952-1955

    The Free Officers republican revolution in Egypt against
King Farouk occurred on July 23, 1952. Seemingly it enjoyed the
instant sympathy of the American Ambassador to Cairo then,
Jefferson Caffery. According to the leading newspaper Al-Ahram,
the new Egyptian leaders got directly in touch with Mr. Caffery
and informed him of the aims of their revolution.(1) Caffery
was then asked to contact the British Ambassador, Ralph Stevenson,
and inform him that the revolution was purely a domestic affair
and that the Free Officers would not tolerate any British interference with it.

    The development of early friendly contacts between the
Free Officers and Mr. Caffery understandably annoyed the British.
George Kirk, an English historian, sardonically comments on this
new friendship and also the favorable American press reaction to
the new Egyptian leaders in this fashion:

> General Naguib...had been quick
> to establish good relations with the
> cordial American Ambassador, Mr. Jefferson
> Caffery; and to many American commentators,
> the Egyptian revolution had seemed to offer
> a heaven-sent opportunity for removing the
> obstacles which had hitherto prevented the
> inclusion of the Middle East in the Western
> Scheme for the containment of Russian ex-
> pansion. Many of the cherished stereo-
> types of the American tradition were re-
> produced in the person of General Naguib--
> the serious soldier assuming the highest
> responsibilities in the state in time of
> crisis; the supplanter of the tyrannical
> king . . . the abolisher of medieval
> titles. . . the buster of trusts and
> privilege . . . and Egyptian publicity
> for its part did not fail to invoke, in

---

[1] Al-Ahram, July 25, 1952, Mr. Caffery was Ambassador to Egypt
from 1949 to 1955. He was already the object of Egyptian respect even before the Free Officers revolution.

favor of its national aspirations,
the Declaration of Independence and
the Atlantic Charter, precedents dear
to American minds. The only obstacle
remaining to the identification of
General Naguib's Egypt with the 'free
world' was, it seemed, the analogue
in 1952 of the red-coated Hessians
of the American Revolution--the
presence of British troops and authority in the Canal Zone and the Sudan;
and an American correspondent reduced
the British case for being there . . .
to a mere survival of 'old-style'
colonialism.(2)

There was no mistake in the fact that the United States--
hoping for a change from the Farouk government opposition to
Middle East defence plans since 1951--was favorable to the new
regime. The Free Officers also hoped for American sympathy and
aid in the difficult task that lay ahead of them in managing
the sad political and economic affairs of Egypt. They also hoped
for American prodding of Britain to satisfy Egyptian national
demands over Suez and Sudan. There was also the ever-present
Arab hope in general that the United States would see eye-to-eye
with them on the issue of Palestine.

In this atmosphere of mutual expectations, a study tour by
some American Congressmen in Egypt at the beginning of August
hailed the new military regime and its forward-looking objectives,
and its proposed sweeping reforms.(3) On August 7, 1952, General
Naguib in a press interview in Cairo made a bid for American arms
aid. He pledged that any American equipment given to Egypt would
not be used for aggression against Israel.(4) According to the
New York Times of August 10, 1952, this was seen by some American
sources as another hint of closer ties to the West. Between

---

[2]Kirk, "The Egyptian Revolution," Peter Calvocoressi, ed., Survey
of International Affairs, 1952 (London: Oxford University Press
for R.I.I.A., 1955), p. 220. The correspondent to whom Mr. Kirk
referred is from the New York Herald Tribune, November 21, 1952.
[3]New York Times, August 10, 1952.
[4]Ibid., August 7, 1952.

August 25 and 27, 1952, the civilian Prime Minister under Nabuib,(5) Ali Maher, conferred with American Ambassador Caffery over military aid to Egypt and the enlargement of the American Point Four Program there.

The official American approval of the new Egyptian regime came in a statement made by Secretary of State, Dean Acheson, in a press conference on September 3, 1952:

> There have been some encouraging developments in Egypt since we last met together, including the reform program announced by the Egyptian Government. We are following events with much interest and we wish Prime Minister Ali Maher and his civilian and military colleagues every success in their efforts to solve the internal problems of their country.
>
> Relations between the United States and Egypt remain most friendly and cooperative. I am hopeful that in the interest of our two countries these relations as well as those between Egypt and all the nations of the free world, will be increased and strengthened. We look forward to an era in which new areas of cooperation and mutual benefit can be brought into being.(6)

On August 22, 1952 the new regime captured a number of "Communists" charged with inciting and instigating riots ostensibly because of the regime's apparent friendliness to the West. Soon, the British and the Egyptians were in the process of solving one of their outstanding problems--the question of the future of Sudan. Throughout August, September and October, numerous conferences took place between the British Ambassador and the new leadership in Cairo over this question. These negotiations were

---

5The Free Officers kept a semblance of civilian government until September 8, 1952, when Ali Maher was asked to resign. Naguib then assumed the role of Prime Minister and proceeded to purge the political parties in Egypt.
6Department of State Bulletin, September 15, 1952, p. 406.

successfully concluded by bringing into force the Self-Government Statute for Sudan on October 22, 1952. This success did not come about without United States prodding and friendly pressure on both governments.(7)

The acceptance of self-government for Sudan was a major compromise on the part of the Free Officers government. For, ever since the nineteenth century Egyptian nationalists spoke of the "unity of the Nile Valley" and claimed Sudan as part of Egypt. Britain, though, had blocked such Egyptian claims and such a unity.

It was hoped by the Free Officers that by compromising on the issue of Sudan (while for the time being de-emphasizing the Palestine question) they would finally accomplish the solution of their top priority demand on Britain: evacuation of the British forces from the Suez bases. Their diplomatic strategy worked, for their willingness to compromise, according to Cremeans, "persuaded British officials, and American diplomats that they were faced with a new kind of regime with which the West might be able to do business."(8) Therefore, and "with the friendly assistance of the United States,"(9) the final agreement between Britain and Egypt over the future of Sudan was signed on February 12, 1953.

The United States was naturally gratified by this development. Two days later, February 14, 1953 the new Secretary of State, John Foster Dulles, sent a congratulatory note to British Foreign Secretary Anthony Eden. It is easy to detect from this note that foremost on Mr. Dulles' mind was an Egyptian military association with the West.

> Achievement of the Sudan accord by
> the British and Egyptian Governments
> is indeed gratifying to the United
> States. . . . This amicable accord
> may well be the first step toward
> the establishment of more fruitful
> associations in an area of critical

7
See J.C. Hurewitz, Diplomacy in the Near and Middle East, Vol. II (Princeton: D. Van Nostrand, 1956), p. 335.
8
Charles D. Cremeans, The Arabs and the World (New York: Frederick A. Praeger, 1963), p. 139.
9
Hurewitz, Diplomacy. . . , p. 335.

importance to the security of the
free world.(10)

Another note was sent the same day to Dr. Mahmoud Fawzi,
Foreign Minister of Egypt.

> The United States is gratified
> that an agreement on the Sudan has
> been arrived at by Egypt and the
> United Kingdom. This is a truly
> important occasion. It affords an
> opportunity for me to express my
> Government's pleasure at the spirit
> in which these difficult negotiations
> were carried out.
>
> My Government trusts that the
> same spirit of good will and cooper-
> ation will characterize the transi-
> tional period preceding the decision
> by the Sudanese people of their future
> status. . . . My Government continues
> to follow with interest and sympathy
> the progressive attitude and energetic
> efforts of the Government of General
> Naguib to meet and overcome the in-
> ternal problems which face the Egyptian
> people. The United States wishes the
> Egyptian Government every success in
> its efforts.(11)

MR. DULLES'TRIP TO THE MIDDLE EAST

Mr. Dulles' concern about the threat of Soviet encroachment
on Western influence in the Middle East was apparent from the
very first few days after he assumed the office of Secretary of
State. For only six days later in an address to the American
nation (January 27, 1953) he stated:

> In the Middle East, we find that
> the Communists are trying to in-
> spire the Arabs with a fanatical

10
11Department of State Bulletin, February 23, 1953, pp. 305-306.
Ibid.

53

hatred of the British and ourselves. That area contains the
greatest known oil reserves that
there are in the world, and the
Soviet interest is shown by the
fact that Stalin, when he was
negotiating with Hitler in 1940,
said that the area must be looked
upon as the center of Soviet aspirations. If all of that passed
into the hands of our potential
enemies, that would make a tremendous shift in the balance of
economic power. And furthermore
this area also has control of the
Suez Canal and that is the portion
of the world. . .which has long
been guarded and called the life-
line which made it possible for
Europe to be in communication with
Asia. There are difficulties at
the present time between the question
of the defense and control of the
Suez Canal.(12)

The difficulties to which Mr. Dulles alluded were partially
solved by the February 12, 1953 Anglo-Egyptian agreement on
Sudan. Nevertheless, relations between Great Britain and Egypt
remained tense after that. The Egyptians, now more than ever,
were becoming impatient with what seemed to them British delaying
tactics in regard to the question of British evacuation of the
Suez canal zone. In fact the same day the Sudan accord was
signed, General Naguib stated in a press conference, that he
hoped the accord would pave the way for immediate talks on the

---

12
Department of State Bulletin, February 9, 1953, pp. 213-214.
One is hard put to discover what Communist 'inspiration' he had
in mind, since he never did explain. It is possible he referred to Communist agitation mainly for home-consumption.
Nevertheless, the frequent reference by American political
leaders to Arab nationalist demands as Communist agitation, was
not only puzzling, but extremely resented by the Arabs. For an
expose of why such misleading references were made, and who in-
stigated and then perpetuated such false misconception of Arab
nationalism, see M. Ionides Divide and Lose, pp. 221-222.

British withdrawal from the Canal zone.(13) Three days later, on February 15, 1953 Foreign Minister Fawzi reported to the press that his Government had officially informed the British Ambassador, Ralph Stevenson, that Egypt was ready for talks on British evacuation. As there was no immediate and satisfactory response from the British Government, the Free Officers resorted to threats of guerilla action against the British forces in Egypt. Finally, the British Government on February 27, 1953 stated its terms before negotiations could be started on the future of the Suez Canal. In these the British insisted on Egyptian agreement to the return of British forces in case of war, and that British or N.A.T.O. technicians should remain behind to oversee military installations there. The Royal Air Force was to be allowed also to share with the Egyptian Air Force eight bases in the Canal zone. It was suggested that if Egypt accepted these terms, substantial American and British economic aid would follow.

Since this seemed to the Egyptians not much progress from the then present British occupation of the Canal area, they refused these terms and a deadlock followed. On March 3, 1953 Ambassador Caffery offered his good offices in the dispute. His attempts failed, and the Anglo-Egyptian situation worsened considerably throughout the months of March, April and May.

Dulles' announcement of a forthcoming trip by him personally to the Middle East might have had a direct effect on the hardening of the Egyptian attitude toward the British. For on March 8, 1953 the Egyptian Foreign Ministry reported that Dulles was planning to visit Egypt in May.(14) This was confirmed a day later by Dulles in his press conference. On the same day, General Naguib declared that Egypt was determined by all means, including force, to secure an unconditional evacuation of British toops from the Suez Canal zone.

Dulles' announcement of his forthcoming trip came after a series of conferences with Foreign Minister Eden, who had been on a visit to Washington since the 4th of March. Eden's trip to Washington, and now Dulles' announcement of his trip to the Middle East, caused uneasiness in Cairo. The Egyptians, it seemed,

---

[13]New YorkTimes, February 13, 1953. In the same press conference, he hailed Ambassador Caffery's role in the accord and stated that he planned to visit the United States soon.
[14]Al-Ahram, March 8, 1953.

were worried lest their unilateral problem with Britain over the evacuation issue would turn into a tripartite discussion which might make British troop evacuation conditional on Egypt joining a Western defence pact.(15) "The Egyptian wariness was further increased," according to Calvocoressi, "when on 14 March General Naguib and Dr. Fawzi received the British Ambassador, accompanied by his American colleague, Mr. Jefferson Caffery. . . ."(16) General Naguib immediately informed the British Ambassador that his Government was not prepared to issue an invitation to the United States Government to join in the talks.(17) Two days later, Nasser also made a statement to the press in which he rejected any official United States role in the Suez talks. Caffery's role, said Nasser, was to be strictly a mediation role, and only then, when asked.(18)

This Egyptian rebuff to the formal involvement of the United States in the Anglo-Egyptian problems delayed the start of negotiations until April 27. The start of these negotiations could be attributed to a somewhat conciliatory statement made by Nasser on April 11, 1953.(19) In it he admitted that the Egyptians could not maintain the Seuz bases unaided; therefore, Egypt would accept British technicians to maintain the bases. And perhaps further baiting Britain to compromise, Nasser stated that since the **Arab** states were all weak and very anxious to strengthen their defences, they could not find better friends than the West to help them do that. Nasser, however, refused to yield on the future use of the base by the West since any commitment of this kind would be premature on Egypt's part, in his view, before getting satisfactory solutions of her problems with Great Britain. He did not, however, bar the use of the base to the Arab states, united militarily since 1950 under the Arab League Collective Security Pact. This largely

---

15Calvocoressi, Survey of International Relations 1953, p. 164. Britain on the other hand was hoping to make an agreement on the troops and installations in the Canal Zone a part of a wider agreement on the defence of the Middle East: In other words, to make British withdrawal conditional upon a new treaty of alliance.

16Ibid.

17Calvocoressi, p. 163. New York Times, March 15, 1953, p. 1. This was reported by Mr. Selwyn Lloyd in a speech in the House of Commons, May 13, 1953. See Denise Folliot, ed. Documents on International Affairs 1953, p. 345.

18New York Times, March 17, 1953.

19Al-Ahram, April 12, 1953. New York Times, April 13, 1953.

paper-pact was mentioned time and again by Naguib and Nasser as--
when and if given Western military equipment--a satisfactory basis
for the defence of the Arab homelands against any threat. London
chose to negotiate possibly to avoid anticipated moral pressure
from Dulles who was soon to arrive in Egypt. The discussions that
started April 27 were broken off though on May 6, only five days
before the scheduled arrival of Dulles in Cairo. Their break was
followed by violent speeches by General Naguib, one of which was
made the same day Dulles arrived. In this he charged the British
with complicating a simple matter: Egyptian self-determination
and independence in a period in which the old style imperialism
was supposedly ended. Moreover, he threatened that if the Egyptian
demands were not accepted, Egypt would use force to get rid of
Britain.

Undoubtedly, the tense atmosphere in Cairo was in part
artificially created by the Egyptians to impress the arriving
Dulles with the urgency of the Anglo-Egyptian situation. Churchill's
speech in the House of Commons in answer to Naguib's statement
pointed this out, and also threatened British use of force in
Egypt in self-defence. In this speech, Churchill denied that he
sent an ultimatum to the Egyptian Government after negotiations
broke down,[20] and commented on Naguib's violent outbursts as
follows:

> It is likely that the outburst
> springs from a desire to impress
> Mr. Foster Dulles. . . . Of course,
> if the boastful and threatening
> speeches of which there has been a
> spate in the last few months, and,
> in some instances, even in the last
> few hours, were to be translated
> into action and our troops. . .were
> to be the object of renewed attacks
> by saboteurs or even by the Egyptian
> Army, which is being aided and trained
> by Nazi instructors and staff officers
> in unusual numbers. . .we should have
> no choice. . .but to defend ourselves.
> I am advised that we are entirely

---

[20] Refers to a Churchill note sent to General Naguib on May 7, 1953,
the contents of which were not divulged, according to Calvocoressi,
p. 166.

> capable of doing this without
> requiring physical assistance
> from the United States or anyone
> else.(21)

The use of the word Nazi made such good political mileage in Western minds that even Churchill could not resist the temptation to use it. Other parts of the speech, in the words of Calvocoressi, "included a nettling reminder of his lifelong sympathy with Zionism."(22)

It was in this kind of atmosphere that Dulles arrived in Cairo, accompanied by Mutual Security Director, Harold Stassen. Dulles spent two and one-half weeks in the Middle East, visiting most of the countries there from May 11-28, 1953. The announced purpose of his trip was made in Dulles' original statement to the press on March 9, 1953:

> As Stalin dies, General Eisenhower...
> has become President of our great
> Republic. . . .President Eisenhower
> is keenly aware of the importance of
> the Near East and South Asia. . .the
> President has, therefore, asked me
> to go personally to the Near East
> and South Asia to show our friendship
> for the governments and peoples of
> these areas. . . . I should like to
> mention, however, the underlying
> approach which will guide me during
> this trip. I am going to get first
> hand information. I shall listen
> carefully to what I am told and con-
> sider the problems presented to me
> with utmost sympathy. I shall not
> bring with me any specific plan or
> program, nor do I expect to ask the
> governments I visit for any decisions.
> I am going to renew old friendships,
> and, I hope, make new ones.

---

[21]Folliot,op. cit., pp. 342-344.
[22]Calvocoressi, p. 166.

> Needless to say, I am looking
> forward to this trip with keen
> anticipation. I shall be the
> first Secretary of State to visit
> these countries. I look upon this
> trip as an opportunity to dispel
> misunderstandings and to develop
> close relations between the United
> States and these friendly nations.(23)

Needless to say, this announced "keen" interest in the area
of the Middle East by the new administration in Washington, and
the high-sounding purpose of Dulles' trip was pleasing to the
governments of the area, including Egypt. In this instance, of
course, it was bound to encourage Egyptian national demands vis-
a-vis Britain. Nevertheless, since Dulles' trip was announced
after a series of discussions with Anthony Eden in Washington,
March 4-9, 1953, as mentioned earlier Egyptian leaders suspected
that Dulles would arrive in Cairo already influenced by the
British point of view on the Suez question.

The Egyptian suspicions seemed to be partially justified,
since when he arrived in Cairo, Dulles issued the following
statement:

> The administration of President
> Eisenhower gave prompt consideration
> of the defense of the Middle East and
> discussed with the British Government
> prior understandings which had been
> reached between the British Government
> and President Truman's Administration.
> We also had discussions relative to
> this matter with representatives of the
> Egyptian Government, both in Cairo and
> Washington.
>
> The defense and well-being of
> this important part of the world are
> inevitably of great concern to the
> United States Government. We came to

---

[23] Department of State Bulletin, March 23, 1953, p. 431. The only
decision one could think of, which Mr. Dulles said he 'would not
ask these governments to make,' is joining a Western defense
system. This was very much on the mind of Mr. Dulles and
Mr. Acheson before him.

the conclusion that there should
be a solution consistent with full
Egyptian sovereignty, with a phased
withdrawal of foreign troops—all
to be arranged however so that the
important base in the canal area,
with its depots of supplies and
systems of technical supervision,
should remain in good working
order and be available for immediate use on behalf of the free
world in the event of future
hostilities.(24)

The passing reference to Egyptian full sovereignty, while
emphasizing the defence of the Middle East, the prior under-
standings with the British Government, the phased withdrawal and
what amounted to a perpetual availability for immediate use on
behalf of the "free world" of the Suez bases—was apparently not
the sympathy Egypt had expected from Dulles. In fact, his statement was basically the British position on the question of Suez.
Therefore, it drew strong Egyptian criticism, and the typical
charge by the Egyptian newspaper, Al-Masri, that Dulles sought
Egyptian acceptance of the British solution to the Suez question.(25) Al-Ahram on May 12 wrote: "There is contradiction in
Mr. Dulles' logic. How could Egyptian full sovereignty be com-
promised with phased withdrawal of foreign troops and the availability of the base for immediate use by even the free world? Is
it possible that to Mr. Dulles the Egyptian sovereignty is only
words, or is it that Mr. Dulles really backs the British designs
in the area? Whichever, the Egyptians have great cause to be
disappointed."

The bitter Egyptian disappointment notwithstanding, Dulles'
trip to Cairo earned him some tongue-in-cheek remarks in the
British press. The London Times' comment is interesting to
quote, since it points out the basic dilemma in which the United
States found itself after the Second World War: to fulfill the
moral expectations demanded from her in the colonial world,
fighting to win complete independence from the European Western
powers; and simultaneously to avoid alienating these powers who
were also America's major allies:

24
  Folliot, pp. 341-342.
25 Al-Masri, May 11, 1953.

The broad purpose of the
tour is to help restore American
prestige in the Near East, which
it was admitted in a message to
Congress last week on the foreign
aid program 'had been deteriorating
rapidly.'(26) In particular the
Secretary of State hopes to be able
to contribute to a settlement of the
Anglo-Egyptian differences over the
Canal Zone. . . . The Secretary of
State will arrive in Cairo armed
with one persuasive argument which
the British are denied--the power
to give or to withold American financial and military aid. It is known
that the administration are determined to use all possible pressure
to remove obstruction to the formation
of the Middle East Command, which is
still a cardinal aim of American
foreign policy. The same arguments
will of course be used in Tel Aviv
as in Cairo to bring about an Arab-
Israel peace-- 'no peace, no aid.'

It is worth noting that the
administration specifies in its new
foreign aid programme submitted to
Congress last week that the military
aid programme to the countries "which
will assist in promoting plans for
peace between Israel and the Arab
nations," and in establishing a regional defence organization.(27)

It was of course the regional defence organization that
was uppermost in Dulles' mind when he arrived in Cairo. But the

------

[26] This is in reference to a statement by Harold Stassen, Mutual
Security Director, on May 5, 1953, describing to Congress his
Mutual Security program for 1954. Department of State Bulletin,
May 25, 1953, pp. 740-742. In it he stated that the United
States had lost prestige in the Middle East due to the loss of
Arab confidence in the United States mainly because of lack of
any solution to the Palestine question.
[27] London Times, May 11, 1953.

timing of his arrival was extremely unfavorable. This was due, first, to the very charged atmosphere over Egyptian disagreement with Britain on the evacuation issue. Second, the new Egyptian leaders had already made it clear before Dulles' arrival, as will be discussed below, that Egypt would not participate in Western defence pacts unless major Egyptian as well as Arab problems were solved satisfacotrily to them. For as long as these Arab regional problems were not solved, the Egyptians, like the rest of the Arabs, felt that their problems were being relegated to the background by the West, whereas defence against the Soviets was over-emphasized. Therefore, they suspected that this defence was aimed mainly at heading off Soviet competition in oil and strate-gic bases disregarding the well-being of the people of the region.

In regard to defence against a hypothetical Soviet menace, Egypt felt secure in the knowledge that before any invading Soviet troops could reach her, they would have to over-run Turkey, Iran, Syria, Iraq, Lebanon, Israel and Jordan, and by that time Western forces would presumably be in the Middle East.

Another reason for Egyptian balking on participation in Western defences was their (and other Arabs) suspicion that Israel might be invited to join such a pact; hence, de facto Arab recognition of Israel.

Finally, the Egyptians argued that if the Western powers were really interested in strengthening the defences of the Middle East, they could do so by giving arms to the already created Arab League Collective Security Pact.

TURKISH EFFORTS BEFORE DULLES' ARRIVAL, AND FAILURE

Turkish diplomats had been active in the creation of a joint defence system in the Middle East since October 1951. This was illustrated by the fact that Turkey was one of four powers, along with Great Britain, France, and the United States that pre-sented Egypt with proposals on October 13, 1951 to join a Western-sponsored pact.(28) The proposals were then rejected by Egypt, but Turkish interest in a defence system including the Arab states on its southern flank persisted. Hence, Turkey again joined the same powers in issuing new proposals on November 10, 1953 in which any Middle East state might voluntarily join the

---

[28] Department of State Bulletin, October 22, 1951, pp. 647-648.

proposed Middle East command. Again, the failure of the Arab states to respond, due mainly to Egyptian opposition, did not completely dampen Turkish interest in the project and Turkey continued to probe Arab leaders on the subject.

Among the Arab leaders who were sympathetic to the idea was Nuri as-Said, then Foreign Minister of Iraq, and to a lesser degree, President Adib Shaishakli of Syria and King Ibn Saud of Arabia. Nuri was of that breed of Arab leaders who grew up with the British (in Iraq) and chose to cast their lot for cooperation with them. His type hoped and believed that the Arabs could ultimately reach full independence through friendly negotiations with the British rather than by revolution and defiance.

Generally speaking, both Hashemite dynasties in Iraq and Jordan were of the same belief as Nuri. Iraq, also, was heavily dependent economically on the oil royalties from the British concerns there, mainly the Iraq Petroleum Company. Colonel Shaishakli's military coup in Syria on November 29, 1951 seems to have had American sympathy from the start. Before long his critics in Syria began to accuse him of being supported by the French-owned Bank of Syria and Lebanon, and by American interests.(29) At the same time, according to Calvocoressi, he was being hailed by Western commentators, "particularly in the United States," as a supporter of Western defence plans in the Middle East.(30) King Saud's sympathy to Western defence plans also stemmed from the fact that the whole economic destiny of his dynasty depended on his maintaining friendly relations with American oil companies there, especially the Arabian American Oil Company (ARAMCO), and with the United States.

Turkish diplomats, therefore, sought to work through these Arab leaders, especially Nuri, to bring about Egyptian cooperation. For this reason Nuri sent Dr. Fadil al-Jamali to Cairo in March 1952. He was a prominent Iraqi leader and then Chief of the Iraqi mission in the United Nations. There he discussed with the government of Hilali Pasha the defence of the Middle East, and also while there, he conferred with the ambassadors of Jordan, Syria and Lebanon.(31)

Egypt, then engrossed with Britain in the Sudan question, die not respond favorably to these overtures. The Iraqi interest,

---

29
30 Calvocoressi, Survey. . .1952, pp. 194-195.
31 Ibid., p. 195 and in the footnotes.
Akhbar al-Youm, March 21, 1952.

though, could not help but arouse Egyptian suspicion that Nuri
as-Said might breach Arab "solidarity" and have Iraq join a Western defence system. This Arab "solidarity" was not against the
defense idea in principle, but rather against it while the Arabs
had outstanding differences with the West. Therefore, while the
Egyptian government maintained correct relations with the Iraqi
government, articles in the Egyptian press began to appear
praising Arab unity and pointedly referring to the possibility
that Iraq might join a Western alliance. For instance, Al-Ahram
wrote on May 2, 1952:

> All Arabs and Arab states should
> be opposed to an alliance with the
> West, especially when there are
> still numerous national problems
> with the Western powers that need
> to be solved. . . . Nevertheless,
> there are indications that Iraq
> might join such an alliance, and
> that Iraq is to be the main line
> of Western defences against Soviet
> invasion of the Middle East, supposedly
> through Iran.

The official negative Egyptian response along with such remarks made Nuri as well as the Turkish government avoid pressing
the issue for the rest of the year. Furthermore, both governments were then awaiting the American Presidential elections in
November, to ascertain the attitude of the new administration in
Washington in regard to Middle East defence schemes. Therefore,
as soon as the Eisenhower Administration proved to have a keen
interest in the project, both governments as well as the United
States became active again in this regard. The Saudi government's
aid was also enlisted, mainly to help influence Egypt. For this
reason, Prince Faisal, Foreign Minister of Saudi Arabia, visited
Washington the first week of March 1953.(32) The Saudi quarrel
with Britain, however, over the possession of the Buraima Oasis
in southern Arabia limited Saudi willingness to cooperate. Turkey
then took the initiative for creating a defence system.

In early March, Turkish Prime Minister Adnan Menderes and
his Foreign Minister Fuat Koprulu went to Paris and conducted,
according to the New York Times, with the French Government of

---

32
New York Times, March 3, 1953.

Rene' Mayer "important discussions" in regard to the Middle East and its defences.(33)   The French Government, according to the report, felt that Turkey was in the best position religiously, historically and geographically, to convince the Arabs of joining Western defences.   According to Wells Hangen, Britain and the United States were also behind the Turkish effort, and hoped that Turkey would succeed in joining the rest of the Middle East with the Balkan and N.A.T.O. alliances.(34)

In a statement to the press in Paris on March 15, Menderes emphasized Franco-Turkish interest in the defence of the Middle East, and stressed the urgency with which the Arabs should view the creation of a Middle East command.

Incidentally, the history of Arab-Turkish relations before and after the Second World War does not justify the French and the general Western feeling that Turkey was in a good position to deal with the Arabs.   On the contrary, any Western remarks to that effect were bound to encourage rather than diminish Arab neutralist sentiment.   For there still was a latent resentment among the Arabs of the past harsh Ottoman rule, and the concept of Islamic solidarity had proved to be politically inoperative since the First World War when the Arabs rebelled and fought against the Ottoman Turks.   Also, Turkey was still involved in a major historical dispute with Syria over a number of possessions on the southern borders of Turkey.   Chief among these were the Hattay province and the port of Alexandretta.   For example, on July 3, 1953 and while Turkey was still hoping to enlist the Arabs into MEDO, a political crisis developed between Turkey and Syria.   This was caused by a speech made by Syria's President Shaishakli in Damascus in which he laid the usual claim to the province of Hattay, the province of Adana, as well as the port of Alexandretta.   The Turkish press reacted violently against this Syrian claim, and Turkish troop movements were reported on the Syrian-Turkish border.   The dispute was also in the headlines earlier, in April 1953.

Turkey also had already recognized Israel since 1951, and developed trade with her.   This fact drastically limited Turkey's effectiveness in dealing with the Arabs.   This point was exploited heavily by the Egyptian press when Iraq and Turkey finally decided to sign a military pact in January 1955.   In fact, Al-Ahram charged then that Turkey was working for International Zionism, backed by

---

33New York Times, March 11, 1953.
34New York Times, April 29, 1953.

65

the West. The purpose, it stated, was to divide the Arabs among themselves by separating Iraq from the other Arab states, and hence weakening them vis-a-vis Israel. With the Arabs divided, Israel could then proceed to force peace on them. Then, of course, there was the predictable feeling of jealousy on the part of Egypt that the Western powers were backing Turkey, a non-Arab state, to lead the Arabs. This naturally threatened Egypt's role as leader of the Arab states. In this regard also, the Soviet Union was diligently reminding the Arabs of past and present Arab grudges against the Turks.(35)

On March 23, a Turkish special envoy, one Fuad Khalousy, arrived in Beirut, Lebanon. His itinerary was to include also Iraq and Egypt. The announced purpose of his trip was to strengthen Turkish-Arab relations. He stated on his arrival that an Arab-Turkish alliance was well desired in Ankara, and for this purpose Menderes would soon visit Lebanon and Iraq. Two days later, an Al-Ahram correspondent learned in a special interview with Turkish Foreign Minister Koprulu that the latter wished to visit Cairo and meet General Naguib. In the course of the interview, and in an obvious bid to woo the Arabs, he completely backed the Arab position on Palestine, and voiced hope for an early Anglo-Egyptian agreement on the Suez bases. But he added that "Turkish foreign policy is a practical one, that aims at providing the Middle East with security, and hopes that the Arab states, and particularly Egypt, would join Turkey in pursuing such a practical policy."(36)

Fuad Khalousy, the Turkish special envoy, arrived in Cairo on April 2, and there he submitted, according to Akhbar al-Youm, a secret note from President Menderes. The nature of the note was not disclosed by Egyptian spokesmen, but it was speculated that it dealt, naturally, with defense. A day later the London Times reported that Eden would go to Ankara on April 7 to discuss with Turkish diplomats concerted efforts in regard to the proposed pact. These discussions were regarded by the Times as continuation of the Menderes-Eden talks in London two weeks earlier, while Menderes was visiting London.

Turkish diplomats also hoped that they would finally cap their efforts successfully with the Egyptians during the coming

---

[35] See for example, an article in Pravda, September 27, 1953, The Current Digest of the Soviet Press, Vol. No. 40 (1953), p. 34.
[36] Al-Ahram, March 27, 1953.

coronation ceremonies of King Faisal of Iraq. These ceremonies, to which all Arab heads of states, as well as the Turkish Prime Minister, were invited and expected to attend, were to take place on May 2, 1953. This was only ten days before Dulles' arrival in the Middle East. Therefore the Turkish Prime Minister pinned great hopes on this meeting with Arab leaders in Baghdad. But by that time a small crisis in inter-Arab relations had developed, which further hardened Egypt's attitude toward any defense gestures, and prompted General Naguib not even to attend the Iraqi coronation ceremonies.

The Arab League members were scheduled to meet in Cairo on March 28. This meeting, which Egypt asked for, was intended to precede Dulles' arrival in Cairo in May. Egypt was then anxious to have the Arab leaders agree on a mutual position regarding the major Middle East questions before Dulles' arrival. For this reason the Egyptian leadership made it very clear that they hoped that the Arab representatives to the Cairo meeting would be either a meeting of Arab heads of states or at least their foreign ministers. Rather, when March 28 arrived, neither the Lebanese, Iraqi, Jordanian nor the Saudi delegation included such figures. Reasons for such absence from a truly important Arab conference in Cairo were far from convincing. For instance, President Chamoun of Lebanon and his foreign minister were visiting Iraq on the heels of Khalousy's visit to both countries. This could not help but create the feeling in Cairo that both countries were working for a foreign power while relegating purely and extremely vital Arab issues to the background. King Hussain of Jordan was on his way to London to offer his condolences for the death of the Grandmother Queen Mary. Saudi Arabia offered no explanation. Egyptian disappointment was bitter, and was vented through the press. In his speech also opening the first session of the League, Egyptian Foreign Minister Mahmoud Fawzi demanded that the Arabs should strengthen the League if they wished it to survive and maintain a strong Arab bloc in these times of crisis.(37) He then added, "the day the imperial powers used to manipulate Arab leaders like puppets should be gone by now, and forever. Any such puppet still found in our midst should be crushed, so that the progress of the Arab nation would proceed apace, and its renaissance secured through strength and unity." A day later, Fawzi again invited Arab foreign ministers to come to Cairo before the arrival of Dulles.

37
Al-Ahram, March 30, 1953.

The storm that arose in Cairo over the Arab League session brought telegrams of apologies from all four Arab states,(38) and one Arab state after the other protested its solidarity with Egypt and its full adherence to Arab unity. Even the Iraqi government was brought into line with the Egyptian view, when on April 12 her foreign minister, Tawfig al-Suwaidi, made the following statement:

> It seems to Iraq now that there is
> no sense in discussing the defenses
> of the Middle East with the Western
> powers. We feel that each Arab state
> should acquire as much military equip-
> ment as possible from those powers
> who are concerned about military
> threats on the Middle East. We feel
> also that the Arabs should strengthen
> their own Arab League Security Pact
> of 1950, and that Iraq will not join
> any pact that might involve her forces
> in fighting outside the territory of
> the Arab states.(39)

Also in the pursuit of this new Arab solidarity, Prince Faisal of Saudi Arabia arrived in Cairo April 14 and President Chamoun arrived there on April 21, 1953.

Nevertheless, when May 2 came, which was the day of the coronation in Baghdad, General Naguib did not go. Instead he sent an earlier note of congratulation through the Iraqi Ambassador in Cario, Naguib al-Rawi. This, of course, was bound to strain Iraqi-Egyptian relations, and this strain eventually reached the breaking point in February 1955 when Iraq finally joined the Middle East pact in spite of Egyptian opposition. As explained above, the Iraqi leadership at that time, and es-pecially Nuri, saw their destiny lying definitely with the West. For the time being, however, Menderes did not meet Naguib, and the major objective of his trip to the Arab world had failed. As he left Baghdad for Ankara after the Iraqi coronation he should have been convinced that at least for the time being, his and other Western powers' approach to a Middle East defence which would include the Arab states, was not workable. A few days

---

38 Al-Ahram, April 4, 1953.
39 Al-Ahram, April 12, 1953.

later on May 7 the Arab League met again. This time its member
states were well represented. As was to be expected, there was
unanimous agreement on a list of Arab national demands that
were to be presented to Dulles on his arrival only five days
hence. These included five major points: a) Complete British
evacuation from Egypt without any prior conditions; b) The right
of the Arabs to defend themselves through their League pact;
c) Enforcement of the United Nations resolutions on Palestine;
d) Opposition to West Germany's reparations to Israel on behalf
of the world Jews, and its repercussions on the balance of power
in the Middle East. (The Reparation Agreement was concluded in
1952); e) The right of the Arabs of North Africa to self-determination.

Obviously, the Turkish failure with the Arabs created a
sense of frustration in Ankara, Washington and London. The
British reacted by suspending the Anglo-Egyptian talks on May 6,
one day after Menderes left Baghdad for Ankara. Five days later
Churchill, as mentioned before, made his violent anti-Egyptian,
anti-Arab speech in the House of Commons. The speech was construed in the Arab world as anti-Arab generally, since in it he
praised Zionism and reaffirmed his historical role in backing it
since the Balfour Declaration of 1917. For this, one Arab state
after the other sent protests to London.

Dulles' reaction was reflected in his statement made on his
arrival in Cairo. As mentioned earlier, this statement proved
very disappointing to the Egyptians. It is also possible that
by the time Dulles arrived, he had given up hope for the creation
of a Western defence system as proposed, and in the words of
Calvocoressi, "there was nothing for him to visit but its
grave."(40) The Egyptian rejection of the defence proposals came
finally in the form of a note handed by Naguib to Dulles on his
arrival to Cairo, May 12, 1953.

THE DULLES REPORT

The final realization on the part of Menderes and Dulles
that the Egyptians would not then join Western defences gave
rise to the idea of an alliance of the 'northern tier' states.

---

40 Calvocoressi, p. 119.

This was to be a pact similar to the Balkan Pact concluded
earlier that year. It was to include those northern non-Arab
Middle East states that border the Soviet Union, and were agree-
albe to creating such a pact on their own initiative. This idea
was accepted, it seems, by Dulles after he left the Arab states
on his way to Pakistan and Turkey. For, on May 22 and while
Dulles was still in Baghdad, the Foreign Minister of Turkey,
Fuat Koprulu, made a major statement to the press. In it he admitted the Turkish failure with the Arabs, than added that he
was anxiously waiting for Dulles' arrival in Ankara to discuss
the possibility of creating a Turkish-Pakistani-Indian alliance.
Therefore, while Dulles was in Pakistan, he emphasized the importance of regional defence, and reportedly influenced Pakistan
in favor of a Middle East defence pact along which lines Turkey
was thinking. Iran under the leadership of Musaddiq was obviously not considered then as a partner.

On May 27 Dulles arrived in Ankara. There, according to
the New York Times, Menderes proposed to him the immediate creation of the northern tier pact, and expected the United States
to allow Turkey a free hand in creating it. According to the
New York Times report, however, Dulles was still cool to the
idea since he was still leaning towards a pact that would include the Arab states as partners. But as this was not then
agreeable to the Arabs, he was seen as favoring informal military and economic pacts with individual states. This partially
explains the fact that the United States never joined the so-
called Baghdad Pact when it was organized in February 1955.
Nevertheless, the Secretary of State did not then stand in
opposition to any new Turkish initiative in this regard.

Reporting to the nation on his trip, on June 1, 1953,
Dulles discussed the diverse forces he had found at work in the
Middle East. The report also reflected the difficult task of
formulating in the area an American policy that would relatively
satisfy these diverse forces, and at the same time remain a
meaningful policy statement. But discouraging as this task
undoubtedly was, and although the report did not provide solutions to the problems of the region, it did include a number of
notable changes from the preceding administration policy.
These changes will be pointed out and analyzed along with general
comments on the report after a brief summary of the report itself.

Dulles began his report by stating that he was received with
warm hospitality wherever he went. He then emphasized the great
strategic importance of that area as the "bridge between Europe,

Asia and Africa." It was also most important, he said, as the source of three great religions. For these reasons the Soviet Union covets it, and for these reasons the United States should not "ignore its fate." The first country he specifically discussed was Egypt and the Anglo-Egyptian dispute over Suez. He voiced hope that "reason would prevail there," and that the tense situation in Egypt would not erupt into hostilities. He then extended a United States offer of assistance in bringing about a peaceful solution.

> The heart of the trouble is not
> so much the presence of British
> troops, for both sides agreed that
> they should be withdrawn, but the
> subsequent authority over and
> management of this gigantic
> base. . . . Experienced adminis-
> trative and technical personnel is
> needed to keep the base in operating
> efficiency and the provision of this
> personnel causes difficulty. The
> matter has an importance which goes
> beyond Egypt, for the base serves
> all Near Eastern and indeed Western
> security.

Dulles' assumption here apparently was that since the Suez Canal was important for the security of the Western world, Egypt should in effect compromise what she deemed her supreme interest --full sovereignty--in the interest of the West. One is reminded of Edward H. Carr's comment that Historian Arnold Toynbee (like Dulles then) was once able to discover that the security of Britain was the supreme interest of the whole world. Dulles went on to say:

> I am convinced that there is no-
> thing irreconcilable between this
> international concern and Egyptian
> sovereignty. We asked, with some
> success, that there be further time
> to find a peaceful solution. The
> United States is prepared to assist
> in any desired way.

Dulles then went on to discuss Israel, Jerusalem and the Arab refugees. He was impressed, he said, by the vision and energy with which the people of Israel were building their new

71

nation. He discussed the international character of the city of Jerusalem, which was "repeatedly emphasized by the United Nations." As for the Arab refugees, he said that at least some of them "could be settled in the area presently controlled by Israel," but most "could readily be integrated into the lives of the neighboring Arab countries," if American aid and other funds were available for irrigation and settlement projects.

He went on to mention his visits to Jordan, Syria, Lebanon, Iraq, Saudi Arabia, India, Pakistan, Turkey, Greece and Libya, and listed the major social and political problems of these countries, and offered United States moral and material aid to help solve them. He concluded his report by discussing six major policy issues and in each case proposing an American solution:

1. Colonialism. The countries he visited were suspicious of colonialism, and the United States was found suspect also "because, it is reasoned, our NATO alliance. . .requires us to try to preserve or restore the old colonial interests of our allies." He recommended, therefore, that "without breaking from the framework of Western unity, we could pursue our traditional dedication to political liberty." He then added:

   > In reality, the Western powers
   > can gain, rather than lose, from
   > an orderly development of self-
   > government. I emphasize, however,
   > the word 'orderly.' Let none for-
   > get that the Kremlin uses extreme
   > nationalism to bait the trap by
   > which it seeks to capture the
   > dependent peoples.

2. Living Standards. Here he proposed ways by which the United States, as well as these governments, could raise the standard of living of their people. American aid "wisely spent. . .will give the American people a good return in terms of better understanding and cooperation."

3. Arab Good Will. Dulles here proposed that the United States should seek to allay the deep resentment against it that has resulted from the creation of Israel. He said the Arabs are afraid that the United States "will back the

new State of Israel in aggressive expansion.
They are more afraid of Zionism than of
communism." The Israelis on the other hand
fear the Arabs. For this reason, he stated,
the United States, Britain and France made
the Tripartite Declaration of 1950. "That
Declaration when made did not reassure the
Arabs. It must be made clear that the
present United States administration stands
fully behind that Declaration. We cannot
afford to be distrusted by millions who
could be sturdy friends of freedom. They
must not further swell the ranks of
Communist dictators."

4. Peace Between Israel and the Arab Nations.
    Dulles suggested here that concessions on
    both sides could achieve peace, and that
    the United States was ready to use its
    influence to promote such a peace. How-
    ever, he did not mention specific con-
    cessions.

5. Middle East Defense Organization. Dulles
    here proposed the abandonment for the
    immediate future of the creation of a
    region-wide military alliance, but did
    not oppose the creation of a northern tier
    pact by those concerned:

> A Middle East Defense Organi-
> zation is a future rather than
> an immediate possibility. Many
> of the Arab League countries are
> so engrossed with their quarrels
> with Israel or Great Britain or
> France that they pay little heed
> to the menace of Soviet Communism.
> However, there is more concern
> where the Soviet Union is near.
> In general, the northern tier of
> nations show awareness of the
> danger.
>
> There is a vague desire to have
> a collective security system. But
> no such system can be imposed from

without. It should be designed
and grow from within out of a
sense of common destiny and
common danger.

While abandoning the region-wide pact, Dulles
suggested that the United States could "use-
fully help strengthen the interrelated defense of those countries which want strength,
not as against each other or the West, but
to resist the common threat. . . ."

6. Friendly Understanding. Here he exhorted the
people of the United States to respect the
thoughts and aspirations of the "proud people"
of that area.

There are a number of points in the report and about Dulles'
trip that are novel and need to be analyzed. In these, there are
significant changes in emphasis from the preceding American policy in the Middle East. First was the fact that this was the
first trip by an American Secretary of State to the area. This
was bound to satisfy the ego of the people of that area, and
also underscore the substantial development of United States
interest and responsibility in that strategic region in the
postwar period.

Second was the new emphasis put on traditional American dedication to political liberty, and how it should be pursued,
"without breaking from the framework of Western unity." This
again would be welcome to Egypt if possible to implement.

A third point in the report that was not fully explained
was how to reconcile the position of those colonial powers who
could not immediately see the "gain from an orderly development
of self-government," with Dulles' emphasis to states asking for
self-government on the word "orderly." One again cannot help
but think of Historian Edward H. Carr's charge that international
morality as expounded by the Anglo-Saxons since World War I
was little more than a convenient weapon against those who oppose
the status quo. Carr felt that since World War I Britain particularly followed the theory of pacta sunt servanda in the inter-
pretation and enforcement of agreements. That is, she insisted
on maintaining the status quo by emphasizing the sanctity of
treaty obligations--which treaties were often signed by her
vanquished opponents under duress.

A fourth point brought out in the report was the proposal of having an impartial American policy in the Arab-Israeli quarrel. The Arabs hoped that of course this would mean a more even-handed American policy as to the Palestine question.

Finally, Dulles proposed the abandonment, as sterile, of the creation of a region-wide pact and the acceptance of the 'northern tier' pact concept.

Generally speaking, Dulles report remained basically the guidepost of American diplomacy throughout the Eisenhower Administration. After its publication, the Arabs developed an attitude of watchful waiting to see if the Eisenhower Administration was serious in its resolve.

The official Egyptian comment on the report came in a statement made by Fuad Jalal, the Minister of National Guidance on June 3, 1953. While cautiously commending most of the report, he took issue with some of Mr. Dulles' comments on the Suez. He singled out the Dulles statement that the Suez had "an importance which goes beyond Egypt," and himself commented:

> It is the duty of every nation
> to defend the peace and security
> of the world. For this reason,
> the United Nations was created,
> and for this reason Egypt joined
> the United Nations. Within this
> context, therefore, Egypt guaran-
> tees the effective operation and
> safety of the Suez Canal, and
> guarantees its use for all the
> world.

A day later, General Naguib commented that the report was "not a bad one." Al-Ahram, however, took Dulles to task. And, since it is the major mouthpiece of the government and exerts a strong influence on the sophisticated Egyptian public opinion, it is of merit to discuss its reaction.(41)

41
Al-Ahram newspaper is usually referred to in Western presses as the "authoritative" Al-Ahram. Its editor, Mohammad Hassanein Haikal, was a friend of Nasser since before the revolution, and at times was used in official and semi-official capacities by the Nasser government. His paper usually spouts the official government opinion.

It is noticeable from Mr. Dulles'
report that two things are clearly
foremost on the American mind--
fighting communism, and the exploitation of the natural resources
in the Middle East. To him the
area's strategic location and its
wealth are to be defended from
Soviet aggression at all costs.

We would have liked Mr. Dulles
to mention openly and as is
apparent, that the imperial powers
are still there, and that they
rely on American arms to keep the
lid on small nations. This, of
course, is the thing that helps
communist expansion, and communist
danger to spread, not outright
Soviet invasion.

It is not enough for Mr. Dulles
to say in flattery that Egypt has
a great future ahead of it. He
should have told the American
citizenry in all honesty that
Egypt has grim days ahead of it
fighting the imperialists armed
with American arms. . . .(42)

These bitter remarks notwithstanding,the Egyptian press
from then on took a cautious attitude in order not to alienate
the United States. This was in hopes that the latter would
assume an active role in mediating the Suez dispute to the satisfaction of Egypt. The official government attitude was even more
careful.

After the Dulles trip and report begins the second phase
of American behind-the-scenes diplomacy to help bring about a
solution of the Anglo-Egyptian impasse. Again it was hoped in
Washington that if the Suez dispute were solved satisfactorily,
the last and major stumbling bloc in the way of creating a
Middle East defence system would have been cleared. Meanwhile,
and in accordance with the Dulles recommendations, the United
States attempted, as much as domestically possible, to be

42
Al-Ahram, June 3, 1953.

"impartial" in the Arab-Israeli issues. Also in the field of
arms supply the United States tried to redress Arab grievances
against what Prince Faisal Ibn Saud once called "the one-way
Tripartite Declaration of 1950." Thus on June 22, 1953 the
New York Times reported that the United States was offering separate bilateral arms aid pacts to the Arab states in a move to
bolster the area's defences. According to the report, the United
States was requiring as a condition that the Arabs would pledge
aid to the Western powers in case of an East-West struggle, and
that such arms would not be used for aggressive ventures. At
least the first condition was then not yet acceptable to Egypt,
and therefore American arms were not given. Also, since Eygpt
was on the verge of war with the British forces in the Canal
zone, any American arms would have been used against the British.
Therefore the United States shied away from offering Egypt such
arms. Egypt, for its part, did not accept the conditions attached
to the arms offer and set the tone for other Arab states to re-
fuse. For this reason, nine months were to pass before one Arab
state, Iraq, was to sign a military aid pact with the United
States. These American format pledges of arms aid to the Arabs
were repeated often in 1953, 1954 and 1955 but without actual
arms delivery to the Arabs. This was due to Israeli and Zionist
opposition, as well as Arab opposition to the conditions attached
to this aid.

Another aspect of the new American approach towards the
Arabs generally was the promise of economic and technical aid
to their countries. American offers though and any possible
gracious Arab acceptance of it, was hamstrung by the unsolved
regional political problems and Arab suspicion of American intentions. Typifying Egyptian reaction, Al-Ahram wrote on
May 15, 1953:

> There is no doubt that our world
> will benefit from the American aid
> if given. But this aid should be
> accepted only with the understanding
> that there will be no American interfer-
> ence in the internal affairs and the
> policies of our countries. Nor should
> it be a prelude for the establishment
> of an American sphere of influence in
> this part of the world. . . . For,
> even though we might be hungry physically,
> we are more hungry for justice and
> integrity. Therefore, besides initiat-
> ing an economic Point 4, it would do
> the United States good to initiate a
> political Point 4.

A special place for Egypt among the Arab States in the
Republican Administration foreign aid planning was first called
for by Harold Stassen, head of the Mutual Security Office. This
was in a special report by Stassen to the Senate in May, 1953.
In it he stated that Egypt should be given a special position, since,
first, she was the leader of the Arab world, and second, because
her new leadership was following steps that would bring Egypt
to closer understanding with the Western powers. Earlier in
March, Eric Johnston was sent to the Middle East as a special
envoy of Eisenhower to study the economic conditions of the
whole area. Johnston's visit gave rise to Arab hopes that size-
able American capital would be invested in their industrial development. On May 18, 1953 Eisenhower sent another special
envoy, Mr. Calbertson, to Egypt. There he met Egyptian indus-
trialists and bankers for the purpose, according to Al-Ahram, of
studying major Egyptian industrial projects which the United
States might aid in executing. Among these, the Aswan High
Dam project was most prominent. And for the first time major
articles about the dam began to appear in Al-Ahram and Akhbar
al-Youm, describing the project, and hopefully speculating on
how it might be executed.

Of course, these American visits were designed also to
soften the Egyptian attitude towards Egypt's participation in
Western defences. But as Dulles' trip failed to enlist Egypt in
a Western defence alliance, the United States economic aid to
Egypt also failed to materialize. From then on, the only major
project which the United States remained probing and hoping to
execute between 1953 and 1955, was the so-called Johnston Plan for
the Jordan River System--a T.V.A. of sorts for Syria, Jordan, and
Israel. This project was rejected consistently by the Arabs for
various reasons that were discussed earlier (Chapter III).

American aid failure to materialize was bound to further
the Egyptian suspicion that American aid offers were made a
sine qua non for Egyptian cooperation, disregarding, if necessary,
Arab and Egyptian political aspirations. It prompted the Deputy
Prime Minister, Gamal Abdel Nasser, to say on November 20, 1953
that even though Egypt had bound itself to accept Point 4 aid
before the new regime came to power, Egypt had received none of
America's assistance in the 14 months of the new regime.(43)

The contrast to Israel was most meaningful to the Egyptians.
From 1945 to 1955, the total United States grants and credits to

_____

43Middle East Journal, VIII (1954),p. 74.

Egypt came to 30 million dollars. Israel on the other hand was
given 370 million. Egypt had over 23 million people then, and
Israel about 1.5 million.(44)

NEW MEDIATIONS AND NEW ALIENATIONS

After the Dulles visit, the United States through its
Ambassador in Cairo, Caffrey, and other channels, resorted to the
old role of mediation between the Egyptians and the British over
the Suez dispute. Again it was hoped in Washington that if a
solution to this dispute was found, like the one over Sudan,
Egypt would join a Middle East Defence Organization (MEDO).(45)
The American effort, particularly Mr. Caffrey's, were in good
measure responsible for the final agreement over the Suez bases
achieved on October 19, 1954. This agreement, though, came after
a long and often interrupted (with threats and counter threats on
both sides) periods of discussion. But while the Anglo-Egyptian
negotiations were going on and off, until October, 1954, another
endeavor was being pursued in the Middle East by Turkey and Pakistan, and sponsored by the United States, that was bound to
affect Egypt. That was the creation of MEDO. Such an organization if concerned only with enlisting Turkey, Pakistan and/or
Iran, would not be of much concern to Egypt. But when it became
known that Iraq, an Arab state, was being asked to join, and
seemed agreeable, Egypt made it her business to interfere.

Ever since the earlier Western attempts at creating a defence system, Iraq was suspected in Egyptian circles of being
the weakest link in the "Arab Unity" chain. Egypt was still
anxious to keep a facade of Arab unity as a front against Britain
in the hope of solving the Suez question as an immediate objective. A united Arab front would later also bring about a favorable solution to the Palestine question. These Egyptian calcu-
lations were shattered by Iraq who, under the leadership of Nuri
as-Said, finally joined MEDO in February 1955. And by that
time the Iraqi government, the United States and the other members of the "Baghdad" Pact were the targets of Egyptian diplomatic attacks as well as open propaganda. In the melee the American good offices in the Suez dispute were lost. Lost, also,
were whatever efforts the Eisenhower Administration had exerted

---

44
  Harry N. Howard, "The Development of United States Policy in
  the Near East, South Asia and Africa During 1955." Part III,
  Department of State Bulletin, April 9, 1956, p. 593.
45
  Henceforth will be referred to as MEDO.

in the Palestine question and its attempt at compromise between
Israel and the Arab states.

MIDDLE EAST DEFENCE ORGANIZATION: A NEW APPROACH

It was soon apparent after the Dulles trip that the countries Dulles had in mind as having "a vague desire" to form a
collective security system were Turkey, Pakistan and Iraq.   Iran
was added to this list after the Musaddiq government was overthrown by General Zahidi on August 19, 1953.   Negotiations between the first two,Turkey and Pakistan, along with the United
States, proceeded soon after the Dulles trip to the Middle East.
Turkey's position was already clear, and her commitment to the
defence idea dated back to 1950.   Pakistan was recruited as a
result of Dulles' trip to Karachi on May 24, 1953.   The New
York Times then reported that Dulles was "successful" in influ-
encing Pakistan in favor of the MEDO idea.   Pakistan, it seemed,
was already favorably disposed to such a pact.   This was demonstrated by the Indian government protests and warnings from the
beginning of the year.   For in January 1953 a committee of the
ruling Congress party in India passed a resolution urging
Washington and London to be informed that the inclusion of Pakistan in a Middle East defence system would be regarded in
India as a hostile act.(46)   Pakistan remained favorable to the
idea.   An American gift to Pakistan of 700,000 tons of wheat in
the spring of 1953, and before the Dulles trip must have also
helped bring about this Pakistani disposition.

The fall of the Musaddiq government in Iran gave rise to
renewed Turkish-Pakistani contacts.   And in September 1953,
informal talks were reported to be taking place between Turkish
and Pakistani officials in Ankara.   In these talks both countries
also voiced hope that the United States would seek to enlist
Iran in MEDO.   In October and November 1953, the Commander in
Chief of the Pakistani army, General Ayub, was in Washington
asking for military aid, and admittedly was discussing with
United States officials the role of Pakistan in MEDO.   Pakistan's
request for military equipment was finally acted upon by the
United States on February 19, 1954.   This activity again brought
strong protests from India who reaffirmed its policy of neutrality.   A similar situation was to develop later when Iraq showed
active interest in MEDO, and Egypt opposed this but for different
reasons.   Hence developed close relations between Egypt and India,

---

46 Calvocoressi, Survey. . .1953, p. 118.

due to their mutual opposition to MEDO. Eventually both India and Egypt signed a treaty of friendship emphasizing their opposition to military blocs. Both also became leaders of neutralism and this leadership helped bring about the Bandung conference of April 1955.

In June 1954 Menderes was also in Washington and he, too, secured defence support aid from the United States on June 5, 1954. Meanwhile, an agreement of Friendly Cooperation had already been signed between Turkey and Pakistan on April 2, 1954, and ratified on June 12, 1954. This Turco-Pakistani alliance was to become the nucleus for the creation of MEDO.

IRAQI MEMBERSHIP IN MEDO AND EGYPTIAN REACTION

As mentioned earlier, Iraqi interest in joining a Middle East defence pact dates back to March 1952. This interest was spurred by the new Republican Administration's "keen interest" in such a scheme. But due to Egyptian opposition, the first approach to Middle East defence died out by the time of the Dulles trip to the area in May 1953. Nevertheless, the then Iraqi leaders remained interested in American arms and were agreeable to overtures aimed at the creation of a Middle East pact. This position, generally unpopular in the Arab world, forced such-minded Iraqi leaders to play a double role, and sometimes a clever one, of trying to keep a facade of Arab unity as long as possible, while working towards the creation of MEDO as discreetly as possible. As explained earlier, the Iraqi leadership at that time felt that the destiny of their country lay politically and militarily with Britain and the West.

Iraq formally and secretly requested American arms in March 1953.(47) This request was hinted at, but not revealed, in a speech by Iraq's then foreign minister, Tawfiq al-Suwaidi on April 12, 1953. While attempting in his speech to please the Egyptians by saying that there was "no sense now in discussing the defences of the Middle East with the Western powers," he added, "we feel that each Arab state should acquire as much military equipment as possible from those powers. . .who are interested in the defence of the area." The latter part of the Suwaidi speech, though, explained what was on his government's mind. It

47
  Hurewitz, Diplomacy. . ., p. 346.

cleverly kept the door open for future Iraqi adherence to the
proposed Western pact while giving the Egyptians and other Arab
states the impression that Iraq had resolved not to do so. It
read, "Iraq will not join any pact that might involve her forces
in fighting outside the territory of the Arab states." In other
words, it was possible for Iraq to join a Western pact, whereby
her forces would be used only in case of an attack on the Arab
states. There was always the possibility, also, that such forces
might be used in an attack on another Arab state. As the statement read, it could also mean that Iraq's forces would not be
used against Israel. In none of the above cases would Egypt,
aspiring to lead the Arab national movement, passively accept
Iraq's adherence to MEDO. And when American arms were finally
given to Iraq on April 21, 1954, with the inevitable non-aggression
proviso, Egyptian propaganda went to work against the Iraqi leaders, Turkey and the United States. For Iraq's acceptance of arms
with this condition, according to James W. Spain,

> ---must have important implications
> for the other Arab states. If as is
> already assumed, it means Iraq has
> 'signed itself out' of any future
> effort against Israel, the other Arab
> states' need for a decision is made
> more urgent. They face the choice
> of letting Iraq go, weakening the
> Arab League, and paving the way for
> other member states to defect, or of
> attempting to bring about enough
> pressure to force Iraq to abandon
> its new Western connection and re-
> submit its foreign policy to the
> direction of the League.(48)

Egypt chose to apply that pressure on Iraq as soon as it was
opportune. This pressure was mainly applied through her powerful
and newly created radio station, the Voice of the Arabs.

The Iraq arms idea, though, was not yet known to the
Egyptians. Even if Egypt had had any hints about the Iraqi dealings, it perhaps was not expedient then to challenge Iraq and the

---

48"Middle East Defense," Middle East Journal, VIII (Summer 1954),
p. 259. That part of the Military Assistance Agreement reads as
follows: "It is the understanding. . .that the Government of
Iraq will use such equipment. . .solely to maintain its internal
security and its legitimate self-defense, and that it will not
undertake any act of agression against any other state.

Western powers who were behind her, at a time when Egypt was still
hoping for British agreement to evacuate her territory, and hoping
for American good offices to secure this evacuation. Besides,
there was a hint in a personal letter from Mr. Eisenhower to
General Naguib early in July 1954 stating that simultaneously with
the signing of an Anglo-Egyptian accord, the United States would
enter into agreements with Egypt to help strengthen the Egyptian
armed forces.(49) Therefore, few direct official comments about
Iraq are noticeable up to October 19, 1954 when the Anglo-Egyptian
Agreement over the Suez base was finally ratified. Meanwhile,
though, the Egyptian leadership did not neglect warning other Arab
states to avoid joining MEDO until Great Britain yielded on the
Suez dispute. At that time, though, Egyptian warnings were mainly
directed against the new Syrian regime of Al-Asali which had overthrown Shaishakli regime in February 1954. For in March 1954, the
new Prime Minister Al-Asali hinted that Syria might join the
Turco-Pakistani alliance of February 1954, thus becoming the first
Arab state to do so.

The Anglo-Egyptian agreement over Suez, entitled "Heads of
Agreement," was signed on July 27, 1954. Upon its ratification
on October 19, 1954, Secretary of State Dulles issued the following statement:

> The signing of the final agreement
> between Egypt and the United King-
> dom on the Suez Base is an event
> of far-reaching importance and an
> occasion for renewed congratulations
> to both countries.
>
> This action. . .marks the success-
> ful resolution of a problem which
> has existed in some form for many
> years. . . . I believe that the
> removal of this deterrent to closer
> cooperation will open a new approach
> to peaceful relations between the
> Near Eastern states and other nations
> of the free world. It is my hope
> that this cooperation may now de-
> velop fully to the mutual advantage
> of all concerned and will strengthen
> the stability and security of the area.

49
   Sydney N. Fisher, The Middle East (New York: Alfred A. Knopf,
   1960), p. 622.

Egypt now assumes new and fuller
responsibilities as the military
base in the Suez Canal passes from
British to Egyptian control. I am
pleased to note that in accepting
these responsibilities, Egypt has
reiterated in the agreement its
adherence to the principle of freedom of transit through the Canal in
Conformity with the 1888 convention.(50)

For a while after this agreement was signed, it seemed as if
Dulles' hope for a "closer cooperation" with the Egyptian government, now headed by Gamal Abdel Nasser since April 1954, might be
realized. The initial agreement over Suez was signed in July
1954. In August the Egyptian government announced that Nasser
planned to visit Pakistan in November. This was seen as a good
omen in Washington. Washington's optimism, though, was short-
lived because a few days later, Nasser made the statement to the
press that any Arab defence pact with the Western powers must wait
for a while until the Arabs overcame the legitimate fear of
Western imperialism. He added that the Arabs would nonetheless
welcome Western military aid to the Arab League Security Pact of
1950, and that the Arabs were capable of raising between ten to
twelve divisions to defend the area.(51) But neither Dulles or
the over-anxious Nuri as-Said was ready to allow for so much time
to pass for the Arabs to "overcome their legitimate fears of the
West," and the latter especially proceeded to join the Turco-
Pakistani pact on February 24, 1955. This was done even though
only one month earlier in a meeting of the foreign ministers of
the Arab League, Iraq had 'agreed' with Egypt that the Arab
Collective Security Pact should be strengthened, and should take
exclusive responsibility for the defence of the Middle East.(52)
"In these circumstances, the sudden volte face of Nuri as-Said
had an air of insincerity and double dealing,"(53) which aroused
the ire of not only Nasser and his government, but Arab nationalists throughout the Middle East. "It was thus," wrote Nasser
later, "that the ill-feeling began between us and Nuri, and between us and America."(54)

50
51Department of State Bulletin, November 15, 1954, p. 734.
52New York Times, August 20, 1954.
   Geoffrey Barraclough, Survey of International Relations 1955-
531956 (London: Oxford University Press, 1960), p. 25.
54Ibid.
   Gamal Abdel Nasser, Where I Stand and Why (Washington: Press
Department, Embassy of the United Arab Republic, 1959), p. 4.

Whether the American-backed Iraqi action was wise, or whether the persistent American policy of viewing the Middle East primarily in terms of defence against the Soviet Union was correct, was hard to forsee at the time. But the subsequent reaction of Egypt, aggravated by the perennial Egyptian and Arab dispute with Israel, and the Western role in the Palestine question, all helped to call up the very Soviet "devil" the West was seeking to deter. From then on Egypt led the forces of opposition in the Arab world to the Western defence schemes and became one of the major proponents in Asia and Africa of the policy of neutralism in the Cold War. Needless to say, such Egyptian action was very pleasing to the Soviet Union who eventually 'leaped over' the MEDO alliance to enter the Arab political scene in the form of economic and military aid from 1955 and on.

CHAPTER V

The Soviet Tangent

Russian attempts in the last two centuries at winning a foothold in the Middle East have been numerous. Long before the establishment of the Soviet regime in 1917 Tzarist Russia looked constantly toward the Mediterranean in search of warm water ports. Throughout the nineteenth century Russia hammered away at the Ottoman Empire in the hope of inheriting parts of it. Russian hopes, however, were invariably thwarted by Britain who time and again upheld the territorial integrity of the Ottomans in the face of these persistent Russian attempts.

The First World War brought an end to the Ottoman Empire. As one of the defeated Central Powers, it was dismembered at Versailles by the victorious Allies. Russia, too, emerged from the war defeated even though she began the war on the Allied side. This was due to Lenin's capitulation to Germany when he accepted the severe terms of the Treaty of Brest Litovsk on March 3, 1918. It was difficult, therefore, for Soviet Russia to claim victory when the war was over. Nor could she claim any of the spoils of the Ottoman Empire that had been promised to her in the Sykes-Picot Agreement of May 1916.

Defeated and ostracized by the victorious powers, the Soviets nonetheless had ideological and subversive goals mapped out for the eventual attainment of world communism. The first and major aim of their foreign policy was the fomenting of world revolution. In industrial countries the working masses were to be incited to revolt against the capitalist regimes and establish communism. But in Asia and Africa there were two major obstacles to that type of revolution. First, there was little industrialization there, and, therefore, there was no proletariat to revolt; second, the European powers had divided these areas into colonial empires, and their presence there stood in the way of any direct contact between the Soviets and the people of these areas. Generally speaking, therefore, the Soviet tactic here was to develop through subversive propaganda anti-imperialist struggles and help organize revolutionary action for the purpose of throwing off colonial rule. And for the time being, Soviet-trained propagandists and revolutionaries were to ally themselves with local nationalists until

independence was secured.(1) Religion was to be used also in
these mostly non-Christian areas, to incite rebellion against the
colonial Christian powers. For this reason, Soviet-trained agi-
tators and diplomatic agents usually professed the faith of the
area to which they were assigned. Religious departments were established within the Communist Party in Moscow, and through these
departments, propaganda in the assigned area, communist training,
and general meetings were arranged.(2)

In November 1918 Soviet strategists called for a general
meeting in Moscow of Soviet communist Moslems to plan for action
in the Moslem world.(3) This meeting became known as the First
Congress of Moslem Communists. It resolved to create a Department
of International Propaganda for the Eastern Peoples, to be attached
to the Bureau of the Moslem Communist Organizations of the Russian
Communist Party. The task of this Department as outlined by the
First Congress was to

> conduct agitation among the peoples
> of the East, explain the Russian
> and the world revolution (to come),
> and gradually bring the revolutionary
> masses to an understanding of the
> idea of world communism.(4)

In order to carry out its activities more effectively, the
Department was divided into twelve sections. One of these sections was to be in charge of agitation in the Arab world.(5)

One year later, on November 22, 1919 the Second Moslem Congress convened also in Moscow, and was addressed by Stalin. In
closing his message to the delegates,he said:

> Let us hope that the banner raised
> by the First Congress, the banner of

---

[1]See generally A. Bennigsen, "The 'National Front' in Communist
Strategy in the Middle East," The Middle East in Transition, ed.
Walter Z. Laquer (New York: Frederick A. Praeger, 1958), pp.
360-369.
[2]Ibid.
[3]Xenia Joukoff Eudin and Robert North, Soviet Russia and the East
1920-1927, A Documentary Survey (Stanford: Stanford University
Press, 1957), p. 162.
[4]Ibid., p. 163.
[5]Ibid.

the liberation of the toiling
masses of the East, the banner
of the destruction of imperialism,
will be carried to the last with
honor by the workers of the Moslem
communist organizations.(6)

Soviet propaganda in the East took concrete form in an
assembly of over two thousand delegates representing thirty-seven
nationalities of Asia and Africa. This assembly met in the city of
Baku on the Caspian Sea from September 1 to 8, 1920. It was
addressed by the Chairman of the Executive Committee of the Com-
intern, Grigorii E. Zinoviev.(7) Like Stalin before, Zinoviev exhorted the assembled delegates to declare a holy war against the
colonial capitalists, and to join with the Soviets in that common
struggle.(8)

According to Laqueur, the designation "Middle East" meant to
the Soviets in the 1920's and 1930's mostly Turkey, Iran and possibly Afghanistan.(9) It is noteworthy, therefore, that in the Baku
Congress there was not one Arab representative present or invited.
The Turkish delegate, Enver Pasha, preposterously claimed the responsibility of representing "the revolutionary organizations of
Morocco, Algeria, Tunisia, Tripoltania, Egypt, Arabia and Hindus-
tan."(10)

The idea of fusing Soviet Moslems with those of the outside
world by attracting the latter to the communist fold seemed to
have been abandoned after the Baku Congress. "The Soviet government evidently feared that, so far from attracting their Moslem
neighbors into the Soviet fold, the peoples of the eastern republics might wish to break away from the union."(11)

6
Ibid., p. 164.
7Walter Z. Laqueur, The Soviet Union and the Middle East (New York:
Frederick A. Praeger, 1959), pp. 8-9; Eudin and North, op. cit.,
pp. 165-167, for full text of Zinoviev's address; an account of
the Baku Congress may be found in George Lenczowski, Russia and
the West in Iran (Ithaca, N.Y: Cornell University Press, 1949),
8pp. 6ff.
The word used by both was Jihad meaning in Arabic "holy war."
9Ibid.
10Laqueur, The Soviet . . . , p. 52.
11Eudin and North, op. cit., p. 81.
Geoffrey Wheeler, "Recent Soviet Attitudes Toward Islam," The
Middle East in Transition, ed. Walter Z. Laqueur (New York:
Frederick A. Praeger, 1958), p. 371.

There also followed, therefore, from then until 1953 a policy of segregation of the six Moslem Soviet republics from their co-religionists in the Middle East. There also followed a period of putting less emphasis on religion, and more use of the "national front" in undermining European rule and influence in the colonial world.(12) But most of Stalin's attention, particularly in the 1920's and 1930's, was directed toward Soviet state interests, rather than fomenting world revolution.

SOVIET-ARAB RELATIONS BETWEEN THE TWO WORLD WARS

Soviet-Arab relations in the inter-war period were extremely nebulous. This was due to the fact that most of the Arab world was under the direct or indirect rule of either Britain or France. And, there was no reason why these two powers should facilitate any contact between revolutionary Russia and their colonial wards. Only with Saudi Arabia and Yemen, two states really independent after the First World War, did the Soviet Union establish diplomatic relations, and some trade.(13)

After the First World War Yemen was the only Arab country that emerged united and independent.(14) The Soviet Union, therefore, was one of two powers that entered early into diplomatic relations

_____

12
  Ibid., p. 370. There is debate among scholars and observers of the Middle East over the compatibility or incompatibility between Islam as a religion and communism. There are those who insist that there are features in Islam that make communism abhorrent to it. Others disagree. For a debate of the two views, see Bernard Lewis, "Communism and Islam," The Middle East in Transition, ed. Walter Z. Laqueur (New York: Frederick A. Praeger, 1958), pp. 311-24; Nejla Isseddin, The Arab World (Chicago: Henry Regnery Co., 1953), p. 368; Nabih Amin Faris, "The Islamic Community and Communism," The Middle East in Transition, ed. Walter Z. Laqueur (New York: Frederick A. Praeger, 1958), p. 351.
13
  Lenczowski, The Middle East . . . , p. 524.
14
  Hijaz--later Saudi Arabia--emerged independent also, but was experiencing a civil war between the Hashemite and the Saudi families. This war ended in Saudi victory in 1926.

with Yemen in 1926.(15)   The Soviet Union then established a Consulate-General in San'a, the capital of Yemen, with one Karim Khan
Hakimoff, a Soviet Moslem, as the head of the mission.   In 1927 the
Soviet Consulate-General was raised to a Legation.(16)   On November 1,
1928 a treaty of friendship was concluded between Imam Yehya, King
of Yemen, and the Soviet Union.(17)

The Soviets apparently were very optimistic about the pros-
pects of their trade and diplomatic efforts in Yemen (as well as
in Saudi Arabia).   According to Laqueur, they regarded both Imam
Yehya and Ibn Saud of Arabia as the future rulers of greater Arabian empires.(18)

Hijaz is the western part of what is today Saudi Arabia.   In
the early part of the 1920's it was the scene of a struggle for
power between Abdel Aziz Ibn Saud, founder of the Saudi dynasty,
and the Hashemite family led by Prince Hussain of Mecca.   The
struggle ended in favor of Ibn Saud who on January 8, 1926 proclaimed himself king of all Arabia.   The Hashemite family was
evicted from Mecca.

Moslem and European powers were hesitant to recognize the
new regime in Arabia.   "But the tune was called by Russian policy
which, still loyal to the anti-imperialist principles of the Bol-
shevik revolution, hastened to accord de jure recognition of the
new regime . . ."(19) in February 1926.   A Soviet Consulate-
General was established at Jidda in 1927.(20)   This was raised to
a Legation two years later, and the same Karim Khan Hakimoff, head
of the Soviet Legation in San'a, also became head of the Soviet
Legation in Jidda.(21)

------

[15] The other power was Turkey.   H. St. John Philby, Saudi Arabia
(New York: Frederick A. Praeger, 1955), p. 344.   Philby, a
Britisher, spent most of his life in the service of the Sauds.
[16] Ibid., p. 299.
[17] Laqueur, The Soviet Union . . . , p. 55; see also Smolansky,
Soviet-Arab Relations . . . , pp. 5ff.
[18] Laqueur, loc. cit.   Laqueur states that the high regard for both
Imam Yehya and Ibn Saud was shared also by many Western experts.
[19] Philby, op. cit.
[20] Jidda in Saudi Arabia.
[21] Philby, op. cit.

The main concern of the Hakimoff missions was to establish
trade with both Arab countries as a wedge to Soviet influence in
Arabia. But by 1938 there was no trade of any significance
transacted, and the Hakimoff missions and the whole Soviet staff
operating in Arabia were recalled to Moscow.(22)

Egypt, the largest and most important of the Arab countries,
became independent from Britain in 1922 but in name only. The
Wafd Party there developed as the largest and most important political party from 1919 until the revolution of 1952. Doubting
the independence of Egypt, Soviet planners shared a pessimism
over the Wafd Party as a vehicle for a national front against
Britain. The Soviets were also suspicious of the fact that such
a large party could be tolerated by Britain while still in full
control of Egypt. Therefore, the Wafd leaders were charged with
collaboration with Britain. Saad Zaghlul, the founder of the
party, was dubbed a traitor and capitulator; and his successor,
Mustafa Nahhas, did not fare better in their estimation.(23)
Subsequently, the Egyptian communist party that had been established in 1920(24) remained illegal and constantly under the
vigil of British and Egyptian authorities. It finally ceased to
exist by 1923.(25) And whichever group inherited its dogma,
according to Lenczowski, remained isolated and very ineffectual
in the political life of Egypt throughout the British presence
there.(26) Generally speaking, this was also the situation of
communism in other Arab countries.

---

[22]Ibid., p. 334. According to Philby, the whole staff were
liquidated on arrival in Moscow due to their failure in Arabia,
with the   exception of one Soviet doctor who disobeyed the
[23]Soviet recall order and took refuge in Saudi Arabia.
Laqueur, op. cit., pp. 52-54. Nahhas, incidentally, led the
[24]Wafd Party until the revolution in 1952.
Laqueur, "The Appeal of Communism in the Middle East," Middle
[25]East Journal, IX (Winter, 1955), p. 17.
Ibid. World War II brought a relative upsurge in Middle East
communism in general. This upsurge, according to Laqueur, was
mainly among the intelligentsia. In 1955 he estimated the
strength of the Middle East communists, including those of
Turkey, Israel and six Arab states at approximately 45,000;
New York Times, May 10, 1954, quoted the U.S.I.A. figure for
[26]the Egyptian communist party as below 3,000 members then.
Lenczowski, op. cit., p. 524.

After the Second World War the Soviet Union in general
attempted to back every move in the Middle East that would under-
mine the presence and the interests of the Western powers
there.(27) This was done mainly through the aegises of the United
Nations.(28) For instance, the Soviets in the Security Council
strongly backed the Arab demand for French and British troop evacuation from Syria and Lebanon when this evacuation was called for
by both countries on February 4, 1946.(29) The United States
then proposed a very mild resolution. In contrast the Soviet
Union proposed an amendment to this which demanded the immediate
withdrawal of British and French troops. And when the original
unamended American resolution was voted upon, Soviet Delegate
Vyshinsky vetoed it.(30)

In the Security Council also, the Soviet Union fully backed
the Egyptian demand for British evacuation of Egypt and Sudan.(31)
Throughout 1946 Anglo-Egyptian negotiations over this issue were
conducted but failed to produce results favorable to Egypt. On
March 3, 1947 Egypt submitted the question to the Security Council.(32) Throughout the debate in 1947 both the Soviet Union and
Poland—then a member of the Council—strongly backed the Egyptian
position. For this, according to Kirk, the Soviet Union was
hailed in the Egyptian press as the friend of Egypt.(33)

In the crucial question of Palestine the Soviet attitude
toward Jewish nationalism (Zionism) fluctuated for various reasons

---

[27]D.J. Dallin, "Soviet Policy in the Middle East," Middle Eastern
  Affairs (1955), p. 341; J.M. Mackintosh, Strategy and Tactics
  of Soviet Foreign Policy (New York: Oxford University Press,
  1963), p. 118.
[28]On fifteen resolutions in the General Assembly of the United
  Nations, proposed between 1952 and 1956 concerning Arab affairs,
  the Soviet Union agreed with the position of the Arab states
  twelve times, abstained once, and opposed twice. In contrast,
  the United States agreed with the Arab six times, abstained
  three, and opposed them six times. In the Security Council, of
  nine major resolutions concerning Arab affairs the Soviet Union
  backed the Arabs nine times, while the United States disagreed
  with the Arabs five times out of the nine.
[29]George Kirk, Survey of International Affairs 1945-1950, p. 109.
[30]Ibid., p. 111.
[31]The Egyptian case remained in the Security Council from 1947 on.
  When the Anglo-Egyptian Agreement of 1954 was finally ratified
  in October 1954, Egypt withdrew her complaint.
[32]Ibid., p. 130.
[33]Kirk, op. cit., pp. 135-136.

from opposition to it inside Russia,(34) to backing of the Partition Resolution on Palestine in 1947, to opposition to Israel.
According to Oles Smolansky, Stalin discredited the possibility
of a Jewish national home or a Jewish state, and attacked Zionism
in the inter-war period as an imperialist and a reactionary movement.(35)

The Soviet attitude regarding Zionists in Palestine after the
Second World War was not more liberal.(36)

In view of the alleged Soviet opposition to Zionism, it came
therefore "as a considerable surprise when Soviet spokesmen in
the United Nations declared their support in 1947 for the idea of
independent Jewish and Arab states in Palestine. . . . "(37)

Laqueur lists various explanations since offered "for this
about-face in the Soviet approach."(38) First, it could have been
a Soviet disappointment with the fledgling Arab national movement.
It could also have been due to a Soviet belief in 1947 that most
Arab governments were pro-British, "whereas the Zionists in 1947
were definitely involved, in propaganda and action, in a bitter
struggle with the British in Palestine."(39) Hence, this Soviet

---

34
Laqueur, The Soviet Union and the Middle East, pp. 33-35; pp.
   103-104; p. 146.
35
Smolansky, The Soviet Union and the Arab East 1947-1957. Unpub-
   lished Ph.D. Columbia University, 1959, pp. 17ff.
36
Laqueur, op. cit., p. 146.
37
Ibid. For expressions of appreciation by Zionist leaders, see
   Zionist Review, May 23, 1947, p. 1, May 30, 1947, p. 5; the
   Arabs were correspondingly dismayed. See Kirk, op. cit., p.
   240 in the footnotes
38
Laqueur, op. cit., pp. 146-147; Martin Ebon, "Communist Tactics
   in Palestine," Middle East Journal, XI (July, 1948), pp. 255-
   269.
39
Notice, for example, an article in Izvestia, May 11, 1950, de-
   nouncing King Abdullah of Jordan, and denouncing the League of
   Arab states as "that offspring of British imperialism, which is
   becoming more and more a tool of the Anglo-American bloc in
   the Near East." Izvestia, May 11, 1950, The Current Digest of
   the Soviet Press, XI, No. 19 (1950), p. 41.

switch could be explained as a method of ending British rule in Palestine as an immediate objective. Third, it is also possible that Soviet leaders shared the general sympathy for the Jewish people due to their extreme plight under the Hitler regime, and felt that something ought to be done for them.

One might also speculate that the Soviets were then of the idea that the new Jewish state might respond more readily to communist anti-imperialist propaganda and Marxist dogma than the conservative Arab leaders and people. This response could legitimately be expected by the Soviets due to the history of communal communist settlements (kibbutz) established by many of the incoming Jews to Palestine before and since the the First World War.(40) It could also be understandably expected by the Soviet Union that the new state of Israel would have to be friendly on two counts: first, Zionist appreciation for the Soviet partition vote on Palestine; and second, because there were over three million Jews in the Soviet Union whose treatment could depend on Israel's behavior toward the Soviet Union.

These Soviet expectations notwithstanding, Israel at best followed a policy of non-identification between East and West from 1948 to late 1951.(41) In November 1951, though, the Israeli government was unofficially reported willing to join the Western-sponsored Middle East Command, a proposal which had been submitted to Egypt the previous month.(42) Israeli neutrality and now possible alignment with a Western-proposed pact aimed at the Soviet Union (contrasted to Egyptian refusal),(43) led to strained relations between the Soviet Union and Israel. Thereafter, Soviet favor began to shift in favor of the Arabs in general and Egypt in particular,since Egypt was the leader of Arab opposition to the Western defence system proposed since 1951. On the other hand Soviet-Israeli relations began to deteriorate in late 1951. This

---

[40] After all, the inspiration for the Kibbutz movement in Palestine (as well as the whole center of Zionist influence) "was Eastern and Central Europe . . . , coinciding with the development of Eastern European revolutionary movements . . . motivated by socialist ideals." Alan D. Crown, "The Changing World of the Kibbutz," Middle East Journal XIX (Autumn, 1965), pp. 423-24.
[41] This Israeli stance could be explained as due to the fact that the Western powers in general, and the United States in particular, were the main contributors to the moral, economic, political and military well-being of Israel.
[42] Calvocoressi, Survey of International Affairs 1952, p. 242.
[43] See Chap. IV.

was reflected in a Soviet campaign against what was called in the Soviet press the criminal acts of "zionist wrecker-doctors" and other "Zionist agents" in the U.S.S.R.(44) Eventually these poor relations reached the breaking point when on February 9, 1953 a terrorist bomb was exploded on the premises of the Soviet Legation in Tel-Aviv. Two Soviet Legation officials were injured and part of the Legation was damaged.(45) The U.S.S.R. immediately severed its diplomatic relations with Israel, and for a while international Zionism became the object of Soviet polemics. The state of Israel also fell under this attack. At the same time the Soviets found this a good occasion to woo the Arabs.(46)

SOVIET-EGYPTIAN MUTUAL OPPOSITION TO MEDO

There is no doubt about the fact that Soviet-Egyptian relations were cemented, and the final Soviet break-through in Egypt came in 1955, on the basis of mutual Egyptian-Soviet opposition to Western Middle East defence proposals. The reason for Soviet opposition to such a Western military alliance in the Middle East is obvious. Egypt's opposition to these Western defence proposals was not due to any particular friendship with the Soviet Union. In reality and until 1954 the Egyptian leadership as seen before was not opposed in principle to an alliance with the West aimed at the containment of the Soviet Union in the area. But regardless of the reasons for Egyptian objections to alignment with the West, the Soviet Union found in this neutralism a most welcome and potent force, undermining the Western position in the Arab world. As shall be discussed below, the Czechoslovak-

_____

44Calvocoressi, op. cit., pp. 149-150 and pp. 171-73. This anti-Zionist campaign was carried on in the Soviet satellites as well.
45Ibid.
46See Chap. II
For example, the Literaturnaya Gazeta of February 17, 1953 wrote, "Following the example of the Hitlerites, the ruling clique of Israel has created a special ghetto for the Arabs, deprived them of the right of freedom of movement, of free choice of residence." The Current Digest of the Soviet Press, V, No. 5 (1953), p. 13.

Egyptian arms deal of September 1955 climaxed what was apparently
a series of individual reactions on the parts of Egypt and the
Soviet Union, independently of each other, to a series of Western
actions and overtures in the Middle East from 1951 on.

As mentioned before, the United States along with Britain,
France and Turkey, presented on October 13, 1951 a set of propo-
sals to Egypt regarding the creation of MEDO. Two days later
Egypt rejected these proposals, hence rejected alliance with the
Western powers on the conditions then offered but not agreeable
to her. This immediate rejection angered the United States
State Department but was received with gratification in Moscow.
Soviet gratification was enhanced when Egypt again, along with
the other Arab states, ignored the new set of principles for the
creation of a pact, issued by the same four powers on November 10,
1951.(47) On November 21, 1951 the Soviet Deputy Minister of
Foreign Affairs, Andrei Gromyko, received the Egyptian Minister
in Moscow, Anis Azer, and handed him the following statement:

> On October 14, this year, the
> press published the proposals of the
> governments of the U.S.A., Britain,
> France and Turkey, . . . to the Govern-
> ment of Egypt. . . . It follows from
> the four-power proposals and declara-
> tions, that the demand of the states
> indicated for the creation of the
> above-mentioned joint command . . .
> pursues the aim of involving the states
> of the Near and Middle East in the
> military measures being carried out by
> the Atlantic bloc under the pretext
> of organization of the 'defence' of
> this region. . . . In this connection
> the Soviet government considers it
> necessary to stress the commonly known
> fact that, from the very first days
> of the existence of the Soviet State,
> the Soviet government has viewed with
> understanding and sympathy the national
> aspirations of the peoples of the East
> and their struggle for national inde-
> pendence and sovereignty. . . . All

47
  See Chaps. I and IV.

> this shows how absurd are the
> statements about some kind of
> threat to the countries of the
> Near and Middle East. . . .
>
> The Soviet government fully
> appreciates the position which
> the government of Egypt has
> adopted toward the above-mentioned
> proposals of the four States.(48)

Similar notes were sent to Lebanon, Iraq and Israel the same day, and to Saudi Arabia and Yemen a day later.(49) On November 24, 1951 a Soviet note of protest was sent to each of the four powers proposing the creation of MEDO.(50)

The Soviet Union reacted unfavorably to any friendly relations between the United States and especially Egypt, among the Arab states, since Egypt is the leading power among them. On the basis of this policy, and due to the fact that the Free Officers seemingly enjoyed American sympathy and support at the start of their revolution in July 1952, the Soviet Union reacted apprehensively to that revolution.(51) This apprehension continued and fluctuated in degree until the new leadership proved, due to circumstances discussed earlier, as adamant in their opposition to Western defence overtures and policies as the Egyptian government of King Farouk before. But this opposition did not in fact become clear until the beginning of 1955 when Egypt began to attack Iraq openly for joining MEDO, and attack the United States and

---

48
Pravda, November 22, 1951, The Current Digest of the Soviet Press, III, No. 41 (November-February, 1951-1952), 20; full text of this note in Denise Folliot (ed.), Documents on International Affairs 1951 (London: Oxford University Press, 1954), pp. 429-31; the same Soviet theme of reminding the Arabs that it was the West, and not they, who had stood in the way of Arab independence since the First World War persisted after the death of Stalin. It was given more meaning after the Anglo-French-Israeli invasion of Egypt in October 1956. See, for example, a speech by Krushchev published in Pravda, January 14, 1957 and quoted in Soviet World Outlook, A Handbook of Communist Statements (Washington: U.S. Government Printing Office, 1959), p. 177.
49
Folliot, op. cit., p. 429 in the footnotes.
50
Ibid., pp. 432-36.
51
Kirk, Contemporary Arab Politics, p. 29.

Britain for "luring" Iraq to join. Meanwhile, that is, from July 1952 until early 1955, Soviet-Egyptian relations fluctuated accordingly.(52) Selected illustrations of this fluctuation will verify the point. The first public comment of Pravda on the Egyptian Free Officers revolution itself came on August 12, 1952. Pravda ruefully wrote,

> The fact that the military
> coup from the very beginning en-
> joyed support from the American
> Embassy in Egypt does not cause
> any doubt. The Americans intend
> to derive a certain advantage from
> the situation which has arisen. They
> hope to make use of this situation to
> speed up creation of the so-called
> Middle East Command.(53)

As also mentioned earlier, rupture in diplomatic relations between Israel and the Soviet Union in early 1953 was an occasion for the Soviet press and official statements to attack Israel, and conversely, flatter the Arabs. And since, in the words of one observer, "any power or political ideology that seeks alle-giance in the Arab world must take a stand on Palestine,"(54) the Soviets took full advantage of this fact and consistently backed the Arab position on Palestine, particularly after 1953.(55) Part of the Soviet strategy was to keep alive the grudges of the Arab states and Arab refugees from Palestine against Israel and the West. This was done naturally to further discourage any possible Arab participation in Western pacts. Writing of this, one Western observer then stated:

> The situation of the Arab refugees
> is made to order for communist agitators
> . . . . The communist line has been

---

52 Laqueur, op. cit., pp. 194-195.
53 Pravda, August 12, 1952, The Current Digest . . . , IV, No. 32 (1952), p. 21.
54 Martin Ebon, World Communism Today (New York: McGraw-Hill Book Co., Inc., 1948), p. 411.
55 See an article by Thomas Hamilton in the New York Times, March 31, 1954, p. 14 on the fact that the Palestine question was be-coming an East-West dispute in the United Nations with the Soviets consistently backing the Arabs.

adapted characteristically to
fit the grudges and sentiments
of the refugees. Thus communist
propaganda suggests that the Western powers are only trying to re-
settle them in order to recruit
them for military ventures. This
line falls on many receptive ears
and strengthens the common resistance to settlement. In spite of
vigilance by camp officials and
local governments a significant
number of communist leaflets are
smuggled into refugee centers. All
of these ring the charges on a fam-
iliar theme: the West is responsible for the refugees' condition;
they must insist on return to their
home, full compensation, and an independent Arab state in Palestine--
in short, a return to the original
Partition Resolution of 1947.(56)

In line with the above tactic the Soviets in January 1954
vetoed a Western-sponsored resolution in the Security Council
calling on the Arabs and Israel to accept the division of the
waters of the river Jordan. This resolution was based on the
proposals of Eric Johnston, and rejected by the Arabs. Commenting on this veto, the New York Times wrote that "Soviet
propaganda has sought to make the Johnston plan unacceptable to
the Arabs by calling it a 'Marshall Plan' for the Middle East.
Hence, this propaganda insists, it is a device of American imperialism."(57)

The death of Stalin abruptly changed the atmosphere of
strained relations between the Soviet Union and Israel. On July
20, 1953 Soviet-Israeli diplomatic relations were resumed.(58)
There was then speculation that with this development there
might be a change in the consistent Soviet backing of the Arabs
in the United Nations on issues concerning Palestine. These

56
Georgiana G. Stevens, "Arab Refugees: 1948-1952, Middle East
Journal, VI (1952), p. 290.
57
New York Times, January 27, 1954.
58
Calvocoressi, Survey of International Affairs, 1953, p. 148.

speculations were alluded to, and possible Arab fears allayed, in a speech by Premier Georgi Malenkov before the Supreme Soviet on August 8, 1953. He stated:

> The assertions of some foreign
> papers that the restoration of dip-
> lomatic relations with Israel will
> lead to a weakening of the relations
> of the Soviet Union with the Arab
> states are void of any foundation.
> The activity of the Soviet Government
> will be directed toward the strength-
> ening of friendly cooperation with
> the Arab states.(59)

What followed in effect after the Soviet resumption of diplomatic relations with Israel was discreet but very meaning-ful and profitable (to Israel) diplomatic and trade activities between these two countries. For instance, a trade agreement was concluded between the two in December 1953, providing for the import of Soviet oil in sizable quantities.(60) According to Laqueur, Israeli imports from the U.S.S.R. were forty times higher in 1954 than they had been in 1950-1951. In June of 1954 the Soviet Legation in Tel Aviv and the Israeli Legation in Moscow were raised to embassy levels, and the Soviet ambassador in Tel Aviv "used this opportunity to present his credentials in Jerusalem . . . , an action that was widely commended in Israel because of the unwillingness shown by most other powers to rec-ognize Jerusalem as the country's capital." In effect the Soviet Union recognized Jerusalem as the capital of Israel, an action vehemently opposed by the Arabs. Israeli relations with other East European countries also improved.(61)

The improved Soviet-Israeli relations did not stop the Soviets at the same time from trying to woo the Arab states. This was done by backing the Arabs on issues (like the division of the Jordan waters mentioned above) discussed in the United Nations. Dealing with both was actually in line with policy set down for this area by Premier Georgi Malenkov in a state-ment to the Supreme Soviet in August 1953, and carried by Al-Ahram, August 9, 1953. In it he declared that the Soviet Union wished for good relations with all nations of the Middle East, including Israel.

---

59 New York Times, August 10, 1953.
60 Laqueur, The Soviet Union . . . , p. 204.
61 Ibid.

Perhaps in the true spirit of revolutionary communism, and the fact that most of the Arabs were still under the yoke of Western imperialism, the Soviet Union consistently backed them against the West in the United Nations. We have seen earlier how this was partially behind the Soviet thinking when they backed the creation of the state of Israel in 1948. That is, the backing of the creation of Israel was a way of ending British influence in the east Mediterranean. Now that Israel was truly independent the Soviets possibly thought it was time to end Western influence generally in the Arab world. In this endeavor they sought to back Arab nationalism consistently in the United Nations, and eventually backed the Arabs with military aid and economic aid.

In the United Nations, therefore, in the General Assembly as well as in the Security Council, the Soviet Union from 1953 to 1956 and after voted consistently in line with the Arabs. This became particularly and understandably true after revolutionary Egypt led the opposition in the Middle East to the creation of MEDO aimed at the Soviet Union. In the General Assembly during the period of 1953-1956, for instance, ten major issues concerning the Arabs were brought up. The first three included resolutions calling for the independence of Morocco and Tunisia, and for keeping the question of Algeria on the agenda of the Assembly. On all three questions the Soviet Union voted with the Arab states. In contrast the United States voted on the side of France. The other seven resolutions were concerned with the tripartite aggression on Egypt in October 1956. The Soviets again championed the Arab cause on all seven occasions. In the Security Council, also, the Soviet Union consistently backed the Arabs on all nine resolutions brought up in that same period of 1953-1956.

SOVIET-EGYPTIAN TRADE

Outside the United Nations actual British and French influence or direct control of the Arab states still stood in the way of easy Soviet contact with the Arabs as late as the middle 1950's. In pre-revolutionary Egypt one barter deal of some significance was reported by Al-Ahram on March 4, 1952. Soviet wheat and petroleum products were exchanged for Egyptian cotton. In view of the fact that cotton constitutes by far the major export item in Egypt, Soviet acceptance of cotton in exchange for their industrial and military commodities facilitated bigger deals to come. This barter deal was to set the pattern for later transactions between Egypt (as well as Syria, which also exports cotton) and the Soviet bloc nations. Apparently, this pattern of trade, aside from its political implications, was becoming an economic necessity for the Soviet bloc also.(62)

The sale of cotton to the Soviet bloc was also becoming a necessity for Egypt. The United States,of course, was never a buyer of Egyptian cotton--rather, a major competitor. This competition had at times very important political implications. For instance, when the question of American aid was raised to help build what the Egyptians considered the very vital project of the Aswan Dam, there was strong opposition by Southern congressmen to this aid. This was mainly because the project would expand Egyptian cotton production, and the aid would in effect stiffen Egyptian competition with America.

Fluctuations in the American policy of agriculture price support, particularly as it concerns cotton, have a serious influence on the Egyptian economy. This is due to the fact that Egypt's economy relies heavily on cotton. Some observers felt that American cotton policy in the 1950's was designed to influence Egyptian politics.(63) Perhaps the following instance might have been an example of this.

Egypt and the United States were at an extremely low point in their relations in August 1955. American agricultural policy was also detrimental to the Egyptian cotton market. John Badeau then wrote:

> Recent American agricultural policy
> has constituted a serious threat to
> Egyptian markets. Because of the
> United States policy of agricultural
> price support, large amounts of Amer-
> ican cotton have been dumped at low
> prices in foreign countries that
> were formerly Egypt's customers. This

[62]H.G. Martin, "The Soviet Union and the Middle Eastern Affairs, VIII, No. 2 (February, 1956), p. 49; see also W.W. Kulski, International Politics in a Revolutionary Age (New York: J.B. Lippincott Co., 1964), p. 344.
[63]Harry B. Ellis, Challenge in the Middle East (New York: The Ronald Press Company, 1957),pp. 166-168.

> naturally led to a loss of
> Egyptian sales and has presented
> the government with a problem whose
> only solution seems to be to find
> new markets. But new markets are
> principally in the communist bloc
> countries. . . .(64)

On August 14, 1955, though, United States cotton price policy was abruptly changed to become very favorable to Egypt. This development prompted the American ambassador in Cairo, Henry Byroade, to call for a press conference to break the good news to the Egyptians.(65) This favorable development perhaps becomes explainable when fifteen days later Dulles broke the unwelcome news to the Western world that Egypt had decided to purchase arms from Czechoslovakia.(66)

Britain was traditionally the major customer for Egyptian cotton. According to Tom Little, Britain used to buy more than one-third of the Egyptian crop before World War II. But by 1955 it purchased only "negligible quantities," and fell to tenth place in the list of the buying countries.(67) Egypt, therefore, was searching for new customers for its major export product. By 1955, according to Al-Ahram, the Soviet Union was already producing enough cotton for its textile factories in Central Asia, and was also exporting some to Eastern European countries. That is, the Soviets, too were fast becoming competitors with Egypt.(68) "But we still have a few years left to fulfill the demands of Eastern Europe before the Soviet Union can fill this gap."(69)

The first Soviet trade agreement with the Free Officers government of Egypt was made in March 1953.(70) This was a smaller barter deal, wheat-for-cotton, than the one made with

---

64
Badeau, Middle East Journal, IX, p. 382.
65
Al-Gumhuriyah, August 15, 1955, p. 1; see footnote above.
66
New York Times, August 31, 1955.
67
Tom Little, Egypt (New York: Frederick A. Praeger, 1958), p. 274. Britain was lost to the United States as a cotton customer, and to Sudan. Canada also used to be a buyer of Egyptian cotton, and was lost to the United States. See Ellis, op. cit.
68
Al-Ahram, April 29, 1966, p. 7.
69
Ibid.
70
Ibid., March 10, 1953, p. 7. Details of the deal were given on March 11, 1953, p. 6.

the Farouk regime a year before.(71) The 1953 deal came at a time
when there was an atmosphere of amity between Egypt, the United
States and Britain. Perhaps for this reason there was hardly any
mention of it in the Western press, adverse of otherwise.(72)
In March 1954 Nasser announced another barter agreement with the
Soviet Union.(73) This was described by Al-Ahram as the largest
deal between the two nations thus far.

In contrast to the 1953 agreement, the above agreement came
at a time when Egyptian-Western relations were at a low point.
Egypt was then extremely bitter at the United States and Britain
for backing Israel on the Suez navigation issue; "luring" Iraq
into MEDO by giving her arms; giving lavish economic and military aid to Israel, etc. On their part the Western powers were
bitter at Nasser (by then in actual control of Egypt) for his
opposition to their policies in the area. Therefore, the Western
press and particularly the British press reacted adversely to the
transaction. While announcing the deal, therefore, Nasser made
reference to the British criticism. He refuted what he called
the British press allegations that he "leans ideologically, politically and economically" toward the Soviets. He added that
"the British press is trying to cover up for its aggression and
occupation of Egypt by discrediting the character of the Egyptian
leadership. This, of course, is an old imperial trick."(74)

---

[71]Ibid., March 4, 1952, p. 1. The 1952 deal was reported worth
approximately 29.7 million Egyptian pounds. The 1953 deal was
worth about 5.5 million. (An Egyptian pound was then equal to
approximately three dollars.
[72]Neither the New York Times, the London Times, nor the Monitor,
mentioned it.
[73]Al-Ahram, March 10, 1954, p. 7.
[74]In an article by Nasser published a few months later in the
United States, he wrote: "In other quarters there has been
talk of 'communist infiltration' in the various Arab and African nationalits movements. It would be unwise for the United
States to take that view of nationalist activities, led by sincere patriots whose only desire is to see their nations free
from foreign domination. Americans recognize this to be the
inalienable right of every man, yet balk at supporting these
nationalists for fear of annoying some colonial power that has
refused to move with the times. It is this procrastination
that gives the communists the chance to take over what usually
starts as genuinely patriotic movements." Gamal Abdel Nasser,
"The Egyptian Revolution," Foreign Affairs, XXXIII (January,
1955), p. 210-11.

The favorable Egyptian fanfare that associated the Soviet deal must have encouraged Soviet diplomats in Cairo to press their advantage. For, while signing the deal, the Soviet Economic Attache, one Alexenko,(75) was reported by Al-Ahram of March 11, 1954 as expressing the hope that this deal would be the beginning of a much more expanded and profitable trade relationship between the Soviet Union and Egypt. The paper then added that experts from the Eastern bloc nations were then on their way to Egypt, also for the purpose of discussing expanded trade relations. "We deem it therefore necessary that our government make a general review of the whole trade pattern of Egypt, and make the necessary changes." Two days later a large Egyptian delegation was reported on its way to Eastern European capitals and to Moscow. On its return on March 28, it announced in Cairo that the Soviet Union and "other Eastern European" countries showed willingness to enter into trade and technical aid agreements with Egypt, either unilaterally or through the United Nations. But these agreements were still under study and discussion.

Egyptian and Soviet relations remained seemingly on a happy note until July 1954, when the Anglo-Egyptian agreement over Suez was finally signed. In view of the fact that the Soviet-Egyptian relations were only a marriage of convenience, the Soviets feared that any rapprochment between Nasser and the West might bring him into MEDO where the rest of the Arab states would follow. Understandably, therefore, the Soviets showed apprehension over the Suez agreement.

Official Soviet comment on the Suez agreement , though, was comparatively restrained.(76) For, while it was obvious from the reaction of many groups in Egypt that the agreement was not popular, as we shall discuss later, the Soviets adopted an attitude of watchful waiting. Their restrained remarks, according to Laqueur, were "expressed more in sorrow than in anger, and putting the main blame on the Americans who had ensnared the Egyptian leaders...."(77) Pravda's article of September 8, 1954 is illustrative of this attitude:

> As is known, an Anglo-Egyptian
> agreement was reached recently

75
76No first name given in the report.
77Laqueur, op. cit., p. 196.
Ibid. An Arabic radio station in Budapest, according to Laqueur, was far more vociferous in attacking Nasser.

on the Suez Canal--an agreement toward which the Egyptian
people, by Nasser's own admission,
have reacted disapprovingly. It
is also known that the United States
acted as 'mediator' in the Anglo-
Egyptian negotiations. The United
States obviously considered these
negotiations and their results as a
deal from which it could gain, im-
posing upon Egypt economic and military 'aid,' which inevitably carried
conditions advantageous to American
monopoly capital, but enslaving to
the countries receiving such aid
. . . . If a real threat to Near
and Middle Eastern countries, including Egypt, does exist, it comes
not from the Soviet Union, but
Western imperialism.(78)

Before we discuss the reaction of Nasser and his government to what they conceived Soviet interference in the internal
affairs of Egypt, it is necessary here to discuss the nature of
the whole course of foreign policy that the Free Officers chose
to follow after 1952. This policy, which Nasser preferred to
call "positive neutralism" and/or non-alignment, could be summed
up in brief as steadfast insistence on complete and full sovereignty for Egypt.(79)

THE NATURE OF POSITIVE NEUTRALISM

The constant factors, it seems, in the foreign policy of
Egypt since the revolution of July 1952 are the search for "full
sovereignty" for Egypt, and leadership in demanding "full sovereignty" for the other Arab states. Two unrelated events occurred
within a few months of the Free Officers' take-over that gave

---

78
Pravda, September 8, 1954, The Current Digest...,VI, No. 36
79(1954), p. 15.
Wilton Wynn's book, Nasser of Egypt, is subtitled The Search for
Dignity. This phrase is also an apt description of Nasser's
foreign policy. William R. Polk calls it a "quest for identity
and dignity." The United States and the Arab World (Cambridge,
Mass.: Harvard Univ. Press, 1965), pp. 248ff.

the new leaders hope for the achievement of this sovereignty.
One was the advent of Eisenhower into the Presidency of the United
States with his seeming interest in "impartiality" in the Palestine
question and just solutions for the problems of the Middle East.
The other event was the death of Stalin in March 1953.

Stalin was the symbol of Soviet aggression in Western thinking. His policies set in motion the urge in Western capitals
for the creation of defence alliances to contain the Soviet
Union. The emphasis on defence was reflected, of course, in
Anglo-Egyptian relations. For instance, it was unthinkable then
to Britain to budge on the issue of evacuation of the Suez bases
as demanded by the Egyptians when the alleged shadow of Soviet
aggression loomed large in their estimation. Now that Stalin was
dead (March 1953), the Egyptians hoped that Britain would change
its position. For this reason the Egyptian press was keenly interested in detecting new trends in Soviet foreign policy under
its new leaders. On April 22, 1953, only six weeks after Stalin's
death Al-Ahram carried under major headlines details of a foreign
policy speech by the Chairman of the Soviet Council of Ministers,
Georgi Malenkov. In this speech he announced forty-eight de-
crees and directives for the Communist Party to follow. Inherent
in these, Al-Ahram noted what might possibly be called the first
signs of the "peaceful coexistence" line of the new leaders of
the Soviet Union. Among these directives to the Party, amity
towards Britain, France and the United States was to be promoted.
The slogan advocating "lessening of tension," according to
Dallin also, was to be used, and the terms "imperialist aggres-
sors" and "warmongers" were ordered eliminated.(80)

As mentioned above, the Egyptians anticipated a break-through
in their impasse with Britain over Suez, on the basis of a relaxation of tension on the global scene. For if the Soviet Union
openly discarded what the Western powers called Soviet "aggressive
designs in the Middle East" as elsewhere, then there would be no
need for the stationing of British troops in Suez. Nor would
Britain be able to point to the Soviet threat as a reason for
remaining in control of Egyptian soil. In line with this Egyptian thinking, Al-Ahram published an interview (on the same day
it reported the Malenkov speech) with the Prime Minister of India,

---

80
David J. Dallin, Soviet Foreign Policy After Stalin (New York:
J.B. Lippincott Co., 1961), p. 138.

Jawaharlal Nehru.(81)   Nehru was then as expectant as were the
Egyptian leaders.   For he then was well aware that Pakistan was
being recruited as a partner in a Western MEDO.   That is why,
as mentioned earlier, a committee of the Indian Congress Party
passed a resolution in January 1953 urging Washington and London
not to include Pakistan in a military alliance which might tip
the balance of power in the Indian subcontinent.(82)

Nehru was questioned by Al-Ahram about the sincerity of the
Soviet move for relaxation of world tension. He answered:

> There is no doubt that the new
> leadership in the Kremlin have
> changed Soviet policies from those
> followed by Stalin. Of course, I
> have no way of being sure. In my
> personal opinion I feel that the
> Soviets genuinely want peace.

Al-Ahram then agreed with Nehru's estimation of the new
Soviet diplomacy. At the same time it charged Britain with
being an aggressor in Egypt "who purposely discards the new
Soviet liberal and peaceful overtures as meaningless for the
purpose of perpetuating its occupation of Suez as well as other
parts of the world." A few days later (April 26), both major
Egyptian newspapers, Al-Ahram and Al-Gumhuriyah, carried in
banner headlines what was referred to as "The Tremendous Changes
in Soviet Foreign Policy."

In the search for complete independence and freedom of
action internally and externally, the foreign policy of revolutionary Egypt fluctuated according to what Egyptian leaders felt
the great powers were forcing upon them. Thus while they were
still feeling the great disappointment after the Dulles trip of
May 1953; and were heavily engrossed emotionally with the Suez

---

[81] The same day, Al-Ahram in an article made a contrast between Malenkov's peaceful gestures and an article by the British paper,
Daily Telegraph, whereby the latter reportedly charged the British government of "appeasing" Egypt, quoting Georges Clemenceau's
statement that appeasement creates the demand for more appeasement.
[82] Calvocoressi, Survey...1953, p. 118. Partly to forestall Pakistan's adherence to Western defence organization, India recognized the full independence of Pakistan on May 15, 1953. This
recognition came on May 15, 1953, a few days before Dulles arrived in Karachi on his trip to the Middle East. See Al-Ahram,
May 17, 1953.

evacuation issue; and extremely bitter against the British and the West in general for various reasons, not least of which was their usual partiality to Israel—Egyptian leaders seemed careful throughout not to lose the very thing for which they were fighting --freedom of action--by falling into heavy moral and political debt to the Soviets. Neither did they seem to lose sight of possible Soviet manipulation of their predicament with the West. For, as Harold Lamb then wrote, now that the countries of the Middle East were independent or on the verge of independence after a long period of imperialism, they would never in any way again invite imperialism, Soviet or otherwise.(83)

The Egyptian insistence on full independence and freedom of action from the West, as of right, without conditions or strings attached, was discussed in the chapters above. We have also discussed how they viewed the Western insistence on Egypt and the other Arab states to join MEDO and make inequitable peace with Israel, as an infringement on Arab rights and sovereignty. Therefore, they opposed these Western policies. Nevertheless, even in their darkest moments with the West, the Egyptian leaders kept the Egyptian Communist Party under surveillance. For instance, when Nasser became Prime Minister on April 18, 1954 he then charged that Egypt was the subject of Western intrigues.(84) A few days before assuming office he also made a statement charging that

> the American insistence on creating
> a pact in the Middle East is going
> to wreck the Arab world and stand
> in the way of its unity. There is
> duplicity in American policies in
> this area. They say one thing and
> do another, and we expected a more
> honorable course from their democ-
> racy. It seems clear that the United
> States is walking with the 'wheel of
> imperialism' so far. The United States
> should hasten in welcoming the Arab
> hand of friendship which has long been
> extended toward her; otherwise, she
> will 'miss the boat.' We began our
> relations with the United States full

---

83 Harold Lamb, "The Mystery of the Middle East," Saturday Evening Post (March 21, 1953),p. 158.
84 Al-Gumhuriyah, April 18, 1954.

of hope for just solutions of the
problems of this area, but this hope
has now vanished or is on the verge
of vanishing.(85)

A day before that, Al-Ahram (April 15) published in great
details and under major headlines an expose of an alleged imperial
plot uncovered against the Arabs. Allegedly, Britain,France and
Israel were plotting to invade Egypt. The result of the invasion
would have been that all three powers would have "evened the
score" against the Egyptian officers in power. The Free Officers'
government would then be overthrown, they hoped,and each of the
three countries would dictate its demands on the Arabs whether in
North Africa, Suez or in Palestine. The Egyptian papers were also
still headlining Vyshinsky's veto and his Security Council statements in favor of Egypt and against the Western resolution favoring Israeli free navigation through the Suez Canal.(86) Israeli
attacks on the Gaza strip were also making headlines practically
every day. On April 10 as mentioned above, five Arab ambassadors
to the U.S. walked out of an official dinner prepared by the State
Department.(87)

All this is mentioned above to illustrate the low point at
which Egyptian-American relations stood at that time. Regardless
of all this, and at a time when the Egyptian government was in
need of Soviet backing and was actually getting it, Nasser made
perhaps the strongest indictment of communist imperialism and the
Egyptian Communist Party throughout his career. This came on the
heels of uncovering a plot against his government on April 28,
1954. The plot was organized by army dissidents allegedly backed
by the Egyptian Communist Party for the purpose of"creating disorder in Egypt."(88) According to the New York Times report,
twelve army officers and forty civilian plotters were arrested.
Immediately, all major Cairo newspapers began attacking the Soviet
Union and its "imperialist" designs in the Middle East.

85
Al-Ahram, April 16, 1954; see also an attack by Nasser on
United States policy in the New York Times, April 14, 1954.
86
See Chap. II
87
This was due to a speech made by a Jewish Rabbi which the Arabs
found offensive. See Chap. II.
88
New York Times, April 29, 1954; Al-Gumhuriyah, April 30, 1954.
See Chap. II.

Egypt's violent reaction to this "communist" plot could have been due also to another facet of Soviet interference in the internal affairs of Egypt. This came in the form of a Soviet note sent to Egypt and other Arab states on March 23, 1954. The Soviet note warned the Arabs that the Soviet Union would consider any Arab adherence to a future MEDO an unfriendly and even a hostile act directed against her. In view of the fact that Egypt was leading the opposition to the pact, and for her own independent reasons, any Soviet reminder to that effect would only have an irritating effect in Cairo.

Nasser's anti-communist speech was delivered on April 30, 1954. It was made to a huge gathering of the membership of Cairo labor unions.(89) The speech is important enough to quote in detail not only because it seemed to further set the record on Nasser's views on Communism and its incompatibility with Arab nationalism, but also because it portrayed the Free Officers' fierce resentment then of any foreign move, or suspected move, that in their opinion might curtail their freedom of action or diminish their full sovereignty.

> The communists are the best allies
> of Zionism in this part of the world.
> In fact, Zionism and Communism are
> indistinguishable as to ideology. . .
> They are both opportunist. . . Notice,
> for instance, its leader in Egypt,
> Al-Bindary, who is also known as the
> Red Pasha.(90) Many of you know that
> he lives a very luxurious life in the
> suburbs of Cairo. He is surrounded
> by a high-living opportunist group
> like him. They all talk of democracy,
> nevertheless, and better life for the
> people.

89
  The speech was headlined by Al-Ahram as follows: "Nasser Exposes Active Communist Plotters," "Communism Is More Dangerous To Egypt Than Zionism," "Communism Is Plotting With Zionism Against Arab Nationalism." Al-Ahram, April 30,1954.
90This was in reference to Kamil Al-Bindary, the Red Pasha, former Egyptian ambassador to Moscow and leading fellow-traveller in Egypt, according to Laqueur, and one of the richest landowners in Egypt. Walter Z. Laqueur, Communism and Nationalism in the Middle East (New York: Frederick A. Praeger, 1956), p. 48.

Nasser went on to discuss how the Communists in Egypt
had opposed the Egyptian revolution in 1952. He stated that only
seven days after the Free Officers took power, the Communists dis-
tributed leaflets charging the Free Officers of being "imperialist
stooges." Then the   Communists did not even know the names
of the Officers who led the revolt, yet they attacked them and their
principles." They did this, according to Nasser, because they
were

> opportunists, whose interest is
> not genuine revolution that would
> really raise the level of life for
> the Egyptian laborer. Their aim is
> more poverty in Egypt so as to augment
> the membership of their group and
> eventually take over power in the
> name of the people.

Nasser charged the Communist Party in Egypt of being finan-
ced by a Zionist by the name of Corbelle, and then questioned
"how could such a party be sincerely interested in the welfare of
Egypt?" He related that he met the Egyptian chief communist, Al-
Bindary, at one time and exposed him and his party as fakers.

> I asked him then to show me the
> program and goals of his party.
> As I read his program, I told him
> that these were beautiful words,
> but how I asked did his party pro-
> pose to implement such a fabulous
> program. He, of course, had no
> reasonable answer and I dismissed
> him.

He went on to warn:

> We came to power to fight exploit-
> ation, feudalism and corruptive
> ideologies. We shall persist in
> doing so, I promise you. The Com-
> munists call for class warfare, and
> war between labor and management.
> But this is not the way to build a
> new Egypt, by dividing its citizens
> against each other. I urge you, the
> Egyptian labor, to work in harmony
> with your employers. So do I urge your

employers to work in harmony
with you and avoid exploiting
you. This is the only way a
new Egypt can be created, free
from foreign domination and internal exploitation.

It is important to note that there was no mention of the
Soviet Union throughout Nasser's speech. Other official Egyptian
attacks on the Egyptian Communists followed the same pattern.(91)
In other words, the Egyptian revolutionaries were then trying to
establish the point that suppressing communism in Egypt was Egypt's
internal affair. Consequently, any suppression of Egypt's communists did not preclude good relations with the Soviet Union.
But whenever the above formula did not appeal to the Soviets, and
at times it did not, their press remarks remained quite restrained.
An illustration of this is Pravda's article of September 8, 1954
cited above, which, according to Laqueur, expressed Soviet "sorrow,"
rather than anger, for the Egyptian leaders who were being "ensnared" by America. Pravda's statement could have been much
harsher on the Egyptians in view of the fact that since the Anglo-
Egyptian agreement over Suez was announced in July, 1954, the
Nasser government had reacted violently against the alleged communists in Egypt (along with the Wafdists and the Moslem Brotherhood groups) who opposed the agreement.(92) But the Soviets were

------

91
See for instance a similar statement by Nasser published in Newsweek (July 20, 1954). A few years later he made the charge: "I
think we must admit that the major responsibility for communist
growth in the Middle East, particularly in Iraq, must be taken
by the Western countries. By supporting undesirable leaders like
Nuri who fought to suppress legitimate nationalist movements, the
West furnished a fertile soil for communism." Life (July 20,
1959); Gamal Abdel Nasser, Where I Stand and Why (Washington:
Press Dept. Embassy of the United Arab Repub., n.d.), p. 4.
92In fact, the Moslem Brotherhood, the Zionists and the Communists
were all lumped together as one "Communist front" by Nasser on
August 22, 1954. On October 27, 1954 there was an attempt on
Nasser's life while he was delivering a speech in Cairo. The
next day over 400 Moslem Brotherhood, Communists, Wafdists, etc.,
were rounded up. New York Times, October 28, 1954. From then
on it was open season in Egypt against the above three groups,
especially the Moslem Brotherhood. The purge finally included
President Naguib, who had been a figurehead since April 1954
when Nasser assumed full control. Naguib was charged with plotting (with the fanatic Moslem Brotherhood and a Wafdist-Communist
front) to get rid of Nasser. He was relieved of the Presidency
and put under house arrest on November 15, 1954. See Al-Gumhuriyah, November 15, 1954; New York Times, November 18, 1954.

shrewder than to cut any "gordian knot" with Nasser for the sake
of the small Communist Party in Egypt. For it was soon apparent
to them that his agreement with the British over Suez did not mean
that Egypt was contemplating joining Western defences. In fact,
the initial Soviet fear that with the Suez agreement Nasser might
join MEDO seem unwarranted in retrospect, since the Egyptian leaders had already taken a number of categorical positions vis-a-vis
the West that were not easy to retract. One was the demand from
the West for a just solution to the Palestine question before
Egypt even considered aligning herself with the West. Another was
the assumption of Egyptian leaders as leaders of Arab nationalism
also. Therefore, before Egypt could ally herself with the West,
equitable solutions for colonial and semi-colonial Arab problems
were to be found. This was far from being accomplished by July
of 1954. By that time also the Egyptians had repeated often
enough to render it hard to retract that the defence of the Arab
states lay mainly in Arab hands, and that the pact of the Arab
League was enough for that defence if the West would give the
Arabs arms. This, too, was far from acceptable to the West who
feared such arms would be used against Israel. Due also to the
above reasons, Egypt was already committed in some degree to the
idea of "positive neutralism" for which Nehru was partially responsible. This philosophy, that was nurtured along with Indian-
Egyptian friendship, reached a high point of maturity when both
leaders, Nasser and Nehru, became co-sponsors and major figures
at the Asian-African Conference at Bandung, Indonesia.

THE ROAD TO BANDUNG

One of the first signs of political cooperation between the
nations of Asia and Africa, according to Dallin, was a conference
convened in 1949 in New Delhi on the initiative of Nehru.(93)
The purpose for the conference was to support Indonesia in its
fight for independence against the Netherlands. In December 1952
on the initiative of the Free Officers government, a conference
in Cairo of twelve Asian and African countries met and discussed
problems common to them.(94) This conference was the beginning

---

93Dallin, Soviet Foreign Policy After Stalin, p. 296.
94These nations include India, Indonesia and Ceylon.

of a large measure of harmony and friendship between Egypt and India. This apparently strange relationship,(95) was strengthened and cemented by Western efforts to create military alliances in the Middle East and South Asia that both Egypt and India opposed for various reasons.

It was already clear to India by May 1953, that is, when Dulles made his trip to the Middle East, that both Pakistan and India were thought of by the Western powers as possible partners to MEDO. (See Chapter II). Nehru objected to joining. His objections, according to Calvocoressi, "were sufficiently well-known and respected to ensure that there should for the present be no serious suggestion of it. But he objected also to participation by Pakistan. . . . His objections were deep-seated and various."(96) They entailed military and ideological reasons, which is not the scope of this discussion to list. Suffice it to mention here, however, that the Indian opposition did not stop Pakistan from probing the matter and finally joining a pact with Turkey early in 1954, as mentioned before. Nor did Indian opposition discourage the Western powers from actively enlisting Pakistan in such a pact.

Egypt was in a similar position to India vis-a-vis Iraq and the West. Her opposition to MEDO also included opposition to other Arab states joining, but for different reasons. Iraq's acquisition of Western arms in 1954, and later joining a pact with Turkey in January 1955 was construed by Egypt as an insult and a challenge, and a covert attack by the West on Arab nationalism and "solidarity." Therefore, Western pursuit of this action encouraged Egyptian sentiment of non-identification in the cold war. Egypt's bitter deadlock with Britain over the Suez Canal evacuation issue throughout the year 1953 and the first half of 1954 added greatly to this neutralist sentiment.

It was therefore natural that good relations were to develop between Egypt and India. These relations were seemingly strengthened in direct correlation to what both viewed as Western intervention in their regional affairs, and pressure to create military alliances. Indian news, therefore, as well as the views of Mr. Nehru, became prominent in the Egyptian press from 1953 on. Conversely, India became an interested and sympathetic party to

---

95
Since any close Egyptian relations with Hindu India might reflect itself adversely in Moslem Pakistan, this Egyptian-Indian friendship would seem unnatural to an Orthodox Moslem.
96 Calvocoressi, Survey...1953, p. 117.

Arab problems.

On May 17, 1953 and while Dulles was touring the Middle
East, Al-Ahram reported that the Indian Prime Minister had accepted
an invitation to visit Egypt, and that he was expected in Cairo in
the lattter part of June, 1953. On May 29, 1953 Nehru stopped in
Cairo to visit Naguib on his way to a Commonwealth meeting in
London. A day later President Naguib told reporters of the Indian
News Agency that "both India and Egypt are working for Asian unity.
Egypt looks to India for Asian leadership."(97) On his state
visit to Egypt in June, Nehru reaffirmed Indian non-alignment policy. "India," he explained, "is not neutral, but is non-aligned.
There is an important difference between the two concepts. We
would like to judge each world problem on its own merit and act
positively without having a predetermined position."(98) This
definition of India's outlook on the world was somewhat the same
as Egyptian leaders gave of their foreign policy and had been
trying to convey to the world after 1953.

The Soviets were obviously enchanted with this "peace tier"
standing in strong opposition to the Western "northern tier" alliance idea. Hence, they encouraged Indian-Egyptian neutralism. In
contrast, the Western powers through their actions and statements
stood in opposition to this neutralism. For this reason also the
Soviets merely watched while India and Egypt continued with their
opposition to Western defence schemes. Falling mostly on receptive ears in Asia and Africa, the Indian-Egyptian philosophy of
non-alignment proved a powerful opponent to American and Western
defence policies. The Western neglect to take serious notice of
it; and at times ridicule and attack the foundations of this non-
alignment(99)---perhaps served only to do more harm to the Western

---

97
98Al-Ahram, May 30, 1953.
99Al-Ahram, June 26, 1953.
Barbara Ward, Five Ideas That Changed the World (London: Hamish
Hamilton, 1959), p. 136, gives a good example of Western subjec-
tivity when she wrote: "There are, in fact, two kinds of neutrality. . . . There is a neutrality, a non-alignment between
military blocs which seem by all means to lessen the conflicts
between them, to suggest solutions, to mediate difficulties. . .
I believe the Swedes . . . use their non-alignment for this purpose. . . . But there is another non-alignment which regards
neutrality as a sort of see-saw in which, by playing one bloc
off against another, now swinging down with Communist support,
now soaring up with Western backing. . . ." For example of an
attack on Indian neutralism and advocation of arming Pakistan,
see F.S.C. Northrop, "Should U.S. Give Military Aid to Pakistan?"
Foreign Policy Bulletin, XXIV (February 15, 1954), p. 5-6.

position in Asia and the Middle East than any good accrued from
defense pacts.(100)

Egyptian neutralism, according to Boutros Ghali, in contrast to European, Indian or Indonesian neutralism, has always
been very harshly criticized.(101) Perhaps the reason for this is
not so much Egypt's aggressiveness, as Ghali had suggested, but
the fact that neither India, Indonesia nor Switzerland, etc., had
aggressive or economically powerful groups in the United States--
like the Zionists--working against their interests, as Egypt and
the Arabs had. One might perhaps be able to find a number of illustrations where Sukarno of Indonesia, for instance, had been at
least as aggressive, in the Western view, if not more so, than
either Naguib or Nasser. On the contrary, throughout the period
under this discussion, the Egyptians felt that they, as well as
the Arabs as a whole, had been the object of Western aggression.
This was manifested to them in the creation of Israel; the evic-
tion of approximately one million Arab natives of Palestine; the
harsh French rule and massacres in North Africa; and the obstinate
British stand in Suez, etc. Nevertheless, Egyptian spokesmen were
seemingly slower to adopt a categorical non-alignment stand than
might be expected, bearing in mind the pressures they felt were
being exerted upon them and the Arab world from the West and
Israel.

The Egyptians in fact continued talking of neutralism indirectly or apologetically as late as January 1955, that is, when
the Turco-Iraqi pact was signed. And whenever the question of
alignment was raised by Nasser or members of his government before
that date, they pointed out the futility of the cold war generally
and the obstinacy of both sides of that European struggle. For
instance, in December 1953, Abdel Khalik Hassouna, Secretary
General of the Arab League stated almost apologetically that there
was-

> "a growing pressure of Arab public
> opinion upon their governments in
> favor of a policy of non-identifica-
> tion with the Eastern or Western
> powers, inside or outside the United

---

[100]Mario Rossi, Foreign Policy Bulletin,XXXV(Nov. 1, 1955),p. 26-27.
[101]Ghali, "The Foreign Policy of Egypt," op. cit., p. 346.

> Nations. . . . Egypt would adopt
> a policy of strict neutralism un-
> less there was a satisfactory solution
> to Arab problems."(102)

On January 11, 1954, while discussion of American arms aid to
Iraq was going on in Washington as a prelude to including her in
MEDO, and echoed bitterly in Cairo, Al-Ahram still talked of
Egyptian neutralism indirectly by quoting a New York Times report-
er, Kenneth Love. It wrote, "Love feels that Egypt is taking
steps to commit herself to strict neutralism in the cold war."
Throughout March 1954 the Soviet Union stood strongly behind Egypt
on the issue of Israeli navigation through Suez. The West was
then backing the Israeli claim. Vyshinsky finally vetoed the
Western resolution in favor of Egypt on March 30, 1954, as mentioned earlier. There followed throughout April, May, June and
July of 1954 a number of low points in Egyptian-American relations.
These events notwithstanding, an assistant editor of Al-Ahram on
July 17, 1954 equally chided "the false propaganda of both sides
of the cold war, and the evil designs of the great powers on the
small ones."

ASIAN-AFRICAN CONFERENCE

In his second Anniversary of the Revolution speech on
July 23, 1954 Nasser made special mention of the Asian-African
bloc of nations.(103) It is probably safe to assume that by the
time Nasser made the above speech he had already been approached
by Nehru over the idea of convening as Asian-African conference.

The original idea, according to Dallin, came in January 1954
when Ali Sastroamidjojo, Prime Minister of Indonesia, proposed
such a convention at a Colombo Powers conference. Nehru was then
cool to the idea "because he saw no point in a conference that
would not include Communist China."(104) The Sino-Indian agreement of April 29, 1954 over Tibet, which "represented the first
announcement of the program known as Pancha Shilla,"(105) pre-

---

102New York Times, December 10, 1953.
103Al-Gumhuriyah, July 23, 1954.
104Dallin, Soviet Foreign Policy After Stalin, p. 296.
105Pancha Shilla is a sanskrit word meaning "five foundations."
    That is, the five principles of peaceful coexistence: mutual
    respect for each other's territorial integrity and sovereignty;
    nonagression; noninterference in each other's internal affairs;
    equality and mutual benefit; peaceful coexistence. Ibid., p. 297.

pared the way for India to discuss the matter of an Asian-African conference with China. This was done according to Dallin, in a conference between the two powers in Stockholm in June 1954. After that, quiet feelers for the idea were sent out to major Asian and African countries.(106) Perhaps Egypt was among them, for as mentioned above, Nasser made special mention of the Asian-African bloc in his July 23, 1954 speech. From the tone of his favorable remarks, Nasser was obviously agreeable to such a conference.

The final arrangements and the decision to send invitations to the Bandung conferees were arrived at after two Asian conferences. One was between Nehru and Ali Sastroamidjojo, Minister of Indonesia on September 25, 1954. The other was a conference of five Asian Prime Ministers at Bogor, Indonesia on December 29, 1954. The five powers were Burma, Ceylon, India, Pakistan and Indonesia.(107)

The United States was not favorable to the convention of the Bandung Conference. This was due in good measure to the fact that the People's Republic of China had been a prime mover behind the conference since June 1954. The Bandung conference was also based on the principles of the Pancha Shilla which were partially the ideas of Communist China and also a reflection of the peaceful coexistence strategy of Soviet Russia. For the above reasons, the United States and the Western powers opposed the meeting in Bandung. But from the Indian and Egyptian view, the United States actions in the Middle East and Indian realm since 1954 were to a good degree responsible for the convening of this conference. These American actions could also be partially blamed for the anti-American and anti-Western tone which the Bandung conference took. For instance, American sponsoring of the Pakistani-Turkish alliance of February 1954, and the extension of arms aid to Pakistan after that might have contributed heavily to the April 1954 Sino-Indian agreement mentioned above and the declaration of the Pancha Shilla. There is little doubt also that the American arms aid to Pakistan helped bring about the Indian invitation to Communist China to a supposedly neutral conference. Perhaps the United States acted partially in retaliation against India when

---

106Ibid.
107See texts of communiques of both conferences in Folliot, Documents. . . 1954, pp. 169-172.

Pakistan was invited to join the Manila Pact (South East Asia Treaty Organization--SEATO), signed September 8, 1954. It is also possible and perhaps no coincidence that Nehru invited Nasser to visit India on September 5, 1954, only three days before the Manila Pact was signed.(108)

The American sponsoring of the Turco-Iraqi Pact of January 1955 had a similar effect on Egyptian non-alignment, as SEATO and other American-sponsored pacts joined by Pakistan had on India. And while the Egyptian government carried the banner of attacking the pact as a Western assault on Arab unity, the Soviet Union stood to gain by merely looking on or perhaps repeating almost verbatim the Egyptian polemics.(109) For the time being, according to Laqueur, the Soviets forgot completely about the Marxist-Leninist doctrines, and profitably backed the national movement in Egypt and India.(110)

The Turco-Iraqi pact was concluded January 12, 1955. Two days later Al-Ahram reported that Nehru and Nasser were expected to meet soon to discuss the new development. The same paper reported on January 19 that the Indian Prime Minister backed Egypt completely in its opposition to the pact and commended Arab resistance to aggressive military designs. In contrast, Pakistan was reported two days later to be behind the pact. Meanwhile, rioting in Iraq against the pact was reported by the Syrian, Jordanian, Lebanese, as well as Egyptian press throughout January and after. Nuri's harsh suppression of these riots earned him even the displeasure of the British press. For instance, the Economist wrote, "It must be confessed that Nuri Pasha . . . in taking the steps that he has taken approaches the technique of dictatorship."(111) And while Egyptian and other Arab sentiment was violent against the Western-sponsored Iraqi pact, reaching the point where Nasser threatened to pull Egypt out of the Arab League Security Pact,(112) and Iraq in effect was outside the League,(113)

---

108 Al-Ahram, September 5, 1954, p. 1.
109 See an article by Welles Hangen, writing from Moscow, on the Soviet press on Middle East affairs then in the New York Times, January 13, 1956.
110 Laqueur, The Soviet Union and the Middle East, pp. 159-168.
111 Economist, CLXXIV (January 22, 1955), p. 255.
112 New York Times, January 31, 1955.
113 Ibid., January 20, 1955, reported Nuri as refusing to go to an Arab League meeting to discuss Iraq's adherence to the pact.

two groups again stood to gain from the whole situation--the Soviet Union and Israel. Both desired and worked toward widening the gulf between the Arabs led by Egypt and the United States.

On February 9, 1955 the Supreme Soviet announced its support of the Five Principles of Peaceful Coexistence (Pancha Shilla).(114) This Soviet action, backing non-alignment, seemed to deserve notice in Cairo. Yet it was barely mentioned. In fact Soviet news was rare in the two major Egyptian papers, Al-Ahram and Al-Gumhuriyah, until September 1955 when the Czech-Egyptian arms deal was announced. Perhaps this was due to an Egyptian attempt at avoiding any iden- tification between their non-alignment manifested at Bandung, and the Soviet encouragement of this non-alignment. Another explana- tion, and possibly the more credible one, is the fact that the Egyptian government and its press became gravely concerned over a new thrust of Western-Israeli and Turco-Iraqi pressures on Egypt and its ardent backer against the Iraqi pact--Syria. These press- ures and Egyptian fears definitely stole the headlines in Cairo, and even the great anticipated participation by Nasser in the Bandung Conference ran a poor second to these new Western pressures. Perhaps if Nasser had still entertained any hopes of Western good- will toward his government early in 1955 they had vanished by the time he left for Bandung in April 1955; and in his view the new military threat to the territorial integrity of the non-aligned Arabs, posed by Iraq, Israel and Turkey, and blessed by the West forced his government to purchase Eastern bloc arms in self-defence.

ISRAEL AND TURKEY

It seems very probable that the notion held by some Western diplomats, that the Arabs could be forced into cooperation with the West through the threat of force and diplomatic pressure was evi- dent in 1955. Iraq, Turkey and Israel were already closely associ- ated with the United States by 1955, in the Arab view. All three exerted heavy military pressure on both Syria and Egypt from February 1955 on, as shall be discussed below. All three might also have been acting on their own and without the backing of the United States or Britain. This, though, seemed farfetched to both Egypt and Syria.

---

[114]Dallin, Soviet Foreign Policy After Stalin, p. 297. (Malenkov resigned the day before this Soviet action).

The year 1954 ended with the Israeli-Egyptian border extremely quiet. This was perhaps a reflection of the tough campaign Nasser conducted against the opponents of the Anglo-Egyptian agreement over the Suez bases, and the expectation by the West and Israel(115) that Egypt might then join MEDO and possibly become more agreeable to peace with Israel. The year 1955 also began with the Egyptian-Israeli border very quiet, and even some attempts by Egypt to relax tensions with Israel. For instance, on January 2, 1955 Nasser announced that he was allowing an Israeli crew, captured aboard the Beit Galim earlier in Egyptian territorial waters to return to Israel.(116) The calm in the Gaza strip borders persisted throughout January. In the interim the above-mentioned Turco-Iraqi pact was signed (January 12). To this Egypt reacted in the violent manner described before. Suddenly a Turco-Israeli military agreement was reported in headlines in Cairo on January 27, 1955.The Egyptian press naturally questioned the motivations for this agreement and inevitably pointed to the indirect relationship which the agreement effected between Arab Iraq and Israel. The Turco-Iraqi pact also brought a new international Zionist clamor, mainly in New York, to enlist Israel in that pact.(117) All this notwithstanding, the borders in Gaza remained quiet for the greater part of February. On February 21, though, David Ben Gurion, the "exponent of an active defence policy," as the London Economist described him, was asked by Premier Sharett to become Defence Minister.(118) That was after fourteen months of retirement.

Commenting on Ben-Gurion's return, a London Times reporter writing from Jerusalem and quoted by Al-Ahram, February 22, 1955, gave a strong hint of things to come on the Egyptian Gaza border. He wrote that Sharett had followed a "policy of restraint" with

---

[115]What was important to Israel, of course, was the hope that if Egypt joined the Western pact, she would be more easily persuaded to accept peace with Israel, and then the rest of the Arab states would follow.

[116]Al-Ahram, January 2, 1955.

[117]The Zionist clamor included the usual slogans about the Arabs being "communist-oriented," and Israel being the only "democracy" in the area. See, for instance, the New York Times, January 23, 1955; and January 28, 1955.

[118]Economist (February 26, 1955), p. 696. This was under an article entitled "Return of Israel's Seer." It was sympathetic to Ben Gurion and his activist policies.

the Arabs for a long time; now that Ben Gurion was in the Defence Ministry, it was hard to say how long Sharett could restrain him, or how long his policy of restraint could last. Al-Ahram then questioned: "There is perplexity in the Egyptian Foreign Ministry as to what all this means, and what Israel means by 'restraint' when there is no trouble on the Gaza borders to speak of?"

Egypt did not have to wonder for long. The next day an Israeli attack on Gaza took place, killing four Egyptian soldiers. Five days later a major Israeli attack on Gaza also took place. This was described by Al-Ahram as "the gravest Israeli aggression on Egypt since the armistice of February 1949."[119] Until that day, according to Lenczowski, no major military engagement on the Gaza strip had been recorded since 1948. The brunt of Israeli attacks, until then, was carried by Jordan and Syria. "On that day, however, an Israeli force estimated at half a battalion attacked and destroyed the Gaza garrison headquarters of the Egyptian army, killing thirty-eight and wounding thirty-one Egyptians."[120] In a speech to the Israeli Knesset,[121] on March 2, Sharett made it clear that Israel was seemingly intent on forcing peace on Egypt. He stated:

> I declare again that Israel has
> a strong desire to be a law-abiding
> State. . . . The obligation con-
> tained in the Armistice Agreement
> to proceed toward a complete and com-
> prehensive peace settlement is a law
> which both sides are obliged to ob-
> serve. If Egypt. . . . declares
> again and again that it maintains

---

[119] Inexplicably, the New York Times saw fit not to print this grave attack at all, which in the judgment of most observers was the one which finally forced Nasser to turn to the Soviets for arms.

[120] Lenczowski, The Middle East in World Affairs, p. 362; Al-Ahram, March 2, 1955, reported that the attack was broadcasted from Radio Tel Aviv three hours before it actually occurred.

[121] Noble Frankland (ed.), Documents on International Affairs 1955 (New York: Oxford University Press, 1958), p. 346.

and has a right to maintain a
state of war against Israel . . .
then Egypt bears responsibility for
the results. These results include
armed clashes . . . and bloody battles
. . . . It is for Egypt to decide.

The next day Nasser answered:

I heard a threat from Israel
yesterday. . . I wish to say on
behalf of you all that we are not
a people who forget a wrong done to
us. . . . The blame for 1948 does
not rest on our shoulders. The Egyptian army did not fight at all in 1948;
it was a victim of betrayal and treason,
of the armistice, and of Israel's
allies. . . .

Today, brothers, we live in 1955,
and today is different from yesterday.
I tell Israel and those who make
threats in Israel's name that there
is an old saying, 'A man lies and
people believe him; he lies again
and people still believe him, he
lies yet again and begins to believe
his own lies.' If Israel thinks that
it defeated the Egyptian army in 1948
. . . then let me tell Israel that we
are ready for her. . . . The causes
which contributed to our defeat in
1948 will not be present again. . . .
The Commander-in-Chief of the Armed
Forces has been instructed to answer
aggression with aggression. . . .
We shall not speak about this matter
again; there will be no further talk,
only action.(122)

These were, of course, strong words for a man whose army

---

[122]Ibid., p. 346-47.

by all estimation lagged behind Israel in equipment and training.
Doubtless much of it was then for home consumption and morale.
But Nasser could not persist in the leadership of Egypt, let alone
Arab nationalist movement on strong words only. This was especially true in the following months when Israel acted consistently
with the line adopted by Sharett. In fact it would seem futile
to list the Israeli attacks on Gaza and the borders of Jordan
and Syria from February 28 until the Egyptian arms purchase from
Czechoslovakia in September. These attacks were ironically reported in most of the Western press as "retaliation," which
further alienated the Arabs from the Western world. In contrast,
the Soviets again championed the Arabs not only against Israel,
but against the new real danger to Syria from Turkey and Iraq, and
the "warmongers" who were backing their aggressive policies in
the Middle East.

TURKEY AND IRAQ VERSUS ARAB NON-ALIGNMENT

The Iraqi Assembly ratified the pact with Turkey on February 6,
1955. A few days later it was reported that Lebanon had been approached by both Turkey and Iraq about the possibility of her join-
int the pact. Both signatories were also actively inducing Jordan
to join their alliance.(123) On February 12, it was announced in
Ankara that President Salal Bayar would visit Jordan and Lebanon
soon.

In opposition to the pact, both Syria and Saudi Arabia stood
squarely behind Egypt. For instance, Prince Saud, Foreign Minister
of Saudi Arabia, stated in Cairo on February 9 (three days after
the Iraqi Assembly ratified the alliance) that "now we know who
are the traitors and liars amongst us, Saudi Arabia is seriously
considering pulling out of the League Pact due to the Iraqi action."(124) Three days later King Saud in Mecca declared that
"any Arab acting outside the League, and whose actions might
wreck the Arab League, is a traitor and a criminal."(125) Two
days after this a new Syrian government was formed under the
Premiership of Sabri Al-Asali whose main policy, according to
Al-Ahram, was "to fight the Turkish pact."(126) A day later the

---

123New York Times, February 12, 1955. For instance the Turkish
    government gave Jordan "three military planes" as an inducement
    124to join, according to the New York Times.
124Al-Ahram, February 9, 1955.
125Ibid., February 12, 1955.
126Ibid., February 14, 1955.

Iraqi Foreign Minister, Fadil al-Jamali, met with the new Syrian leader, and according to Al-Ahram, the latter refused to join. The same day the New York Times (February 15) reported that the Turkish Government paper charged Saudi Arabia with bribing Jordan not to join the pact. The same day, also, Nehru stopped in Cairo on his way to London, and met with Nasser. Their communique, after a reported two and one-half hour conference, repeated the Pancha Shilla, and put new emphasis on peaceful coexistence, rather than military alliances, to secure world peace.(127)

Diplomatic activity in the Middle East went on in this feverish pitch throughout February and March and to a lesser degree, after. Israel then made her move on February 28, 1955 when she attacked Gaza. The immediate reaction to this Israeli action was the proposal of an All-Arab military alliance on March 6, 1955 by the three Arab states opposed to the Iraqi pact.(128) The British move against this came two days later when Eden declared in Parliament that Britain would join the Turco-Iraqi pact.(129) The same day Al-Ahram and Al-Gumhuriyah (March 9) reported under major headlines an "Official American Dangerous Note Sent to Syria," informing her that the United States stood in complete opposition to the proposed Syrian-Egyptian-Saudi defence pact. According to the report, the United States informed Syria that "America views the Arab League only as a cultural organization, and not the basis for military alliances." The above note was understandably not publicized by the United States government. Nevertheless, a similar Turkish note to Syria was reported two days later, March 11, by the New York Times. According to this report, Turkey protested to Syria that the proposed Arab pact was "aggressive and designed against her and Iraq." The Syrian reply refuting the Turkish allegations brought another Turkish ultimatum to Syria, while rejecting the Syrian reply as unsatisfactory. The Syrian government publicized this ultimatum along with other Turkish actions designed "to prepare the way for Turkish invasion of Syria." A day later Turkish troops were reported on the Syrian frontier. The Syrian Foreign Minister, Khalid Al-Azm, then met with the ambassadors of the four major powers and informed them of the dangerous situation inherent in the Turkish troop movements

---

127 Ibid., February 16.
128 Al-Ahram, March 7, then wrote under major headlines, "Israel Unites the Arabs." March 10, 1955, p. 1.
129 New York Times, March 9, 1955. Britain finally did enter the pact on April 4.

close to the Syrian border.(130)   There was no apparent Western
move to warn Turkey regarding her aggressive actions--assuming
these actions had not been condoned by the West.   In contrast,
the Soviet Union moved inside and outside the United Nations to
defend Syria.   On March 29, the U.S.S.R. raised the issue of
Turkey's threatened aggression against Syria at the U.N.   The
Soviet press was also very vocal in attacking Turkey, Iraq and
the Western governments that were backing their actions.(131)
On April 17, 1955, also, an official statement by the Soviet
Foreign Ministry on the "Security in Near and Middle East" was
published.   This, too denounced Turkey, Iraq and the West for
their aggressive designs on the non-aligned Arabs.   The statement
then repeated:

> The Soviet Union considers that
> relations between states and their
> real security can be ensured by the
> practical application of the well-
> known principles set forth in the
> declaration; (declaration of the
> U.S.S.R. Supreme Soviet on February
> 9, 1955 (announcing support of the
> Five Principles of Peaceful Co-
> existence, mentioned above)), equal-
> ity, non-interference in internal
> affairs, non-aggression, respect for
> the territorial integrity of other
> states and sovereignty and indepen-
> dence.(132)

Whatever motive the Soviet Union had in protecting Syria
seemed immaterial to Syria and Egypt at the time.   Rather, the
press in both countries then portrayed the Soviet Union as the
protector of Arab integrity.   On March 28 a Syrian Member of
Parliament, Faisal Al-Asali, then in Cairo on an official visit,
discussed with the Egyptian press the welcomed Soviet protection.
He stated that "Molotov met in Moscow with the Syrian Ambassador

---

130
   Al-Ahram, March 24, 1955.   The Syrian fears of Turkish invasion
   and the Turkish troop movements on the Syrian borders were not
   reported by the New York Times.   Only when the U.S.S.R. moved
   to warn Turkey about her actions did this become headlines in
   the Times.   The Soviets, of course, were reported as the aggress-
   ors.   See New York Times, March 28, 1955.
131
   Laqueur, The Soviet Union. . . , pp. 257-59.
132
   Pravda, April 17, 1955, The Current Digest . . . , VII, No. 16,
   p. 19.

and informed him that the Soviet Union would not stand by to allow
Turkey to threaten or infringe upon the sovereignty of Syria.
Molotov meaningfully added to the Syrian Ambassador that Turkey
should remember that she, too, has borders with the Soviet Union.(133)

The Soviet threat apparently did not stop Turkey from further
menacing the Syrian border. On March 30 Turkey ordered further
troop movements to the Syrian border. This Turkish move, according to the New York Times (March 31) "alarmed" the United States,
Britain and France.(134) In view of the fact that Syria had
been shrilly charging Turkey with aggression and troop movements
for over a week; and in view of the fact that Western "alarm"
developed only after Soviet threats to Turkey began--this "alarm"
seemed unconvincing to the Syrians and Egyptians. It was therefore
more in anger than in jubiliation that the Egyptian papers announced
on April 3 that the United States had officially informed Turkey
that "the United States does not agree with her methods and strong
measures with Syria."(135)

On April 1 Nasser made a major foreign policy statement.(136)
Here in part is what he said:

> We in Egypt still stand on what we
> said more than two years ago that
> the defence of the Arabs should be
> accomplished by the Arabs themselves.
> We oppose military pacts and believe
> more than ever in positive neutralism.
> We have to strengthen our armed forces
> though to stop Israeli aggressions
> that are occurring daily in Gaza . . .
> It must be remembered by the West that
> the major reason for us and other Arab
> states not joining their military pacts
> was Palestine. . . .

He went on to state that the Arabs had cooperated with the
West in two world wars, yet their "reward" was British and French
colonialism, "worst of all the loss of a whole Arab country to

---

133See also a speech made in Cairo by Syrian Foreign Minister Khalid
Al-Azm on Soviet offers of protection to Syria. Al-Ahram, June
12, 1955.
134According to the N.Y. Times the three Western powers were "alarmed
at the strong measures Turkey was taking to prevent Syria from
joining an all-Arab pact."
135Al-Gumhuriyah, April 3, 1955. See the N.Y. Times, March 31, 1955
on the American disagreement with Turkish "methods" with Syria.
136Al-Ahram, April 1. This speech was made to the Egyptian Armed
Forces.

Zionist colonialism." He agreed that communism might be a danger, "but actual Western occupation is far more dangerous."

> We told Dulles in 1953 that before
> we join a Western alliance we must
> be equal. And to be equal we must
> be fully independent. Otherwise if
> we join we will be but lackeys and
> figureheads and reduced to a new
> imperialism. We would have nothing
> to say but yes and no, and lose our
> personality and dignity. . . . Our
> major concern today is creating out
> of Egypt and the Arabs a dignified,
> free and independent nation. . . .
> We have, since we came to power, in-
> formed our diplomats that we are for
> three things: we are for self-deter-
> mination; we are against imperialism
> in all its forms and wherever it
> occurs; we are for peace. . . . In-
> stead of dealing with honest Arab
> nationalists the Western powers dealt
> with Nuri. . . . I shall never again
> subject the Arab nation to foreign dom-
> ination if I can help it.

It should be pointed out again the emphasis Nasser put on "dignity" and "complete sovereignty" for Egypt. The above statement also points out the fact that whenever Nasser spoke, he spoke also in the name of the Arabs. His words were definitely appealing to Arab nationalists. It was this appeal which had made him a hero by that time in the eyes of millions of Arabs. Consequently, this enabled him to appeal directly to the Arab masses, and with obvious success, ignoring at times their governments' stands on a given issue.(137)

Nasser left for Bandung on April 9, leaving behind him an atmosphere of crisis in the Middle East. He stopped on his way to

---

[137]The Egyptian radios—Voice of the Arabs and Radio Free Egypt —were widely listened to, and hurting the Iraqi administration of Nuri and the West.

Indonesia for a five-day visit to India.(138)   From there he
left with Nehru for Burma where they met with the Chinese Prime
Minister, Chou En-Lai. This was the first meeting between Nasser
and the Chinese leader,and the latter immediately extended him an
invitation to visit China.(139) His stature increased in the
eyes of Arab nationalists in correlation with the dignity he
was accorded by the great leaders of Asia en route to, and in
Indonesia. This was perhaps the first time in many decades,
if not centuries, that an Arab leader was received with the
dignity Nasser was searching for.

There is no mistake in the fact that the Bandung Conference was a major propaganda victory for the Eastern Bloc in the
cold war. At least four leading voices in Bandung, aside from
Communist China, were outspoken against the West. These were
Egypt, India, Afghanistan and Indonesia. Each one of these
powers had in its view a legitimate gripe against either the
United States in particular or the West in general.(140)   But
while British and French imperialism were not saved from Nasser's
attacks at Bandung, he avoided mentioning the United States by
name in his major speech at the conference.(141)

While Nasser was at Bandung, another Syrian crisis developed.
This one involved American covert pressure on that Arab country.
On April 22, the Assistant Commander-in-Chief of the Syrian Armed
Forces, Adnan Malki, was assassinated while watching a soccer
game in Damascus.(142) Seemingly Malki was an outspoken opponent
of the Turco-Iraqi pact. One of his assailants was captured and
allegedly confessed that he was working for the illegal Syrian
Nationalist Party. Upon raiding the headquarters of the above

---

138
    As expected, he received a rousing welcome in New Delhi.   Two
    days before he left for India, India and Egypt signed a treaty
139of friendship. New York Times, April 7, 1955.
140Al-Ahram, April 15 and 16, 1955.
    See William Spencer, Political Evolution in the Middle East
141(New York: J.B. Lippincott, 1962), pp. 171-72.
    His major speech was published in full by Al-Ahram, April 20,
1421955. Nasser remained in Indonesia until May 2, 1955.
    See, for instance, Barada, Al-Nahar, Al-Ahram,Al-Gumhuriyah for
    daily reports on the Malki assassination for over two months
    in both countries after April 22, 1955; see also Lenczowski,
    The Middle East. . . , pp. 308-309.

party there followed daily reports in Syrian and Egyptian papers
that the United States' C.I.A. was involved in the affair.(143)
Eventually, and after a series of trials in Damascus that lasted
until the end of June 1955, 140 members of the suspected Nationalist Party were given various jail terms. The official Syrian
government report which was published throughout Syria and Egypt,
charged the United States' C.I.A. of instigating the affair.(144)

In the middle of May 1955 Iraq also began to pressure Syria.
Like Turkey before, Iraq sent an ultimatum to Syria on May 15 and
for the same reason. That is, according to Iraq, the proposed
Syrian-Egyptian-Saudi alliance was an aggressive alliance directed
against Iraq. In view of the fact that Israel was then daily
attacking Egypt in the Gaza strip, and Turkey had troops already
stationed on the borders of Syria, Nuri's move at that time made
him sink to a new low in the eyes of the Arab world.(145)

As mentioned above, the diplomatic and military pressure on
Syria was correlated with strong Israeli military pressure on Egypt
in Gaza.(146) In an apparent desperate effort to defend Egyptian
territory Nasser relied on fedaiyeen (volunteer commandos) sabo-
tage raids, as his military equipment was no match for the modern
arms Israel had. These fedaiyeen raids were billed in the Egyptian
press as great successes, probably for home consumption. In
reality, though, they only served to intensify the Israeli "re
taliation."(147) The battles in Gaza, always inside the Egyptian

---

143.
144 Ibid.; Lenczowski, op. cit., p. 308
    The New York Times which had ignored the affair entirely since
    the assassination of Malki, reported it on July 1, 1955, mainly
145 to write that "the United States denied the charges."
    Preposterously, the New York Times reported on May 18, 1955
    that Nuri maintained that Arab public opinion sanctioned Arab
146 military ties with the West. New York Times, May 18, 1955.
    Read Chap. XIV of Commander E.H. Hutchison, Violent Truce,
    pp. 111-23 as to Israel's daily aggression on Egypt. Hutchi-
    son was an American military observer on the United Nations
147 team in Palestine.
    See the Economist (June 11, 1955), pp. 944-45 on this point.

line, grew fiercer and longer. For example, on May 22, 1955, an
Israeli attack on Gaza lasted over two hours. A four-hour battle
took place on May 31.(148) On August 23 an Israeli attack lasted
six hours, resulting in heavy casualties on both sides. The day
before Dulles hinted at the Egyptian arms deal with Czechoslovakia,
three Israeli attacks occurred, etc.

All this seemed to verify the Egyptian government belief
that Egypt had no choice but to purchase arms from the Soviet
bloc. That deal was consummated in strict secrecy. It was
first announced by Dulles in a press conference on August 30,
1955. It seemed then to be a casual announcement of a normal
trade transaction. Yet the strong Western and Israeli reaction
to this deal--which in the views of the Egyptians and most Arabs
seemed their right and possibly even long overdue, but to the
West and Israel seemed upsetting to the "balance of power" in
the Middle East--(149)was to pave the way to the invasion of
Egypt in October 1956. The following chapter will therefore discuss the crises that followed the arms deal, and the play of power
politics that led to the invasion of Egypt, and almost to a major
world war.

---

[148] Nasser then met with General E.L.M. Burns, Chief of the United
Nations Armistice Commission, and suggested the erection of
barbed wire on the Gaza borders to forestall Israeli attacks.
On June 7, Al-Ahram reported that Israel refused Nasser's
suggestion, conveyed to her by General Burns. Al-Ahram, June
7, 1955.

[149] Geoffrey Barraclough and Rachel F. Wall, Survey of International Affairs 1955-1956 (London: Oxford University Press,
1960), pp. 78 and 90. The English authors still spoke of the
balance of power "as registered in the 1950 Tripartite Declaration" as being upset by the arms deal. The fact was, of
course, there never was a balance of power in the area; rather,
Israel was receiving arms freely from the West from 1950 to
1978, and the Declaration operated like a one way street.

133

CHAPTER VI

Suez War: Failure of American Diplomacy

The Egyptian-Czechoslovakian arms deal was the result of,
rather than the cause of an atmosphere of crisis in the Middle
East. It was an atmosphere that for the Arabs dated back perhaps
to the loss of Palestine in 1948 and even before that. As mentioned above, the Palestine question created a crisis of confidence
between the Arabs generally and the West. It was brought about by
a strong Arab sense of moral injustice done to them by the West--
mainly the United States and Britain--which they were unwilling to
forget.   The Egyptian arms deal was only a measure of self-defense against a moral and physical attempt at coercing Egypt, as
the leading Arab state, to accept an"unjust" fait accompli in
Palestine and in other Arab colonial problems. It was received
with shock by the West, and was seen by Israel as upsetting its
"balance of power" in the area. As seen before, the Israeli view
of the balance of power was different from what the Arabs felt was
close to an equilibrium. The Western outcry that followed the
deal and heightened the crisis atmosphere in the Middle East,
eventually to produce the invasion of Egypt, only substantiated
in Egyptian thinking the "plot theory" behind the creation of
Israel in the area. That is, that Israel was created and fos-
tered by British imperialism mainly to stand in the way of Arab
nationalism and thwart it.(1) A component of this theory was also
that Israel would be an outpost for British influence close to the
Suez Canal, and would be a future staging theater of operations
against Egypt--that is, in case the latter attempted at a later
date to fully control the canal. This theory was naturally substantiated in Arab mind when France, Britain and Israel were involved in joint invasion of Egypt in October, 1956.

The Czech arm deal was negotiated and consummated in secrecy.
It was first hinted at in a Dulles press conference in Washington
on August 30, 1955. Reporting on that conference the New York Times

---

[1] In his Address to the Nation on the third anniversary of the
Egyptian revolution, Nasser stated: "Israel in the Middle East
represents the Western colonial powers. It is the implement
they use to control us and keep their hegemony over us. It represents a colonial plot to keep the Arabs weak and divided, besides the loss of Arab Palestine." Al-Ahram, July 23, 1955.

wrote:

> . . . the Secretary explained that
> he had received indications that the
> Soviet Union had offered to supply
> military equipment to Egypt.
>
> These indications were unofficial,
> but they bore the mark of reliability
> . . . . He pointed out that the Arab
> states were, of course, sovereign and
> independent and could do as they
> wished.(2)

The paper added that there was also an indication of this in
the French newspaper, Les Echos, a few days earlier.

The above report was neither confirmed nor discussed in Cairo.
In fact, the two major Egyptian papers, Al-Ahram as well as Al-
Gumhuriyah ignored the matter for almost the full month of Septem-
ber.

Egyptian silence on the arms deal becomes more understand-
able when one ponders the reaction that was taking place, especially in New York City papers. The New York Times again took the
lead in the United States to portray the deal in the worst possible
light. According to Alfred Lilienthal,

> When the story of the Czech-Egyptian
> arms deal broke out in September 1955,
> every New York newspaper, with the
> exception of the World-Telegram, re-
> sponded with a sickening irresponsibil-
> ity toward our (American) national
> welfare and the truth. The complete
> refusal of these information media to
> relate cause and effect of the arms
> barter compounded American misinforma-
> tion as the crisis intensified.
>
> Headlines were warped--editorials
> were slanted. From the New York Times
> to the Daily Mirror, the one cry was
> for peace on Israeli terms, and the
> Egyptians were assailed as guilty ag-
> gressors.

---

[2] New York Times, August 31, 1955.

> The New York Herald Tribune
> talked of the danger of war,
> attributing the crisis to a
> 'long series of border incidents,
> together with the Arabs' steady
> refusal to accept the fact of
> Israel's statehood.' After thus
> exculpating Israel from any fault,
> this editorial continued to rewrite
> history. . . . Even the usually re-
> liable Alsops indulged in such fan-
> ciful aberrations as "the Russians
> are challenging us in an area which
> we had always thought an American
> monopoly. . . ."(3)

Lilienthal goes on to explain the significance of this type of American press reaction on American-Egyptian and Western-Arab re-lations:

> As one can discover in traveling
> around the United States, the Sunday
> 'News of the Week in Review' of the
> Times is looked upon as a sort of
> news bible. It is important to note,
> therefore, the bias contained in the
> Review's treatment of Middle East
> events. . . . For another example:
> "On important occasions over the past
> few years, the West has sided with
> the Arabs against Israel. These con-
> cessions have not satisfied the Arabs,
> however. They want the West to pull
> out of the Middle East entirely, in-
> cluding French North Africa. They
> also want the Western Powers to back
> them fully in their battle against
> Israel."

The news media also attempted to portray Nasser as a com-munist. As mentioned earlier, Nasser perhaps foresaw this even-tuality a year before, when he denied that any present or future

---

3
See Chap. XIII of Alfred M. Lilienthal, There Goes the Middle East (New York: The Devin-Adair Company, 1957), pp. 216-38.

dealings with the Soviet bloc would have any ideological over-
tones.(4) Nevertheless, to Britain, France and the Zionists,
Nasser became the object of hostility and press attacks.(5) Reports unfavorable to the Egyptian government flowed to Washington
(as well as London and Paris), that were eventually believed by
many Americans. Needless to say, the whole process of misinforma-
tion had a consternating effect on the Egyptians. Discussing this,
Ionides wrote:

> There must be some reason, they
> (the Arabs) presumed, why Eisenhower
> and Dulles were acting as if the Egyp-
> tians and the Syrians had absorbed
> communism with the help Russia was
> giving them. The Americans had em-
> bassies and intelligence organizations
> in every Arab capital, and there were
> countless newspapermen in the area.
> From every part of the Arab Middle
> East. . .Washington and the Western
> capitals must surely have been bom-
> barded, ever since Nasser took Russian
> aid in 1955, with reports that Arab
> nationalism was a bourgeois movement,
> not communist, that it was the help
> of Russian power they wanted, not her
> communism, that Russia was not even
> pushing her communism at them. . . .
> What happened to all these reports
> when they reached Washington? Obviously
> there must be some point in the flow of
> information where a series of reports
> in the opposite sense was being injected,
> for an assessment so contrary to the
> actual facts and reports could not possi-
> bly spring ready-made out of thin air.
> If contrary reports were being injected,
> someone must be creating them, uttering
> them, pushing them into the stream. That

4
See preceding Chapter.
5The Economist, July 7, 1956--that is, even before Egypt national-
ized the Suez Canal on July 23, 1956--confessed that "some sections
of the British press have been more anti-Nasser than the Egyptian
press has been anti-British." Economist, p. 40. Western polemics
were naturally more intensified after the nationalization of the
canal on July 26, 1956.

could only be a party who stood
to gain, if these untrue reports
were accepted as true by the American Government.(6)

Ionides then went on to speculate:

> Those who stood to gain could
> only be those whose ends would
> be served if the American Govern-
> ment, like the British, came down
> in hostility to Arab nationalism
> as a whole and, like the British
> took to dividing the Arabs against
> themselves on false lines of fissure,
> and thereby incurred general Arab
> hostility. No American or British
> statesmen or politicians would
> knowlingly incur general Arab hostil-
> ity. . . . There were only two can-
> didates for this role: Russia and
> the Zionists. The Russians could
> hardly have a means of inserting re-
> ports into the stream designed to
> set the Americans against the Arabs.
> The Zionists could and all past ex-
> perience showed that they did.

The first time there was an official Egyptian discussion and
confirmation of the Czechoslovakian deal was on September 27, 1955.
In a public speech on that day Nasser explained what was referred
to in Al-Ahram and Al-Gumhuriyah as the "Story Behind the Arms
Deal."(7) In effect he reviewed the numerous Egyptian efforts for
over three years to acquire arms from all three Western countries,
and how all three "kept avoiding giving us a straight answer."

> As usual, the West demanded from us
> conditions that were not compatible
> with our sovereignty, and therefore
> we refused their arms. Meanwhile
> Israel was acquiring arms from Britain,

---

[6] Ionides, Divide and Lose . . . pp. 221-222; see also a similar
statement by Emile Bustani, March Arabesque (London: Robert
Hale, Limited, 1961), p. 95.
[7] Only after Nasser's mention of it did Pravda make any mention of
the arms deal, two days later. Current Digest of the Soviet
Press, III, No. 3 (November 9, 1955), p. 16.

France, Belgium, Canada and other
places. France wanted to bargain
with us over the fate of Arab North
Africa for her arms. We refused
. . . . America made the condition
that we join a military alliance
with her, and we refused; hence,
we got not one piece of equipment
from America. From Britain we acquired all kinds of promises but no
arms. . . . Eventually Czechoslovakia
answered our call for arms, on a
strict trade basis, cotton for arms,
and without any strings attached. We
accepted their terms readily. . . .

He went on to say:

We used to read in the foreign press--
whether British, French, or American--
gleeful reports that the Israeli army
could easily defeat the Egyptian army
and all the Arab armies combined. We
used to read glowing reports about
how Israel is far better armed than
all the Arabs. We ask, how did Israel
acquire these arms when these same Western powers are the ones who made the
Tripartite Declaration of 1950 equaliz-
ing arms deliveries to the Middle East?

We have said time and again that
we will use arms only for self-defence
against Israel. Obviously the West was
not interested in that endeavor, either----

And perhaps to further avoid Western attempts to explain his action in ideological terms, he stated,

I repeat, the Czech arms deal was
a purely trade transaction, and without
any strings attached. It is designed to
end colonialism in our land, not to open
it for any new colonialism. . . . It is
clear from the Western clamor that what
they are really worried about is that
their spheres of influence, their colon-

140

ialism would be ended with the
arms deal. For our part we say
this area should be and will be
the sphere of influence of its
people

The moral position of the West was further weakened in Arab
eyes with the spectacle of both major Western powers, Britain and
the United States, attempting hastily to curry favor with Egypt as
soon as the arms deal became known. Perhaps, to the Egyptian leaders this was only a reinforcement of the axiom that nothing
succeeds like success. It gave them an assuredness they had perhaps never known before. This was reflected in official statements emanating from Cairo. Thus Nasser told a number of British
reporters in Cairo on October 2, 1955, that "Egypt will never beg
again. We shall defend ourselves from now on with arms, not statements and declarations emanating from foreign capitals."(8) And
while the Western powers suddenly became attentive to Egyptian requests, the stature of Nasser grew accordingly in the whole Arab
world. This new Western attention, as shall be illustrated below,
was unconvincing to the Arabs in whose view the West had already
taken a number of negative categorical stands vis-a-vis Arab problems. Therefore, any sudden Western change of heart on these
questions could only bring derision as well as cockiness in Cairo.

The new assuredness in Cairo also had its reflection on the
news from the Egyptian-Israeli border. In the last week of August
and the first ten days of September 1955 Egyptian fedaiyeens
(commandos) allegedly penetrated deep into Israel. According to
Al-Ahram they dynamited the Tel Aviv radio station just outside
the city on September 1.(9) It was due to these "daring attacks"
of the Egyptian commandos, according to the Egyptian press, that
Israel finally "pleaded with General Burns, Chief of the Mixed
Armistice Commission, to have him intervene with Egypt to stop
these raids. In return, Israel promised not to further attack
Gaza."(10) In reality, the same day Israel did sign an agreement
promising to ease the tension on the Gaza border. When three days

---

8
Al-Ahram, October 2, 1955.
9
Ibid., September 1, 1955.
10Al-Ahram, September 3, 1955, p. 1; see Security Council Official
Records, Tenth Year, Supplement for July, August and September
1955, pp. 5-8 on Israeli requests to Burns, and the Security
Council to stop the Egyptian "fedaiyeen" attacks.

141

later a small Israeli attack occurred, Israel, according to Al-Ahram, apologized for the incident. On September 21 it was reported that Israel was then willing to pull her forces 500 meters back from the demarcation line. This was a request which Nasser had already proposed to General Burns on June 5, 1955.(11)

The next day, however, Israel attacked and occupied the Auja demilitarized zone, a small strategically located area half-way between the Gaza strip and the Gulf of Agaba on the Egyptian-Israeli border. It was also the headquarters of the United Nations Armistice Commission. Eventually, and with persistent demands from General Burns, Israel finally evacuated the Zone on October 3, 1955.(12) Generally speaking,the Ben Gurion government(13) from then on followed a policy of selective, diplomatically timed attacks on Egypt, Jordan or Syria, rather than the casual daily excursions into Arab territory, as shall be illustrated later.

The British and American reaction to the arms deal was characterized by haste. A day before Nasser officially confirmed the Czechoslovakian arms offer, it was reported that the United States had already offered the sale of arms to Egypt on credit, apparently to forestall the Soviet bloc arms deal. According to the New York Times report (September 26, 1955), the harried American offer was protested by Britain who held that no American offer should have been made under the threat of Egypt bargaining with the Soviet bloc. A day later the same paper confirmed the reports that the United States agreed "in principle" to sell Egypt arms, and was weighing specific items. It seemed to the Egyptians as if the American willingness to sell arms to Egypt now was a tacit admission on America's part that there never was a balance of military power in the Middle East. Nevertheless, the same day also, Lincoln White, the official spokesman for the White House, confirmed the American offer. Eric Johnston and Ambassador Byroade in Cairo both met with Nasser the same day reportedly for the purpose of dissuading him from buying Czechoslovakian arms.(14)

All the above American efforts, notwithstanding, Nasser announced on September 27, that he was accepting the Czechoslovakian

---

[11] Middle East Journal,XIX (1955), p. 443.
[12] For a full Burn's report on this, see Security Council Official Records . . . September 1955, pp. 8-14.
[13] Ben Gurion had been in office since August 15, 1955.
[14] New York Times, September 27, 1955.

arms offer. The American arms offer was not accepted, according to Al-Ahram, partially because "the amount offered was too small; hence, it is not expected that Egypt will ignore the Czech deal." A day after the Nasser announcement Dulles and Macmillan conferred in New York City and issued a joint statement "to correct the impressions," according to the New York Times, that the United States had offered arms to Egypt.(15) This manner of conducting Western diplomacy became almost a pattern of British-American behavior with the Nasser government. The most outstanding illustration of this was the promise of both these governments to Nasser by December 1955 to help finance the Aswan Dam, and later reneging on this offer. This Aswan Dam project and above-mentioned Western offer will be discussed below.

Another facet of this type of Western diplomacy which further helped bring about the Suez war was that whenever Egypt, during the next twelve months, disagreed with their policies on the Middle East, Nasser was charged with blackmail. The analogy to Hitler and "appeasement of dictators," etc., were used more often.(16) There was no doubt that the Egyptian government, now that the Soviet Union was committed militarily and economically to aiding them, had more leeway for political bargaining with the West. Now that they had more room for political maneuvering, they naturally became more difficult to deal with from the Western point of view.

On September 29, Under Secretary of State George Allen flew to Cairo, again reportedly to dissuade Nasser from going through

---

[15] New York Times, September 28, 1955. Text of their statement in Ibid., p. 4.

[16] Utley, op. cit., p. 189. Freda Utley quotes Nasser as stating in an interview with George Weller, of the Chicago Daily News: "Dictator or liberator, it is how you look at it. Lincoln used to tell the fable of a shepherd who prevented a wolf from eating his sheep. To the sheep he was a liberator. But to the wolf he was a dictator." Utley, p. 188; U.S. News and World Report (September 21, 1956), pp. 56-62; Economist (July 7, 1956), p. 40. See Anthony Eden, Full Circle: The Memoirs of Anthony Eden (Boston: Houghton Mifflin Co., 1960), pp. 480-81 and 519-20, giving the analogy of Hitler and appeasement of dictators when talking of Nasser in 1955 and 1956. See also a Toynbee interview on Nasser with the New York Times, December 27, 1964. He stated: "I have noticed quite a prejudice against Nasser in this country. Americans seem to assume he is a dictator, a bad man. I do not agree with that."

with the arms deal.(17) The same day Dulles and Macmillan met with
Molotov in New York City to protest the Soviet bloc arms deal.
Mahmoud Fawzi, Foreign Minister of Egypt, also met with Molotov,
and Fawzi later warned that Egypt would not allow interference with
her sovereign right to purchase arms for her defence on the world
market. This view was reiterated by the Soviets. Pravda wrote:

> The Soviet government believes that
> every state has the right to defend
> itself and to purchase weapons for
> its defence from other states on a
> normal commercial basis.... The
> Soviet government has informed the
> Egyptian and Czechoslovak governments
> --as well as the British and U.S.
> governments. . . of its point of view
> as described above.(18)

On October 1, Nasser met with George Allen and the ambassadors
of the United States, Britain, France, the Soviet Union and India.
He later declared that "our trade and diplomacy is based on freedom
of action. Egypt is fully sovereign to trade with any country she
feels like trading with, just as Britain is trading with the Eastern
bloc."(19)

On October 2, 1955, Nasser made a major speech to the Military
Academy in Cairo. In it he violently attacked the United States,
Britain and France for a "great treachery the Egyptian Intelligence
Service just exposed." While speaking, he was waving two documents
at the crowd, one allegedly British and the other French, which
"proves beyond any doubts"(20) that the three Western powers have
been arming Israel with heavy military equipment for months, and
that all three knew about and encouraged Israeli invasions of Gaza
from February 28, 1955 on. The French document, according to Nasser,
exposed the heavy British and French military aid to Israel. The
military equipment was supposedly NATO assigned American arms, and
that the United States was well aware of, and in agreement with

---

17
18New York Times, September 29, 1955.
Pravda, October 3, 1955; The Current Digest of the Soviet Press,
19No. 44 (1955), p. 10.
20Al-Ahram, October 1, 1955.
Al-Gumhuriyah, October 3, 1955; New York Times, October 3, 1955.

this French and British action since the end of 1954.(21) The gist
of the British document was that the British government, as well as
France and the United States, were also aware of the Israeli attacks
on Gaza, and that these attacks were actually conducted with the
full collusion of these governments. This was done, allegedly to
"soften" Egypt vis-a-vis her position with regard to the Turco-Iraqi
pact, North Africa, etc. Nasser stated:

> Here is an example of some of the
> equipment which Israel has secured
> from Britain: 20 Meteors, 50 Mus-
> tangs, 20 Mosquitoes, 7 (?) trans-
> port planes, 100 Sherman tanks, 15
> Churchill tanks, 100 weapon-carriers,
> and 70 pieces of field artillery.
> This official French document also
> says that other transactions are
> being concluded between Britain and
> Israel. . . . . This is what is
> contained in the French document,
> which naturally did not report
> what France had herself delivered
> to Israel.(22)

Nasser's allegations were inadvertently confirmed by no less
than the Israeli Defence Ministry the next day. In a speech by
the Director-General of the Israeli Defence Ministry, Shimon
Peres, the latter stated:

> Two years ago, before he went to
> Sdeh Boker, the Defence Minister
> David Ben Gurion drew up a pro-
> gramme for the arming of the Israeli
> defence forces. Thanks to the
> generous attitude of the French

21
See Robert J. Donovan, Eisenhower, The Inside Story (New York:
Harper and Brothers, 1956), p. 389. This is comparable to the
West German shipment of heavy arms--tanks, bombers, etc.,--that
was exposed in 1965. The German action was also effected with
the full knowledge of the United States. For the full story
on this German action, see Arab Observer, February 15, 1965,
pp. 4-11.
22
Frankland, op. cit., p. 373.

145

Government, which provided us
with the guns and tanks seen on
Independence Day, and thanks to
the full support of the Treasury
. . . , more than two-thirds of
this programme was accomplished
in the past two years.(23)

Peres then added that the Egyptian arms deal required the
acquisition of more tanks, guns, etc., by Israel.

We acquired modern aircraft, which
gave us a new air superiority. Together with these planes we bought
a considerable quantity of spare
parts. . . . With regard to the
acquisition of arms, we have provided Israel with superiority over
the Arab states.(24)

The above statement seemed to confirm once again two points:
Israeli arms superiority over all the Arab states combined; and
the fact that Israel was freely acquiring arms from the West regardless of the 1950 Tripartite Declaration.

Nasser's charge that Western arms were freely going to
Israel was partially confirmed by the British Foreign Office also.
On October 8, it issued a statement which did not categorically
deny the sale of arms to Israel. Rather, it protested that "the
figures quoted . . . are inaccurate and most are grossly exag-
gerated."(25)

The Western clamor, though, against the Egyptian-Czech arms
deal persisted unabated. It was also correlated with a similar
outcry by Israel, and the Zionists. The Editor of the New York
Times ominously warned that the Egyptian arms deal might be the
beginning of Soviet "intervention" in the Middle East. On October
6, five American Jewish leaders protested the deal. On October 9,
two rabbis decried the deal in New York City sermons. On
October 13, another group of American Jewish leaders conferred

---

23Ibid., pp. 373-74 (quoting from Summary of World Broadcasts,
  Monitoring Services of the British Broadcasting Corporation).
24Ibid.
25Ibid., p. 376.

146

with Dulles over the deal. On October 14, fifteen United States Representatives urged the United States to supply arms to Israel. On October 31, Governor Thomas Dewey of New York attacked the arms deal. He was later joined by Harry S. Truman.(26) Thus, again the grave Palestine question and the whole delicate Middle East situation became a political football inside the United States.

The above pressure on the State Department was also correlated with official Israeli demands for Western arms. On October 19, Sharett in a speech in Jerusalem urged the West and world Jewry to help arm Israel to offset the danger of Egyptian "aggression."(27) He added that Israel was entitled to a security pact now with the United States. Few days later Sharett flew to Geneva to see the Big Four Foreign Ministers who were then meeting there. His trip, according to the New York Times, (October 23, 1955) was for the purpose of explaining "the war dangers" resulting from the Egyptian arms deal. While at Geneva an Israeli attack on Gaza occurred on the Al-Auja demilitarized zone. These were designed, in the Egyptian view, to draw world attention to the "troubled" Middle East, and perhaps dramatize the urgency of the Israeli "need" for arms. The Ben Gurion speech to the Knesset on November 2 was viewed by the Egyptians in the same light. In it Ben Gurion stated that Israel desired peace "with all our hearts," and "good neighborly relations."(28)

The same evening, however, an estimated three thousand Israeli troops attacked the Egyptian village of Sabha deep inside the Egyptian border beyond the Al-Auja demilitarized zone. The Egyptians admitted to 50 dead, and boasted that over 200 Israeli invaders were left behind, dead, after 17 hours of battle.(29) Nasser then charged, "Ben Gurion asks for peace in the morning, and invades Egypt in the afternoon. It is obvious to any naive observer that he wants to mislead world public opinion, and prepare the spade work for his mad aggressions."(30)

The United States reation to the Sabha invasion added to the Egyptian consternation. A statement by the State Department issued on November 5 declared that :

------

26 New York Times, October 4, 6, 9, 13, 14 and 31, 1955 on the above pro-Zionist clamor.
27 Ibid., October 19, 1955.
28 Frankland, op. cit., pp. 379-81; Al-Ahram, November 3, 1955, headlined the speech naively as "Ben Gurion Wants Peace with the Arabs."
29 Barraclough and Wall, op. cit., p. 97.
30 Al-Ahram, November 4, 1955.

                    . . . the United States has noted,
                with deep concern, the increasing
                tempo of hostilities between Israel
                and Egypt. According to our informa-
                tion there have been violations . . .
                by both Israel and Egypt. . . . The
                United States deplores resort to force
                for the settlement of disputes. . . .
                Assistant Secretary Allen informed the
                Ambassadors of Israel and Egypt of the
                attitude of the United States......(31)

The next day the Egyptian Ambassador to the United States,
Ahmed Hussain, protested to Assistant Secretary Allen the American
statement, since the statement implied equal guilt of both Israel
and Egypt, when it was Israel who had invaded and ruined the Egyptian village of Sabha. And while the Egyptian protest was not
mentioned by the New York Times, for instance, it did publish a
lengthy comment by Hansen Baldwin the same day, November 6, warning that the Soviet Union was "moving into" the Middle East to
fill the vacuum caused by the cuts in British strength in the
area.

On November 9, 1955, possibly one of the last glimmers of
hope in Arab capitals for an "equitable" Western-backed solution
of the Palestine question came about. This was in a speech by
Eden at the Guildhall in London.(32) In it he suggested a "compromise solution" of the Palestine question based on the United
Nations partition   resolution of 1947. After backing the
United Nations efforts to supervise the borders of Israel and the
Arabs, and attacking the Egyptian arms deal and the "Soviet action";
and regretting the failure of the Eric Johnston missions and his
irrigation schemes for over two years, he concluded:

                    As I have said, we have tried, for
                a long time past, to find common
                ground for some kind of settlement.
                I think that the time has now come
                when the acute dangers of the situa-
                tion force us to try again. We must

---

31 Department of State Bulletin, November 14, 1955, p. 786.
32 For the full text, see Frankland, op. cit., pp. 382-85.

> somehow attempt to deal with the
> root cause of the trouble. . . .
> Our countries would also offer
> substantial help--financial and
> other--over the tragic problem
> of the refugees.(33)

He noted that the Arabs would be willing to discuss terms with
Israel, based on the 1947 and subsequent United Nations resolutions. However, the Israelis based their position on the Armistice Agreement of 1949, to include the present territories they
occupied. Eden deplored that the United Nations resolutions were
being ignored, and felt that it was in the interests of both sides
to work out a compromise. He then offered his government's fullest
cooperation in that endeavor.

A similar statement, but not so detailed, was issued by the
American State Department the same day. This one was mainly concerned with stating American opposition to any aggression in the
Middle East, and declared the American backing of peaceful solutions
in Palestine.

Eden's and the American State Department's hopes for a "compromise" and a peaceful solution for Palestine were dashed within
less than 24 hours. The same day Sharett arrived in New York City
for a three-day speaking tour. Upon arriving, he declared that
Eden's speech was an open support for the Arabs, and that Israel
would not yield any of her territory to any one short of war.(34)
A few days later Ben Gurion "scathingly rejected"(35) the Eden
suggestions in a speech to the Knesset.(36) Eden was also subjected
to attacks and charges by Zionist and pro-Zionist Members of Parliament in the House of Commons.(37) This Israeli reaction to Eden's
compromise suggestion was correlated with a similar campaign in the
United States.

33
Frankland, op. cit., pp. 384-85.
34
Barraclough and Wall, op. cit., p. 97.
35
Ibid.
36
For a text of his attack on Eden, see Frankland, op. cit., pp.
385-88.
37
The London Times also misconstrued Eden's suggestion, perhaps
to jump on the Zionist "bandwagon." It stated that Eden meant
by his compromise that Israel should give the whole of Negev to
the Arabs. The Negev makes up more than half the territory of
Israel. London Times, November 14, 1955. As part of the pressure on Eden, Al-Ahram reported on November 16 that over four
thousand Jewish-British soldiers demonstrated in London against
Eden's suggestion. Al-Ahram, November 16, 1955.

In contrast, Nasser, in reaction to the Eden speech, made the following statement:

> Eden's efforts and his suggestions
> are the first just and honorable
> Western suggestions of the solution
> of the Palestine question within re-
> cent memory. The Arabs are agreeable
> to negotiate on the basis of these
> suggestions and on the basis of the
> U.N. resolutions. . . . It should
> be remembered by Israel, that the
> mere Arab acceptance of the principle
> of the partition of Palestine now is
> a major compromise on the part of
> the Arabs.(38)

The American announcement that Israel could purchase arms from the United States ironically came two days before the Eden suggestion for peace in Palestine.(39) This poor correlation between Western policies in the Middle East—as well as the poor correlation between the State Department policies and the politicians in the United States, became an outstanding feature of Western diplomacy in the Middle East. It has, no doubt, since 1917 been a major cause for the creation of an extremely difficult situation in Palestine, and was to contribute heavily to the Suez War in 1956. This vacillation by the United States between what was politically expedient internally, and what the best judgment of American (and British) statesmen recommended in Palestine, particularly, plagued the policies of both Western powers since the start. And while world Zionists played on and to a good degree caused this vacillation, there were seemingly two losers in the Middle East—the Arabs and the West.

The American vacillation between what seemed diplomatic policy statements for the Middle East, and subsequent action to the contrary, also covered the economic sphere. Thus while the State Department and other agencies of the government negotiated over, and finally promised aid for the Aswan Dam project in Egypt, for instance, a sudden volte-face would occur in Washington. The abruptness of such a switch in policy, coupled with the hastily contrived excuses for a given change, reduced American diplomacy,

---

[38]Barraclough, op. cit., p. 97.
[39]Current History, XXX (1956), p. 53; Al-Ahram, November 7, 1955.

in the Arab view, to an irresponsible state. And what seemed to
have incensed the Arabs more than the changes in American policy
itself, were the excuses given for the changes. An outstanding
illustration of this type of "diplomacy" was the case of the
Aswan Dam project.(40)

ASWAN DAM PROJECT

According to John S. Badeau:

> A competent observer of Middle
> Eastern affairs recently remarked,
> 'the trouble with Egypt is that she
> is trying to undergo three revolu-
> tions at once: the American Revolu-
> tion to run out the Redcoats; the
> French Revolution to depose a King
> and build a Republic; and the Social
> Revolution—to remake an entire
> economy.' It will take a very large
> hero indeed to fulfill such a multi-
> form role.(41)

After 1952 the Free Officers diligently attempted to accomplish what seemed at times a hopeless situation, given the extremely distressing position in which Egypt was left by the Farouk
regime. And while Nasser was "a man in a hurry," as he once described himself, his economic revolution was considerably slowed
down due to the political complications discussed above. Naturally, any Egyptian hope in 1952 for economic aid or investment
would have been centered around Washington and London, since the
Soviet Union had not yet chosen trade and aid as a means of competition in the cold war.

Among the projects high on the priority list which the Free
Officers hoped to accomplish was the Aswan High Dam. By tracing

---

40
  Senator William Fulbrignt pointed out in 1957 on the floor of
  the Senate that two events led to the entry of the communist in-
  fluence in the Middle East: arms given by the Soviet bloc to
  Egypt in 1955; and the withdrawal of the United States offer to
  help build the Aswan Dam in Egypt. Congressional Record, August
  10, 1957, p. 13393.
41
  John S. Badeau, "A Role in Search of a Hero: A Brief Study of the
  Egyptian Revolution," Middle East Journal, IX (Autumn, 1955), 384.
  Badeau served at one time as the President of the Amer. Univ. at
  Cairo.

their early excited comment about it, and their related hopes for
accomplishing it, it would be accurate to state that the new
Egyptian leaders viewed its accomplishemnt as a measure of the
economic success of their revolution.

On June 20, 1953, Al-Ahram carried a lengthy article based
on an interview with Egypt's Commander of the Air Force, Ali Sabri.
In it he related the history of the Aswan Dam idea and the early
interest of the new regime in accomplishing it. According to Sabri,
the idea dated back to the Farouk regime, "which did not have the
vision to pursue it." The idea originated with an Egyptian engineer
named Adrian Daninous. "It was brought to my attention in August
1952, and I took the blueprints to the Revolutionary Council.
The idea was immediately accepted." At the end of 1952, Daninous
was sent to Italy, France, Britain and the United States to help
generate technical and financial interest in the project. Ten
international engineers finally met in Cairo in "early 1953" and
"all reported to the Revolutionary Council that the project is
feasible." The project would take about seven years to build and
needed approximately 180 million Egyptian pounds--about 500 million
dollars--in foreign aid. The urgency with which the Egyptians
viewed the fulfillment of the Aswan Dam was, of course, no guarantee for American financial aid. In fact, two weeks later Al-
Ahram (July 6) discussed why American financial aid to Egypt was
lagging. It was "because the conditions attached to it are not com-
patible with the principles of the Egyptian revolution." The paper
also added that "in any case, there are British attempts to influence America not to give aid to Egypt." The latter remark was
due, of course, to the fact that Britain and Egypt were then still
at odds over the Suez evacuation issue.

The next mention of the project in Al-Ahram was on October 7,
1953. It then carried an interview with the then Egyptian Minister
of Finance, Abdel Jalil Al-Umari. Al-Umari had then just arrived
back from a month's tour of Europe and the United States. He
stated:

> I have made contacts with the United
> States government for the purpose of
> economic assistance in financing vari-
> ous Egyptian industrial projects; chief
> among them was the Aswan High Dam. All
> American circles have shown positive re-
> sponse in this regard. We expect to be
> able to borrow from the International
> Bank for Reconstruction and Development

152

(henceforth to be referred to as the
World Bank) to fulfill some of these
projects. . . . America, particularly,
seems to be positively oriented towards
aiding the Aswan Dam project.

This optimistic report also coincided with the Eric Johnston
trip to the Middle East on October 15,1953, where he went particularly to discuss, and perhaps to offer economic aid for various
projects. As mentioned earlier, also, Johnston's arrival coincided with the Israeli attack on the Jordanian village of Qibya,
which weakened the appeal of any American aid to the Arabs generally, if offered. Hence, there was no progress made over the possible American financing of Aswan.

Throughout the first half of 1954 the political and diplomatic
climate in Egypt and in Western capitals was such that any financial aid to Egypt was unlikely. For this reason, there was hardly
any mention of the Dam project or Western aid for it, in either
Al-Ahram or Al-Gumhuriyah throughout this period. But almost immediately after the initial Anglo-Egyptian agreement over Suez was
signed on July 28, 1954, discussion of the Dam began to appear.
On July 31, Al-Ahram reported that two experts, one American and
the other French, were on their way to Cairo for the purpose of
"studying the project and all its ramifications." "It was hoped,"
according to the report, "that work will begin on the project this
year." In a major article by the same paper on August 25, it
stated that "there are very good indications that the World Bank
will participate in executing the project."

However, adverse political developments intervened again,
and Egypt began to drift toward "non-alignment." This drift was
accelerated after the Turco-Iraqi pact was signed early in 1955.
But Nasser's strong opposition to the pact rendered him, in the
Western view, not so much non-aligned, as on the "wrong side of
the track." For this reason, as we have seen above, Egypt, as well
as Syria, felt subjected to various diplomatic and military pressures from a variety of "Western" quarters. Nasser's participation
in the Bandung Conference further diminished the probability of
Western economic aid to Egypt, and again the Aswan Dam project remained dormant. That is not to say that Egypt did not continue
to seek a Western economic aid for its accomplishment. For instance, at the height of the clamor over the Turco-Iraqi pact,
signed January 15, 1955, Al-Ahram reported on January 26 that the
Egyptian Minister of Economy, Al-Kaisuny, was conducting financial
negotiations with a delegate of the World Bank, one John D. Wild.

Nevertheless, these negotiations never materialized, and no financial agreement over the Dam was ever realized. Thus, little mention of the project was to be found in the Egyptian press until the arms deal was announced.

Dulles announced his knowledge of the Egyptian arms deal on August 30, 1955. There followed the American and British attempts, discussed above to dissuade Nasser from going through with the deal. American arms were hastily offered to Egypt, and were refused. Then Dulles stated also that there must be a way of stopping one state (presumably Israel) from attacking the other in the Middle East, even using joint Western efforts for the purpose.(42) A month later Eden suggested also that there must be a just solution to the Palestine question, even at the expense of territorial loss to Israel. Meanwhile, Eric Johnston was in Jerusalem and Cairo, seemingly concerned with the fate of Arab refugees. The Soviet Union then offered financial and technical aid to Egypt, perhaps for the first time in its history. In a press conference in Cairo, and in an apparent attempt to outbid any Western offers, Soviet Ambassador Solod declared that the Soviet Union had decided to offer financial and technical aid to all Arab countries that might ask for it.(43)

Needless to say, such hasty Western reactions encouraged the Egyptian press to hint at further Soviet aid offers, perhaps to hasten Western aid commitments to Egypt. Thus, on October 11, 1955, Al-Ahram hinted that the U.S.S.R. was willing to build the Aswan Dam. The next day it wrote that the Soviet "offer" to build the Dam "threw a great scare into Washington and London." Doubtlessly, such intimations were also used to put pressure on the Soviet Union to commit itself to real aid in the project. For, it would be reasonable to assume that the Egyptians were not anxious to have the Soviets score propaganda victories in Egypt over the West, that would cost Russia only words. But while these hints went understandably unchecked, but also unverified either by Nasser or Solod, they seemed to have worked on the United States and Britain, producing what seemed as possible favorable results for Egypt.

For one thing, the State Department withstood for a while Zionist and Israeli clamor for the immediate delivery of American arms to the latter. There was also the American Zionist demand, refused by the United States, to sign some kind of a military alliance with Israel. The State Department also opposed the British view and pressure to have the United States join the Baghdad Pact (MEDO).

42
New York Times, October 5, 1955.
43
New York Times, October 11, 1955; Al-Ahram, October 11, 1955.

154

Instead, the United States was content with declaring its verbal and economic backing of the pact, and the acceptance only of a "military and political liaison" with it. Then on November 18, discussions opened in Washington between Egypt and the World Bank over the financing of the Aswan Dam.(44) The Egyptian delegation was headed by Minister of Economy, Al-Kaisuny. These negotiations seemed to have gone well from the start. On December 2, 1955 Al-Ahram quoted Al-Kaisuny as stating that things were going extremely well in Washington. On December 9, the same paper discussed the conditions which Egypt hoped would be accepted by the United States and the World Bank, so as to make any offer of aid acceptable:

> Egypt is asking for 200 million dollars each from the United States government and the World Bank. Reports indicate that the Bank has already agreed to lend Egypt the money. It is expected also that the United States government will ask Congress for the setting aside of 200 million dollars to be spent as requested by Egypt, but not dependent on a yearly allocation from Congress.

Speculations as to Congressional acceptability to a long term aid offer went on. Finally, the following American statement was issued on December 17, 1955:

> During their stay in Washington, Mr. Kaissouni(45) and his colleagues have been carrying on discussions with the management of the World Bank and representatives of the United States and the United Kingdom Governments concerning possible assistance in the execution of the High Aswan Dam project.
> The United States and British Governments assured the Egyptian Government through Mr. Kaissouni of their support in this project. . . . Further, Assurances have been given to Mr. Kaissouni that the Governments . . . would, subject to legislative authority, be prepared to consider sympathetically

---

44
Middle East Journal, X (1955), p. 66.
45
A variation of the spelling of "Al-Kaisuny."

in the light of then existing circumstances further support toward
financing the later stages to supplement World Bank financing.

Final understanding with the
British and American Governments
and the World Bank will await Mr.
Kaissouni's consultation with the
Egyptian Government.(46)

This agreement was billed by the Egyptian press as a success
for the Egyptian delegation. In fact, though, it fell short of the
original Egyptian expectations. Since, if Nasser accepted the
offer as it stood, he would in effect be promising Britain and
the United States what they considered "good behavior" on the part
of his government for at least the next seven years. This was, of
course, the period expected for completion of the Dam. In fact,
the statement of the agreement seems to be explicit about this.
But it has already been established that what Nasser believed was
legitimate Egyptian interests was not always what the Western
powers believed to be so. Hence, it would seem reasonable to ex-
pect Egypt to hesitate before accepting these Western conditions
for the aid offer.(47)

Another reason for the Egyptian hesitation was pointed out
later by Al-Ahram, June 21, 1956. This concerned the World Bank
loan. It wrote that the Bank loan was also contingent on the Bank's
prerogative to be consulted before Egypt incurred any further
large loans from other sources.

Other factors led to the Egyptian hesitation. One was the
Soviet offer to participate in financing the Aswan Dam. Others
were political reasons including new British attempts to recruit
new Arab members for the Baghdad Pact and new Israeli actions on
the borders of Egypt and Syria.

BRITAIN AND ISRAEL

The United States was also behind the Eden suggestion for

46
47Department of State Bulletin, December 26, 1955, pp. 1050-51.
For justification of Egyptian hesitation, see Fisher, op. cit.,
p. 630.

peace in Palestine that was rejected by Israel.(48)   This action
temporarily aroused Arab hope for a just solution in Palestine.
However, this did not last long.   For Britain simultaneously re-
verted to the policy of enlarging the Baghdad Pact membership.
This was done, seemingly, even though the United States was not
convinced of the wisdom of expanding the pact in the autumn of 1955.
In contrast to Britain who insisted on the pact as the best
Western policy in the Middle East, the United States,

> . . . was increasingly mindful of
> neutralist feeling. On November 6,
> 1955 Dulles had met Tito at Brioni
> (Tito was already a friend of Nehru
> and Nasser, and another proponent
> of "neutralism"). . . . Washington
> showed little enthusiasm for the treaty
> (MEDO) which Nehru had described, as
> recently as December 5, as 'deplorable
> from the point of view of peace and
> security.'(49)

France was also beginning to doubt the wisdom of the pact
by the end of 1955.(50)   Nevertheless, Britain renewed its efforts
in this regard in December, 1955.   On December 6, 1955, General
Gerald Templar, Chief of Staff of the British army, was sent to
Amman, Jordan, for the purpose of enlisting Jordan into the pact.

On December 9, 1955, the Jordanian cabinet of Said Al-Mufti
met for a five hour session with the Templar party.   It soon became apparent that the Al-Mufti government was opposed to joining
the pact.   For, on December 13, four Jordanian Ministers submitted
their resignations as a protest against the Templar "pressure" on
Jordan to join.   A day later, Said Al-Mufti himself resigned, and

---

48
  See for instance, a message from President Eisenhower to a
  Zionist meeting in Madison Square Garden stating that peace in
  the Middle East had to be based on a just solution to the
  Palestine question. Al-Ahram, November 16, 1955.
49
  Barraclough and Wall, op. cit., p. 282.
50
  In December, 1955, Mendes-France called the pact a "blunder."
  New York Times, December 21, 1955.

riots broke out throughout Jordan against the Baghdad Pact.(51)
On December 15, 1955 the New York Times reported over forty persons
killed in Jordan by the Jordanian army (the Arab Legion) in an
attempt to quell the anti-Baghdad Pact riots.(52) These riots lasted
over ten days. As a result, even the British Economist confessed
later on December 24, 1955, that:

> In terms of popular sentiment, Jordan
> is almost certainly with Egypt and Syria
> and against Iraq on the defence issue
> . . . . In a small country obsessed by
> fears of Israel, it was inevitable that
> an arrangement which is part of the
> Western defences against Soviet Russia
> should have little appeal beside the
> Egyptian-Syrian alliance which is pri-
> marily directed against Israel.

The above statement seems to indicate that Jordan would have
opposed the pact with or without Egyptian influence. The fact is
that the Egyptian press played down the Jordanian events. This
was perhaps due to the fact that these events coincided with
Egyptian negotiations with the United States and Britain that
were going on in Washington over the financing of the Aswan Dam.
These negotiations were going well and finally reached fruition
on December 17, 1955. as mentioned above. However, the "ineptness"
of the British policy there, as Barraclough characterized it, was
blamed on Egypt.

The oppostion of Jordan to the Baghdad Pact was taken in
Britain as an Egyptian blow to her in an area where there had
been traditionally strong British economic and military influence.(53) As this attitude reflected itself on the Aswan Dam
financing, the British offer of December 17, 1955, was in doubt

---

51
In a press conference a week after his resignation Said Al-
Mufti discussed the British strong-arm methods against Jordan:
"I told General Templar as he arrived that the Jordanian people
were against the Baghdad Pact. He answered me in English,
'Don't worry.' I told him I would not consent to any forceful
measures in this regard. . . . I realized later that the British were working through one of the Ministers of my cabinet,
Hazza Al-Majali, who was in favor of the pact. I immediately resigned. . . . I must state that the people of Jordan have every
reason to be proud of their King Hussain. For he, too, like me,
was under British pressure to join." Al-Ahram, December 23, 1955.
52The Arab Legion was then led by a Britisher, General John Bagot
Glubb. New York Times, December 16, 1955. Al-Ahram, December 17,
1955, reported over fifty dead.
53Eden, op. cit., pp. 385-87.

in London almost as soon as it was announced. After the Jordanian events, Nasser was indicted in the British press as the sole
perpetrator of British troubles throughout the Middle East.
Britain was also beginning to resent what they felt was American
aloofness from the Baghdad Pact, allegedly in the interests of
relations with Egypt and her allies, Syria and Saudi Arabia.(54)

In this atmosphere of new friction between Britain and Egypt
with her Arab allies, Israel executed another major raid into
Syria. On December 11, 1955, an Israeli force estimated at eigh-
teen hundred soldiers wiped out the Syrian outposts at Butaiha on
the northern shores of the Sea of Galilee.(55) Fifty-six Syrians
were killed. This Israeli action might have cost Israel more in
world sympathy than she anticipated. For aside from the routine
Security Council censureship of the attack, Israel even lost some
ground momentarily with its Zionist public opinion. For instance,
even Senator Herbert H. Lehman of New York warned Israel to show
restraint and respect for the sanctity of each human life.(56)

The Israeli attack on Syria might have strongly influenced
Jordanian non-receptiveness to the Templar mission, and Jordan's
final refusal to join the Baghdad Pact. It also temporarily reinforced the American non-commital, until then, to act on the Israeli request for arms. It was directly responsible for the formation of an Arab joint military command, ostensibly bringing together the armed forces of Egypt, Syria and Saudia Arabia.(57)

Nasser began the year 1955 at a low point in popularity and
influence. He finished it, according to Wynn, as the unquestion-
able leader of the Arab world.(58) It was a measure of recognizing this fact that in March of 1956, leaders from both France and
Britain were to go to Cairo. Both Western nations were then embroiled with various colonial problems that rendered them vulnerable
to Egyptian broadcasts. Britain was then suppressing the Mau Mau
rebellion in Kenya, and Cyrus was fighting for its independence.
Also for Britain there were Arab national troubles in Aden and the
Trucial Coast area (Oman, Qatar, Emirates and Kuwait, later) on
the Persian Gulf. Iraq, too, Britain's only Arab ally, was iso-

_____

54
55Barraclough, op. cit., p. 284; Eden, op. cit., pp. 374-375.
56Lenczowski, The Middle East in World Affairs, p. 362.
His warning though came in the course of an Israeli bond drive
57in New York City. New York Times, December 15, 1955.
58Ibid., December 27, 1955. (Text of communique on p. 3.)
Wynn, op. cit., p. 133.

lated from the Arab world and vulnerable to the Egyptian nationalist
line. France was embroiled in war in Algeria. Both France and
Britain tended to blame most of their troubles on alleged Egyptian
incitement and inflammatory radio programs.

Eden's Middle East foreign policy was also subject to various
pressures inside and outside Britain. For instance, Labor leader
Hugh Gaitskill, in the usual British imperial manner, was demanding
in January, 1956, that Eden invite the Soviet Union to a conference
on the Middle East.(59) This the British government still hesita-
ted to do, since it would imply recognition of the Soviet Union as
a contending power in that area. Naturally, it did not occur to
liberal Gaitskill, of course, to demand liberal and unimperial solutions of the area's problems accepted by its natives!!!

The Baghdad Pact was also the subject of attacks by various
Americans. For instance, ex-Secretary Dean Acheson charged that
the pact split the Arab states against each other and gave the Soviet
Union "opportunity for mischief." Acheson doubted the military
value of the pact and urged the United States not to press the nations of the Middle East to join.(60) Tito's numerous denuncia-
tions of the pact finally brought British protests to Belgrade.(61)

In answer to these adverse pressures, Eden flew to Washington
at the end of January, 1955 to discuss the problems of the Middle
East with the State Department. The main object was to synchronize
Western diplomacy vis-a-vis the new Soviet challenge in the Middle
East, and to formulate a specific program for common action with
full American participation. Seemingly, Eden was hopeful that the
United States would immediately accede to the pact to relieve the
pressure on British policy there. Instead, their communique only
declared that the pact was a "bulwark against Soviet penetration."
Meanwhile, it was made clear to Eden that the United States would
only join the Baghdad Pact when "it can be seen to contribute to
the general stability of the area."(63) As for the Arab-Israeli
border problems, Eden suggested the stationing of Western troops
on these borders. The United States opposed this also, and the

---

59
Such an invitation, Gaitskill argued, would stop the Soviets from
manipulating Arab-Israeli quarrels to their advantage. New York
Times, January 25, 1966. He also demanded that Israel be armed.
60Ibid., January 13, 1956.
61New York Times, January 8, 1956.
62Barraclough, op. cit., p. 285.
63Baraclough, op. cit.

final communique only expressed support for the efforts of General Burns and the United Nations observers in Palestine, and a new emphasis was put on the 1950 Tripartite Declaration as a deterrent to any aggression. There was also a mention of agreement on some joint measures to be taken in case of aggression, and that France was being invited to participate. France did participate on February 6 in a new set of discussions in Washington, but these talks brought no clear-cut Western agreement on a line of action.(64)

The mere mention of the stationing of Western troops on the borders of Israel and the Arab states aroused the suspicion of the Arabs. The Egyptians also resented the fact that the Western powers persisted in discussing the fate of the Arab world without inviting the states of that region to these discussions. Al-Ahram then wrote on February 7, 1956:

> It is bewildering, and very indicative
> of the mentality of the Western powers,
> that they sit down to discuss the fate
> of the Middle East, as if it was still
> a pawn of old style imperialism. This
> is done in disregard of the fact that
> these nations are independent. . . .
> Egypt will not agree to any policy
> arrived at without its full participa-
> tion, and resents the mention of sta-
> tioning any troops on its soil. . . .

A day later Nasser also warned the great powers to change their tactics of deciding the fate of the smaller powers in their capitals. His warning was repeated by the excluded Soviet Union a few days later. On February 14, the Soviet Foreign Ministry issued the following statement:

> The participants in the Washington
> conference assert that the measures
> they have planned with regard to the
> Near and Middle East countries have been
> caused by 'the state of tension' in re-
> lations between 'Israel and her Arab neigh-
> bors.' In so doing they try to create the
> impression that the tripartite declaration
> . . . of May 25, 1950, entitles them to take

64
Dulles at a press conference on February 28, 1956 confessed that there was no formal agreement, but "exchange of views as between the three members of the tripartite pact of 1950." See Barraclough, op. cit., p. 286.

arbitrary action outside the United
Nations.

This is not the first time that
attempts have been made to impose
upon the Near and Middle East countries the will of certain foreign
circles. . . . It is precisely for
the implementation of these military
plans that the notorious Baghdad pact
has been concluded. . . . (65)

The statement went on to warn that any "arbitrary actions" by
the Western powers in the area "cannot fail to arouse the Soviet
government's legitimate concern." Such actions "would be a gross
violation of the United Nations Charter and the national sovereignty
of a number of countries."

Thus, in the absence of any agreement by the Western powers
for any action in the Middle East, and the refusal of Arab states
to accept dictated Western policy, and now the Soviet warnings
that they too had legitimate reason to be concerned about events
in the area, the situation in the Middle East became highly com-
plicated. Adding to the complication was the internal pressures
on the British and American governments to clarify their Middle
East positions and perhaps correlate them.

Dulles, though was vacillating between outright refusal to
join the Baghdad pact--thus weakening the hand of Britain and her
MEDO allies--and making statements to the Senate Foreign Relations
Committee, for instance, favoring the pact. In answer to queries
by the Committee on February 25, he commended the pact as a "de-
fensive" alliance against the Soviet Union, and denied the charge
that it was aimed at disrupting harmony in the Arab World.(66)
His vacillation covered other spheres of American policy in the
Middle East. This indecision became an outstanding feature of the
Eisenhower administration policies until the invasion of Suez in
October, 1956, and was probably a major contributor to that debacle.
For it was to become increasingly difficult for America's imperial
allies, as well as Israel and the Arabs to interpret American policy
on a given issue. It was also becoming increasingly difficult for

---

[65] For a full text of this statement, see Frankland, op. cit., pp
53-56.
[66] New York Times, February 26, 1956.

162

Congress to follow the logic of the State Department uncertainties.   For this reason the Eisenhower Administration was subjected to a barrage of attacks, particularly by leading Democrats.

Another example of poorly correlated Western policies in this area was the attitude toward arms shipment to either Israel or the Arabs. As seen above, the West reacted hysterically to the Czech arms shipment to Egypt on the partial grounds that it would create an arms race. In fact, though, Western actions appear to give the impression that the West, not the Soviet bloc, was making an arms race possible. First, the West, as stated above, offered Egypt arms to forego the Czech deal. Then they refused publicly to give arms to Israel. The Israeli attack on Syria on December 11, 1955 seemed to have the temporary effect of curtailing Western arms delivery to Israel.

On January 2, 1956, though, the New York Times reported that British arms "were on their way to Egypt." This understandably brought Israeli complaints and strong British Labor Party demands, mentioned above, on the Conservative government to give arms to Israel (see footnote 59). On February 16, a number of American tanks were given clearance by the State Department to be sent to Saudi Arabia. These were stopped two days later by an order from President Eisenhower under Zionist pressure.(69) Two days after that, this "embargo" was lifted under Saudi pressure.(70) This oscillation, naturally reflected heavily on American moral and political leadership, not only in the Middle East, but throughout the world. On February 23, Al-Ahram reported a number of British jets of the Meteor type on their way to Israel. The same paper speculated that the American embargo on the large Israeli arms request was expected to be lifted soon. Eventually this embargo was lifted, and in April, 1956, substantial amounts of American arms were going to Israel indirectly through France.(71) This,of course, brought the expected Egyptian outcry. Arms shipment to Israel was allowed even though Dulles testified before the Senate Foreign Relations Committee on February 24, 1956:

> While realizing that the introduction
> of large quantities of Soviet-bloc arms
> could upset the balance of arms within

69
  See text of the suspension order in Department of State Bulletin,
  February 27, 1956, pp. 325-26.
70
  New York Times, February 22, 1956.
71
  Barraclough, op. cit., p. 300.

the area, we do not believe that a
true peace can be based upon arms alone
. . . . It is natural that in the circumstances they (the Israelis) would
wish to increase their military cap-
abilities. However, Israel, due to its
much smaller size and population, could
not win an arms race against Arabs having access to Soviet-bloc stocks. It
would seem that Israel's security could
be better assured, in the long run,
through measures other than the acquisition of additional arms. . . .(72)

The above sentiment was repeated by President Eisenhower in a
news conference on March 7, 1956.

Lack of common policy was also reflected by the three Western
powers in their attitude toward the Baghdad pact. As mentioned
above, Britain remained of the opinion that the pact was the best
Western policy for the Middle East.(73) This opinion was not
shared fully either by the United States or France. In fact, the
French Foreign Minister, Christian Pineau, on March 2, 1956, came
as close to attacking the pact as diplomatically possible.(74)
Simultaneously, therefore, the attitude of the West varied in regard to the subject of neutralism. In this respect, also, there
was oscillation within the Eisenhower Administration itself, as
illustrated below.

Britain was, of course, fully committed to the pact, and therefore opposed the notion of "positive neutralism." France was
wavering in its commitment to the idea of the pact, and perhaps
more opposed to it than not. The United States was also wavering
in its attitude. This American vacillation, according to a New
York Times survey of April 9, 1956, incurred the "enmity" of the
Baghdad pact states because the United States would not join, and

---

72Department of State Bulletin, March 5, 1956, pp. 368-69.
73For this reason, Indian and Egyptian neutralism was most abhorrent to Britain, and both countries fell under British charges.
Al-Ahram, March 29, 1956, reported that India warned Britain that
she might abandon the Commonwealth if Britain persisted in its unfriendly policies toward her.
74New York Times, March 3, 1956.

the "hostility" of the Egyptian-led Arab states because the United States backed the pact. This wavering permeated the ranks of the Eisenhower Administration.

Generally speaking, the Egyptians felt that Eisenhower was closest in sympathy to their point of view, while Dulles was viewed differently.(75) Therefore, and judging from the Egyptian press, the Egyptians, in the first few months of 1956, seemed to have been involved in a contest with Britain over winning the backing of President Eisenhower for their Middle East point of view. Conversely, Eisenhower was viewed with further disfavor in Zionists circles. Perhaps correlated with this also was the Israeli "retaliation" policy on the Arab borders. For instance, Eisenhower made a statement on April 4, 1956, declaring that he was sympathetic to Arab national aspirations. This naturally made the headlines of both major Egyptian newspapers.(76) A day later an "incident" occurred inside Gaza. The battle between Egypt and Israel lasted for seven hours the first day and continued for three more days. There were sixty-three Egyptian casualties.(77)

BRITISH LAST ATTEMPTS

Perhaps in their frustration to reach an agreement with the United States over a British-inspired common course in the Middle East, the British government finally attempted direct diplomacy with Egypt. On March 1, 1956, the British Foreign Minister, Selwyn Lloyd, arrived in Cairo for an "explanatory mission" of the Baghdad pact.(78) The communique that was issued two days later, though, was not encouraging. In reality, it could not have been otherwise. For, while Lloyd was still in Cairo, another blow to British prestige in the Middle East occurred that was again interpreted in London as the work of Egypt.

On March 2, 1956, King Hussain of Jordan summarily dismissed

---

[75] Al-Ahram, April 5, 1956, quoted Eisenhower as declaring his sympathy to the Arab national aspirations, a day before, and stating that there was some misunderstanding between him and Eden over Middle East questions.
[76] See footnote 75 above.
[77] Al-Ahram, April 5 and 6, 1956. Egypt sent a strong note of protest to the Security Council on the 6th of April.
[78] This mission also took him to India, and both Nasser and Nehru were still fundamentally opposed to alliances. See Barraclough, op. cit., p. 195.

his British Chief of Staff of the Arab Legion, John Bagot Glubb.
Glubb had been suspected in Egyptian and Jordanian anti-Baghdad
pact circles as the one who had engineered the Templar mission,
which had led to riots and heavy loss of life in December, 1955.
His dismissal, therefore, was widly acclaimed in the Arab press.

But rather than revising the British policy vis-a-vis the
pact and Arab nationalism in general, London convinced itself further that Nasser was the only culprit.(79) It followed also in
British logic that if this were the case, then Nasser must go in
order for British policies in the Middle East to succeed. This
"logic" had been a pattern of British and Western myopic thinking
in the Middle East—to look at the results rather than the causes.
It was also a pattern of Western disregard to the forces of Arab
nationalism.(80)

France also followed the British line of thinking. On March
10, for instance, Al-Ahram complained that ex-Governor General of
Algeria Jacques Soustelle testifying before the National Assembly
in Paris, charged that Nasser was the "actual leader of the Algerian National Liberation Front."(81) Perhaps in the actual belief
of such an aberration Foreign Minister Christian Pineau went to
Cairo on March 14, 1956. The result of his mission (as well as
Lloyd's) was to enhance the prestige of Nasser in the Arab world,
rather than "solve" the national uprising in Algeria.(82)

Perhaps as a last resort, the British government decided to
discuss the subject of the Middle East with Soviet leaders. As
mentioned above, Israel and Egypt were involved in a major clash
from April 5 to April 10, 1956. Eden then suggested to the United

---

79
  Lloyd left Cairo for Bahrain where he was met with over ten thou-
80 sand demonstrators who stoned his car. Al-Ahram, March 4, 1956.
  Glubb's testimonies, articles and writings in Britain later, did
  not help the Foreign Office change its views on Nasser. Rather,
  he reinforced its phobia that Nasser was the main culprit. See,
  for instance, Glubb, Britain and the Arabs, Chap. XXIII, entitled,
  "The Poison of Asps."
81
  The Front was the Algerian rebel movement against the French rule
  there.
82 Al-Ahram, March 17, 1956, thus bragged that "there is present today a world power in the Middle East. . . created by Gamal Abdel
  Nasser. . . . "

States that Western forces should be sent to the area. Eisenhower, however, favored working through the United Nations. Dag Hammarskjold (Secretary-General of the United Nations) was asked to go to the Middle East and survey the situation on the Israeli borders. The American-sponsored United Nations resolution which suggested the Hammarskjold trip was also backed by the Soviet Union. Responding to the British proposal of sending Western forces to the Middle East, the Soviet Foreign Ministry issued a major statement on April 18, 1956. It reflected what was most on the mind of the Soviet Union, then. The statement suggested that the Baghdad pact, being "the cause of the deterioration of relations between the Arab states and Israel as well as Turkey," should be scuttled in the interest of peace and international security(83) It scored the "attempts to make use of the Arab-Israeli conflict for intervention from outside . . .," and declared that the Soviet Union "will render the necessary support to measures of the United Nations aimed at exploring ways and means for strengthening peace in the Palestine area, and implementing corresponding decisions of the Security Council."

According to Barraclough, "even in the United States, it was admitted that Moscow was backing the United Nations," and that the Soviet Union in the estimation of some observers was in a better position than the Western powers to deal with the Palestine question.(84)

A day after the Soviet statement scoring the Baghdad pact was issued (April 18), it was reported by the New York Times that the United States had decided to join the Economic Committee of that pact. While this was hailed, according to the report, by Britain and the pact membership, it was naturally received with consternation in Cairo and Moscow.

The Soviet statement was issued while Bulganin and Khrushchev were on their way to Britain for a visit that lasted from April 18 to 27. The publication of the above statement was perhaps timed in such a way as to set Soviet conditions for any bargain with Britain over the area. Perhaps a possible one would be British foregoing the Baghdad pact in exchange for Soviet foregoing its new Arab "friendship."

83 Frankland, op. cit., p. 59
84 Barraclough, op. cit., p. 278.

The above statement followed another Soviet statement of four days earlier in which the Soviet Union suggested a conference on the Middle East. In it, according to Al-Ahram (April 14, 1956), the Soviet Union would participate with the Western powers and "other nations that are concerned." The tone of bargaining, and the fact that the Soviet statements did not mention specifically Arab participation in the proposed conference, did not go unnoticed in Cairo.(85) The American adherence, though, to the Economic Committee of the Baghdad pact and the British jubilation over it, saved Moscow the embarrassment of questioning by Cairo, and perhaps saved Cairo the possibility of having Britain and the Soviet Union strike a bargain detrimental to Arab interests. Such a bargain was then definitely feared in Cairo.(86)

The outcome of the joint British-Soviet discussions brought no real satisfaction to the West. In the communique that was issued at the end of these discussions, both governments innocuously pledged that,

> The two governments will do their utmost
> to put an end to the armaments race in
> all parts of the world, and thus to free
> the peoples of the world from the threat
> of a new war.(87)

In contrast to dissatisfaction in London, there was a sigh of relief in Cairo. For Al-Ahram candidly wrote on April 25 that "we the states of the Middle East and the Arabs at this junction, count

---

85Al-Ahram then meekly questioned what is meant by "other nations..."
86April 22, 1956, Al-Ahram wrote apprehensively: "There is an atmosphere of barter in the Anglo-Soviet discussions. These involve the German problem, general disarmament, the Middle East, etc." A day later it quoted "high Arab diplomatic sources" that bargaining in London is going on. Two days later, the paper came close to openly denouncing the London discussions. It wrote: "As Egypt has said time and again, the destiny of the Middle East is to be decided by its people, not by any one else anywhere...."
87New York Times, April 27, 1956.

168

any disagreement among the two European camps a mercy to our national cause. For experience has taught us that whenever they agree, they agree to our detriment, rather than for our good." A day later, and in major headlines, both major Egyptian papers jubilantly announced the "failure" of the Soviet-British talks.

Calm seemed to prevail in the Middle East after the above talks ended. In fact there was seemingly some type of a thaw in Egyptian relations with the West, and even with Israel. For instance on April 27, it was announced in Cairo that France had decided to sell small arms to Egypt. The same day and in major headlines, Al-Ahram reported that Eisenhower called for the friendship of all the states in the Middle East. On May 2, the same paper reported that Egypt and Israel had agreed on the creation of numerous observation posts on their borders.

Nevertheless, the British failure with the Soviets to curtail arms shipments to the Arabs was ominously viewed in Israel. The Israeli "fears" were legitimized on May 6 when Jordan and Egypt signed a military agreement designed ostensibly to coordinate and eventually unite their armies.(88) A day later a major Zionist conference convened in Tel Aviv. This meeting coincided with another meeting in Paris of the big three Western foreign ministers on May 3-7, 1956.

Speculation in Cairo was going on from early April that Zionist pressure might finally succeed in forcing the West to allow shipments of large amounts of arms to Israel. On May 10, the headlines in Egypt reflected a new crisis in Egyptian-Western Relations. "A New Dangerous Plot by the West Against the Arabs Hatched in Paris," Al-Gumhuriyah wrote. "The Unveiling of a New Western Intrigue," Al-Ahram wrote. The gist of the alleged plot was that the three ministers had agreed that France particularly would give Israel large amounts of NATO arms. A day later Al-Ahram scored what it called Dulles' "duplicity." It charged that "while Dulles publicly declares that Israel's best salvation is not in arms, he secretly allows France to give large amounts of American NATO arms to that country." From then on there was a new prominence of British and French colonial troubles in the Egyptian press. On May 17, Nasser announced his recognition of the People's Republic of China. A day later it was announced that the Political Committee of the League of Arab States was meeting in Cairo to discuss similar action by other Arab states. Another blow to American policy in the Far

---

[88]New York Times, May 6, 1956. In truth, Israel did not have to fear such development. Those perenial Arab alliances always proved to be only paper-pacts.

East was, therefore, in the air. On May 20, Nasser made a major foreign policy statement in which he warned that "Egypt shall befriend he who wants our friendship, and show enmity to whoever insists on provoking us." The same day the Arab League states decided to bring the Algerian question to the Security Council.(89)On June 4, Al-Ahram threatened that Egypt "will not renew the Suez Canal concession when that concession expires on the midnight of November 16, 1968. It is expected that this will be announced officially in the next two days." This was the first time, as far as could be ascertained, that the Suez Canal concession was publicly discussed. In view of what happened later, that is, the nationalization of the canal in July, 1956, it might have been the first clue that Egypt was thinking along those lines.

Aside from similar signs of the worsening Egyptian-Western relations, the months of June and July witnessed glaring examples of the absence of a common policy within the Eisenhower Administration. This was in regard to the American attitude toward "neutralism", the "neutral" nations, and the related field of American economic aid.

Discussing the general relationship between the American attitude toward neutralism and American economic aid, Norman Graebner wrote in 1956:(90)

> Nothing illustrated so strikingly the intellectual barriers preventing the Administration (Eisenhower) from formulating an imaginative foreign aid program as did its stand on neutralism. . . . Asian nations require Western capital for their economic development, but they harbor an inordinate pride and are determined to seek their own destiny. Any effort to infringe on their liberty of action quickly reveals how bitterly they resent any attempt to push them around.

On June 6, 1956, President Eisenhower in his press conference recognized the fallacy of demanding military alliances from newly independent nations as the price of American aid. He reminded his audience that America herself was once neutral and isolationist--

---

[89] Such questions as Cyprus, Kenya, Algeria, the ouster of Glubb, etc.
[90] Norman Graebner, "Foreign Aid and American Policy," Current History, XXXI (1956), pp. 212-17.

for over a century and a half—and added that neutralism does
not mean anti-Americanism. This Eisenhower "understanding"
was cheered in Cairo, the next day in headline form. Vice-President Richard Nixon seemed to confirm this new attitude toward
neutralism in a commencement address at Lafayette College a few
days later. He stated that the new nations needed time to build
their countries internally, and solve their regional problems,
before looking toward the solution of cold war problems. He concluded by stating that "the uncommitted nations are not going to
be frightened into alliances with the West by military power,
nor can their allegiance be purchased by dollars."(91)

On June 9, Dulles, though, made the following statement in
a speech at Iowa State College:

> The principle of neutrality pretends
> that a nation can best gain safety for
> itself by being indifferent to the fate
> of others. This has increasingly become an obsolete conception, and except
> under very exceptional circumstances,
> it is an immoral and shortsighted conception.(92)

In a speech at Manila on the tenth anniversary of the Philippine Independence, July 4, 1956, Nixon made his volte face in
regard to neutralism. He stated:

> We have heard recently a great deal of
> discussion of the attitude that goes
> by the name of neutralism. We in the
> United States can understand the attitudes of such powers. For over a century we tried to avoid being identified
> . . . . But we learned from hard experience that politics that worked well
> in the nineteenth century were completely
> inadequate in the twentieth. . .(93)

91
Quoted by Graebner, Ibid.
92"Is Neutralism Immoral? What Republicans Think," Foreign Policy Bulltein, XXXV (August 15, 1956), p. 180-184.
93U.S. News and World Report (July 6, 1956), pp. 70-72. Perhaps
it was a mistake to invoke the name of God when talking of politics, particularly to a Philippine audience. Pres. McKinley
supposedly invoked the name of God when he decided on the conquest
of the Philippines. See remainder of quotation, infra.

Like Dulles before, he went on to differentiate between neutrals "under very exceptional circumstances," and other neutrals:

> But there is still another brand of
> neutralism that makes no moral distinc-
> tion between the Communist world and the
> free world. With this viewpoint we have
> no sympathy. How can we feel toward
> those who treat alike nations that be-
> lieve in God and honor religion and
> morality, and nations that boast of
> atheism.

This halting search for a common American attitude toward "neutrals" naturally reflected itself on the economic aid sphere. In the case of Egypt it was the Aswan Dam project that was at stake. As mentioned before, the United States had committed itself to help finance the Dam in December, 1955. This commitment wavered in 1956. There is no doubt that various political considerations, inside and outside the United States, influenced the final withdrawal of Dulles'offer. These included the opposition of Southern congressmen to "building up facilities for the growing of Egyptian cotton so it may undersell the cotton of our own Southern states."(94) Other causes might be British, French and Zionist pressures on the United States to withdraw the offer.(95) This action of Dulles might also have been prompted by Dulles' anger with Nasser for "playing footsie with the Moscow rulers," in the words of one David Lawrence.(96) But whatever the real reasons, the manner in which it was handled could not have been but a deliberate blow to Egyptian pride, and a slap to Nasser, personally.(97)

On July 7, 1956, Al-Ahram quoted a "high source" in the State Department stating that America was still ready to help finance the

---

94
95U.S. News and World Report (September 7, 1956), p. 144.
96Lilienthal, There Goes the Middle East, p. 179.
97U.S. News and World Reports (July 27, 1956), p. 128.
Speaking to the lower house of India's Parliament, House of the People, on August 8, 1956, Nehru stated: "More than the decision the way it was done hurt Egypt's pride and self-respect and disregarded the people's sentiment." Quoted in Foreign Policy Bulletin, XXXVI (September 15, 1956), p. 6.

Dam. On July 17, the Egyptian Ambassador in Washington, Ahmed Hussain, arriving from Cairo, stated that Egypt had decided to ratify the special financial agreement with the United States over the Dam project. "Egypt was ready to do so," he stated, "even though there are some points which were never clarified by the American State Department. Chief among these is the pledge for a long range commitment to finance the project."(98)

On July 19, Hussain met with Dulles and was curtly told that the United States had changed its mind regarding the Dam. The same day a statement was released to the press on the withdrawal of the American offer of assistance to Egypt.(99) It declared that developments since December, 1955 (the original offer date) had not been favorable to the success of the project. It cited as one reason for the withdrawal that "agreement by the riparian states has not been achieved, and the ability of Egypt to devote adequate resources to assure the project's success has become more uncertain . . . ." A day later Britain followed the American lead and withdrew its offer also.

Aside from the abrupt American change of policy,(100) the statement also cast doubt on the Egyptian economy which naturally angered the Egyptians. It also came at a time when Nasser was meeting with Nehru amd Tito at the Brioni Conference which for Nasser was a high point of his career.(101)

Seven days later on July 26, and in an atmosphere of great expectations in Egypt and the Arab world, Nasser made a well-pub-

---

98
99Al-Ahram, July 18, 1956.
99Department of State Bulletin, July 30, 1956, p. 188.
100Seven months later, before the Senate Joint Committee Hearings on the Eisenhower Doctrine, former Ambassador to Egypt Henry Byroade admitted under Senator J.W. Fulbright's questioning that he had first learned about the cancellation from the Egyptian press, not from the State Department. U.S. Congress, Senate, Hearings Before the Committee on Foreign Relations and Committee on Armed Services, 85th Cong., 1st Sess., Pt. 11, p. 717. Eden also complained later that "We were informed but not consulted and so had no prior opportunity for criticism or comment," regarding Dulles' abrupt change of mind. See Eden, op. cit., p. 470.
101The Brioni Conf. began July 12 and lasted until July 21. The American actin occurred while he was in Belgrade. He left Belgrade for Cairo with Nehru. The action couldn't help but be construed as an insult to neutralists, Nehru and Tito also.

licized foreign policy speech in Alexandria.(102)   Before a
crowd of over two hundred thousand Egyptians, he announced the
nationalization of the Suez Canal Company.

What followed after that and for the next three months was
a war atmosphere in London, Paris and in the Middle East.   Events
within these months centered around the Western efforts to "inter-
nationalize" the canal, and Egyptian efforts to keep it.   Suffice
it to mention here that all these Western efforts failed.   This
failure led to the Israeli invasion of Egypt on October 29, 1956,
the British-French invasion a day later, and the failure again of
Western diplomacy in the Arab world.

102
Without explanation, the day was declared a holiday for the
people of Alexandria.

Chapter VII

American-Arab Relations in the Inter-war Period: 1956-1967

The development of Egyptian and general Arab neutralism by
1955 was a measure of the failure of U.S. diplomacy in the Arab
East. It represented America's failure to be impartial in the
Palestine question. It represented America's failure to assume
moral leadership vis-a-vis British, French and Zionist colonial
issues with the Arabs after World War II. It represented a lack
of sympathy and understanding of the basic demands of the Arab
national movement. This lack of understanding (or perhaps lack
of wanting to understand) is part of what John K. Fairbank once
called the "key problem" for American foreign policy after the
Second World War. In his book, The Problem of Revolutionary Asia,
(1950) he exhorted the United States "to find and support" these
Asian leaders who had the vision and the dynamic idealism to lead
their nations into independence and progress. It is obvious that
at least in the Middle East, this course the United States did
not choose to pursue. In fact the United States by 1956, rather
than "finding and supporting" such leaders, was viewed as the
major obstacle in their path of independence and progress, and
the major perpetrator of their woes by such in the Arab world and
by the Arab masses. By then it seemed to most Arabs that America
was interested to see Britain leave Egypt only to have the United
States, Britain and France come back under the guise of a Western
"defence" system. This "defence against the Soviets" was viewed
suspiciously by most Arab nationalists as the West's way of keeping
the Arab East as their private imperial domain disregarding the
sentiments of the Arab national movement. American policy in
regard to French colonial enterprises in Tunis, Algeria and
Morocco was mute at best, sympathetic to France at minimum, and
antagonistic to the Arabs in reality. After all, it was American
NATO weapons that the French were fighting with to subdue Arab
nationalists in North Africa. Moreover, whenever an Arab nationalist leader like Nasser complained of this, he was charged with
"meddling" by policy-makers in Washington. And when finally the
Eygptian government under Nasser-leading the Arab nationalist move-
ment-was practically forced into neutralism and purchasing arms
from the Soviets in 1955 to protect itself (against Israel),
rather than Washington changing its course, it declared open war
on Nasser. It was in the spirit of "how dare Nasser?" that Dulles
reacted after the Czech arms deal became public in August 1955.
It was in the same spirit that he abruptly cancelled American
verbal commitments to help build the Egyptian Aswan High Dam

project. He spared no verbal attacks or derogations on Nasser and his policy of non-alignment. In that atmosphere, the Soviet Union was bound to move in and pick up the maximum pieces of the shattered Western diplomacy in the Arab world. They moved inside the United Nations to play verbally the role of the protector of the Arab national cause. Inside Egypt and Syria they moved to sell arms and offer technical know-how to build cherished projects which these states long had on their drawing boards. Part of the Western inertia of fallacy was that the more these Arab states welcomed aid from the Soviets, the more Washington, London and Paris charged them with being "communist." It was, therefore, natural that Israel was able to convince Britain and France to invade Egypt in October 1956. The atmosphere in the West generally was ripe for this type of old-fashioned imperialism. All that they were waiting for was the "excuse." And Nasser gave them that excuse in nationalizing the Suez Canal in July of 1956.

The Suez invasion is another climactic point of the failure of Western diplomacy generally in the Arab East. It marked some forty years of Western duplicity, deceit and total partiality for the Zionist cause in Palestine. It marked more than a century of viewing the Arab East as an exclusive Western preserve, in disregard of its native sentiments. This view was not altered after the Suez invasion of 1956, but intensified.

The immediate result of the attack on Egypt in 1956 was a drastic depletion of American and Western prestige in Arab eyes. And regardless of the fact that Eisenhower irately ordered the stoppage of that invasion and later ordered the total evacuation of Egypt by the invading powers, much of the credit in Arab eyes was then given to the Soviet Union. For it did not seem convincing to the Arabs that American policy-makers who declared war on Nasser prior to that invasion would now truly come to his rescue. In fact the Eisenhower stiff reaction against Western and Israeli invasion of Egypt was out of line with the Dulles policies toward Nasser before that invasion. No wonder then that Arabs as well as the British, French and Israelis remained perplexed by that Eisenhower reaction for many years after Suez.

Nevertheless, the lessons of Suez did not materially alter American-Arab relations. This was because the factors that brought about Suez remained present after 1956. After 1956, America's sympathy and backing of Israel was intensified. After 1967, the United States was viewed not only as sympathetic to Israel, but perhaps as a major partner to her aggressive designs on the Arabs. Ever since, it seemed to most Arabs that Israel finally succeeded in totally equating her interests in the Middle East with those of the United States.

After 1956 the earlier American tendency to suspect and fight progressive Arab regimes and revolutions was also intensified. This was evident in the American policy vis-a-vis the Iraqi republican revolution of 1958; the Yemeni republican revolution of 1962; the Algerian War of Independence of 1954-1962; and finally the Palestine Fath revolution after 1967. Nasser and his type in the Arab world, naturally, remained the culprits in Washington's eyes. It was Nasser who was behind one coup and the other throughout the Arab world! It was he who "opened the Middle East to Soviet penetration!" etc., etc. Having sustained such a myopic view of the Arabs and their national leaders, it was easy to see how Israel again succeeded, now with the United States itself (rather than with Britain and France as in 1956) in having America stand guilty of open complicity with Israel against the whole Arab world. And regardless of U.S. policy-makers' protestations of "impartiality" in the Middle East, these protestations were somehow not convincing to the Arabs. And whether the so-called energy shortage would alter America's posture in the area is still too early to speculate.

AMERICA AND THE IRAQI REVOLUTION OF 1958

As seen earlier, Nuri's interest in joining MEDO culminated in having Iraq join the Turco-Pakistani pact in February, 1955. This was done even though Nuri just one month earlier gave Egypt, Saudi Arabia and the rest of the Arab League to believe that the Arab Collective Security Pact should be strengthened and take exclusive responsibility for the defence of the Arab area. Nuri's action aroused the ire of not only Nasser and Saudi Arabia but general Arab nationalists. This action is singled out by Nasser in one of his writings as the one that brought about "ill-feeling between us....and America."(1)

Subsequent to the Iraqi adherence to the pact, Egypt and also Saudi Arabia feverishly attempted to isolate Iraq from the rest of the other members of the Arab League to forestall any further breaches by other Arab states to join "foreign pacts." It was due perhaps--at least partially--to this violent reaction by both that the United States never joined the pact. According to Lenczowski, the "failure of the United States to join the pact was

---

1
Where I Stand, p. 4, also quoted earlier in Chapter IV.

due partly to America's reluctance to burn the bridges in her relations with Egypt and partly to the protests of Israel, who
attacked the pact as hostile to herself." Of course one could
easily speculate that historically the latter's protests were the
more effective of the two on America's actions. Nevertheless, the
failure of America to join did not lessen Egyptian attacks on
Iraq and the pact. Britain joined the pact on March 30, 1955, and
it too fell under Egyptian polemics. These attacks on Nuri of
Iraq made him more vulnerable to his internal dissenters. For it
is rarely mentioned that the pact was also very opposed from
within Iraq. Lenczowski rightly stated the case when he wrote in
1957 that Nuri's policies in regard to MEDO were "not favored by
the masses, the students, and the intelligentsia outside the
bureaucracy. . . . No amount of persuasion seems to win converts
among the people. . . . Consequently, the key to stability will,
in the long run, be found in the government's ability--and willing-
ness--to effect much-needed reforms."(2) This "long run" was not
to be. For on July 14, 1958 the Iraqi coup against Nuri and the
Hashemite Royal family took place, and Iraq subsequently withdrew
from the pact in March 1959.

As mentioned earlier, the United States persisted even
after the 1956 Suez War to explain Arab affairs in terms of Soviet
attempts at "domination" or "penetration" of the Middle East.
Hence, the declaration of the Eisenhower Doctrine on January 5,
1957. In it Eisenhower stated, for instance:

> The reason for Russia's interest
> in the Middle East is solely that
> of power politics. Considering
> her announced purpose of communizing
> the world, it is easy to understand
> her hope of dominating the Middle
> East.

In this doctrine he asked Congress to authorize economic
and military aid, including the employment of United States troops
to "protect the territorial integrity and political independence
of nations requesting such aid, against overt armed aggression
from any nation controlled by international communism." Congress
approved this policy on March 9, 1957.

The Eisenhower Doctrine is a prime example of the myopic

---

[2] Lenczowski, p. cit., p. 264-265.

American view of the Middle East.(3) It could also be viewed as part of that inertia of fallacy that was overtaking Washington either consciously or unconsciously. But regardless, this Doctrine supposedly "vindicated" itself when it was used later in 1958 in Lebanon.

The Lebanese crisis of May 1958 was occasioned, according to Professor Harry N. Howard, "by the evident determination of President Chamoun to maintain himself in his high office, in violation of the Lebanese Constitution."(4) It was part of an almost perennial disturbances between Lebanese Moslems and Lebanese Christians since France left that country. It was obviously an internal crisis that had little if any connection with "international communism." In fact the United States originally saw it also as a simple Lebanese internal affair. Yet when on July 14, 1958 the Iraqi coup d'etat took place, fifteen thousand American marines began landing in Lebanon the next day. This is the gravity with which the United States viewed the Iraqi revolution. Britain also began landing troops in Jordan. Needless to say, Egypt, then united with Syria in the United Arab Republic was in for most of the Western charges of instigation. After the success of the Iraqi coup, the American view of Iraq was never the same. It too, became the object of ostracizing in Washington ever since, and since 1958 one rarely sees either official or non-official American references to the Iraqi leaders without the use of the adjective "radical."

In retrospect one could seriously question the Dulles policy of alliances in the Middle East. More even in question is the success of MEDO as a regional security arrangement. After the Iraqi withdrawal, it is hard not to judge it as a failure as a security device, And also a cause for further polarization and friction between the states of the Middle East themselves. It might eventually have had some usefulness in the field of economic and technical cooperation to those states that remained in it. That seems to be all. But if one object of American policy in the Arab East was to bring the bulk of the Arab states closer to America, then the pact was definitely a failure.

---

[3] See also Eisenhower's comment about the doctrine, that it was intended to "block the Soviet Union's march to the Mediterranean, to the Suez Canal and the oil pipelines, and to the underground lakes of oil which fuel the homes and factories of Western Europe." Eisenhower, Waging Peace (New York: 1965), pp. 182-183.
[4] "The Regional Pacts and the Eisenhower Doctrine," The Annals, May 1972, p. 91

AMERICA AND THE YEMEN REVOLUTION OF 1962

There is no doubt that until the revolution of September 1962 Yemen was one of the most backward countries in the Arab East and perhaps the world. The Zaidi Imamate kept the country literally in the dark ages. Until 1962 there were no schools to speak of in Yemen, no hospitals, no roads or modern communications. The machinery of the Imam's government did at best belong to antiquity. Until 1962 it was invariably referred to as "remote" Yemen, or at times the "Tibet of the Red Sea."(5) The fact is, though, Yemen is not that remote. It lies astride the most strategic and most plied modern routes of trade and commerce.

As mentioned earlier in Chapter I, Yemen became independent after World War I. Between the two world wars the United States developed a measure of goodwill with Yemen, thanks to the efforts of two Americans – Charles Crane and Karl Twitchell. Outside of some mining activity on the part of these two, little or no American relations developed between Yemen and the United States. In fact, diplomatic relations between the two countries were not established until May 11, 1946.

After World War II, Yemen joined the League of Arab states. In February 1948, discontent broke out against Imam Yehya's despotic and reactionary rule. This was led by a group led by one Abdullah al-Wazir backed by one of the Imam's sons and a group that called themselves the Free Yemen Party. The Imam and three of his sons were murdered in this coup. Al-Wazir was elected by his followers as the new Imam. He was still opposed, though, by Ahmad, the oldest son of Imam Yehya. Both parties appealed to the Arab League states for recognition. King Ibn Saud strongly opposed recognition of the new regime and his influence carried the day in Cairo. Eventually the forces of the "legitimate" Ahmad entered San'a victorious on February 13, 1948, but not without the active help of Saudi Arabia and the British airforce (R.A.F.).(6)

Britain remained at odds with the new Imam over boundary lines in southern Arabia. That is why Imam Ahmad was very anti-British. In fact, British-Yemen relations from 1949 on were marked with hostility invariably verging on the brink of open warfare. Thus Yemen throughout the 1950s echoed Nasser's attacks on the West and leaned more and more towards "non-alignment." It too took a

---

[5] Sanger, p. 242.
[6] See Middle East Journal, Vol. II, 1948, p. 328.

very strong position in the councils of the Arab League against
Iraq joining MEDO. For this reason in March 1958 Yemen joined the
United Arab States Federation comprising Syria, Egypt and Yemen.
Yet Ahmad's alliance with revolutionary Egypt was bound to under-
mine the autocratic authority of the Imamate in Yemen. In April
1959 and again in March 1961, Imam Ahmad just missed being assassinated by republican plotters. This dampened his fervour for
Nasser and he pulled out of his Federation with Egypt in 1961. In
December 1961, another abortive assassination plot took place
against Ahmad. By then he was openly charging Nasser with meddling
in his affairs. In retaliation, Nasser openly attacked Imam Ahmad
on December 23, 1961, as an agent of imperialism and reaction.(7)
Three days later, Egypt broke diplomatic relations with the Imam.

American political and economic relations with Yemen after
the Second World War were extremely nebulous. Perhaps this was
due to the fact that the United States was then interested mainly
in creating military pacts against the Soviets, and Yemen was
viewed as either too backward and isolated, or too anti-British to
be of any use. Yemen therefore was not even approached to join
MEDO. Yemen though became a staunch backer of Egypt and her neutralist policies, and violently opposed MEDO and Iraq's adherence
to it.

The September 1962 Yemen Revolution had many aspects that
fit harmoniously into the continuum of the march of Arab nationalism. The clash of modern Arab nationalism and traditionalism had
been in evidence on many issues after World War II. This clash
though remained on the ideological level until the advent of the
Yemeni Revolution. This event brought the clash to the military
level also, and Egypt finally committed over 50,000 of her troops
to firm up the republican revolution there. And for better or for
worse, the Egyptian cause in Yemen was far more popular to the
Arab masses than the cause of Saudi Arabia and the old regime,
both backed by the sympathy of the United States.(8)

On September 19, 1962 Imam Ahmad was reported dead of natural
causes at the age of 71. Crown Prince Al-Badr was proclaimed his
successor. Eight days later, though, there was a revolution in
Yemen against the Imamate led by elements of the Free Yemen party

---

7
In a speech marking the 5th anniversary of the withdrawal of British and French troops from Egypt after the 1956 Seuz invasion.
8
Boutres-Boutres Ghali, "The Foreign Policy of Egypt," Foreign Policies in a World of Change, edited by J.E. Black and K.W. Thompson
(New York, 1963), pp. 340-341.

and other liberal army groups. Finally an army officer, Abdullah Sallal, emerged as the leader of the revolution. It was then believed that many of the Royal family members including the new Imam Al-Badr, along with numerous princes outside the country were still alive and very much demanding the continuation of the Imamate in Yemen. Al-Badr and many tribal loyalists sought refuge in the mountain area to the north close to the Saudi frontier and also inside the Saudi frontier. King Saud, like his father before him in the 1948 Yemen revolution, was understandably opposed to revolutions and regicide. Thus it became very evident from the start where he stood in the Yemen crisis that followed. The United States that had extremely cordial oil relations with the Saudi Arabian monarchy since the 1930s made it also clear in time where her sympathies lay. The United States also had had very bad relations with Nasser in the past, and any endeavor that might smell of Nasserism since 1954 was opposed by Washington almost automatically. Historical evidence would seem to indicate, though, that revolution in Yemen was bound to come whether Nasser backed it or not. Perhaps he only accelerated it. Britain, also, being a southern neighbor of Yemen, and worried about maintaining her colonial position in Arabia would naturally back the acquiescent conservative forces in Arabia. Hence Britain too opposed republicanism in Yemen. In this situation, Nasser had the choice of either accepting the strangulation of the new republic in Yemen, as happened in 1948, or acting in defence of the republic. And he chose to act.

One day after the declaration of the establishment of the new regime in Yemen, Nasser (along with the Soviet Union) declared his recognition. Other "progressive" Arab states followed suit. No recognition, though, came from the United States or Britain in the following days or weeks, even though the Sallal government appealed publicly for international recognition.(9) A few days after the revolution, the Royalists began their attacks on republican outposts in the north of Yemen close to the Saudi frontier. For this reason, Sallal ordered general mobilization on October 4, 1962. Three days later there were reports that the Republican forces were fighting Saudi Arabian forces on Yemen's northern frontier.(10) The same day, October 7, the deputy Premier of Yemen

---

9
The republican Minister of Foreign Affairs Muhsin al-Ayni appealed for international recognition in a statement in Cairo, September 30,
10 1962. Al-Ahram, October, 1962.
Middle East Journal, Vol. 16, 1962, p. 141.

warned that United States' delay in recognizing the new Yemen "might jeopardize" American interests in the country.(11) Meanwhile, Royalist power augmented with Saudi (Western) arms, became evident in the north. Nasser had to act or leave Yemen to its fate. On October 8, it was reported by the Yemen Foreign Minister that Egyptian instructors were helping train the Yemeni republican forces.(12) Saudi and Egyptian intervention in the Yemen revolution was on, and was to last for five years. Meanwhile the Yemeni question became not only a hot war inside Yemen, but also part of the cold war inside and outside the United Nations; with the Arab progressives backed by the Soviet bloc on one side, and Arab conservatives backed by Britain and the United States on the other.

The recognition of the new regime in Yemen gives a good example of contrasts between the United States and the Soviet Union policy for the area. Granted the United States had vested and economic interests in the Arabian peninsula. But the assumption that these interests could only be served by backing conservative, if not reactionary forces in the Arab world seems to be mistaken and harmful not only for the Arab national movement but also for the American interests in the long run.

As mentioned above, the Soviet Union recognized the new regime in San'a a day after it took over.

In contrast, the United States seemed in no hurry to recognize the Yemeni republic established in September 29, 1962. On October 5, 1962 President Kennedy held talks in Washington with the Crown Prince of Saudi Arabia, Faisal. These talks were described as "cordial and frank" discussions on the "world situation."(13) Yemen was not mentioned but no doubt was a major topic of discussion. Perhaps these discussions had their effect on American non-recognition of Yemen then and later, and for two and a half more months. On October 17 President Kennedy held "frank and cordial" talks with the Crown Prince Al-Rida of Libya "on the world situation."(14) Finally on December 19, 1962 it was announced in Washington that the United States had decided to recognize the new regime in Yemen. Even then, it was clear from the statement that the United States was doing so after a set of

---

11 Ibid., p. 142.
12 Ibid.
13 Department of State Bulletin, October 29, 1962, p. 641.
14 Department of State Bulletin, November 5, 1962, p. 689.

conditions had been, or were promising to be met by the new regime. The statement reads partially as follows:

In view of a number of confusing
and contradictory statements which
have cast doubts upon the intentions
of the new regime in Yemen the United
States Government welcomes the reaffir-
mation by the Yemen Republican Government of its intentions to honor its
international obligations....

The United States Government also is
gratified by the statesmanlike appeal
of the Yemen Arab Republic to Yemenis
in adjacent areas to be law-abiding
citizens and notes its understanding
to honor all treaties concluded by
previous Yemeni governments. This,
of course, includes the Treaty of
San'a concluded with the British
Government in 1934, which provides
reciprocal guarantees that neither
party should intervene in the affairs
of the other across the existing international frontier dividing the
Yemen from territory under British
protection.

Further the United States Government
welcomes the declaration of the United
Arab Republic signifying its willingness to undertake a reciprocal disengagement and expeditious phased removal
of troops from Yemen as external forces
engaged in support of the Yemen royalists are removed from the frontier
and as external support of the royalists is stopped.

In believing that these declarations
provide a basis for terminating the
conflict over Yemen. . .the United
States has today (December 19) decided to recognize the Government of
the Yemen Arab Republic and to extend to that Government its best

184

wishes for success and prosperity.(15)

Here, of course, the United States seemed to be clearly
protecting the interests of both Britain and Saudi Arabia as conditions for recognition of Yemen. Later in the conflict, American sympathy was further evidenced on behalf of Saudi Arabia and
Britain as both were partners in the attempt to strangule the
Yemeni republic. For this reason Yemen broke diplomatic relations
with England February 17, 1963.(16) On February 26, 1963 there
were reports of Yemeni-British troop clashes on the Beihan-Yemen
frontier, and Yemen sent a complaint to the Security Council.
Ralphe Bunche was then sent to Yemen on March 1, by Secretary
General U Thant on a fact-finding mission. On April 29, 1963 the
Secretary General reported to the Security Council on Yemen. He
stated that since 1962 he had been consulting with the governments
of Saudi Arabia, the United Arab Republic and the Republic of
Yemen to assist in avoiding further worsening of the situation in
Yemen, due to intervention. As a result of the fact-finding mission of Mr. Bunche and an independent mission by Ellsworth Bunker
of the United States, he reported he received assurances of their
acceptance of identical terms of disengagement in Yemen.

> According to the terms of disen-
> gagement, the Government of Saudi
> Arabia would terminate all support
> and aid to the Royalists of Yemen
> and would prohibit the use of Saudi
> Arabian territory by Royalists for
> the purpose of carrying on the
> struggle in Yemen. Simultaneously
> the United Arab Republic undertook
> to begin phased withdrawal of its
> troops sent there at the request
> of the new government.(17)

A 20 km demilitarized zone on each side would be established,
U Thant reported, where a U.N. military observation mission would
operate. He stated that he had asked Major General Carl Carlsson
von Horn, Chief of Staff of the United Nations Truce Supervision
Organization in Jerusalem to go to the three countries concerned

---

15
16Department of State Bulletin, January 7, 1963, pp. 11-12.
17Middle East Journal, Vol. 17, 1963, p. 143.
United Nations Yearbook, 1963 (New York: Columbia University
   Press, 1965), pp. 63-67.

to discuss terms relating to the nature and functioning of U.N.
observers in Yemen. All parties seemingly were then agreeable,
according to the Secretary General, to have an observation team
operate for two months in Yemen. On May 27, 1963 he reported
again to the Security Council that about 200 observers were
needed for the operation. On June 8, the Soviet Union asked for a
meeting of the Security Council to act on the Secretary General's
reports, and on aggression in Yemen.(18) He then attacked "foreign
imperialist interference" in the domestic affairs of Yemen. The
Soviet delegate stated that he would, generally speaking oppose
the sending of U.N. troops there except for the fact that the
United Arab Republic, Yemen and Saudi Arabia had agreed to that.
This was so since:

> Recent years had shown....that
> the dispatch of United Nations
> forces was a method used by the
> imperialist powers to establish,
> under the flag of the United Nations,
> their own control over specific re-
> gions.

The United States was then also in favor of sending such a
mission to Yemen. Eventually a United Nations Yemen Observation
Mission (UNYOM) was sent there and began functioning in Yemen on
July 4, 1963. Saudi charges and Egyptian counter-charges of bad
faith did not lead to any troop withdrawal, and UNYOM had to extend its mission time and again. Meanwhile open warfare was raging
in Yemen. It is hard, of course, to pin the blame on either side,
but in a report by the U.N. Secretary General to the Security Council
on January 2, 1964, U Thant seemed to indicate that Saudi Arabia
and the Royalists were more guilty of breaching the original agreement on disengagement. In that report he stated that the Royalists "were still getting some kind of Saudi support, while UNYOM
tended to confirm that there had been substantial net withdrawal
of United Arab Republic troops from Yemen during the period under
review, amounting to some 4,000."(19) The Yemen war went on. On
August 25, 1965 both Saudi Arabia and the United Arab Republic
signed the so-called "Jiddah Agreement."(20) This agreement also
broke down, and the "Haradh Conference" of Yemeni factions followed in 1966. This too broke down and war continued in Yemen until 1967. Partially as a result of this Saudi engagement, King
Saud lost his throne on November 2, 1964, when his half-brother
Faisal took over. Faisal, though, continued Saudi engagement with

---

18 Ibid.
19 Ibid.
20 Ibid., p. 65.
  See Lawrence Mosher, "Nasser's Drive for South Arabia," The Reporter, February 9, 1967, pp. 24-27.

more vigor. Some observers seem to believe that the Jiddah Agreement failed to disengage the parties, particularly Egypt, due to an announcement in early 1966 by the British Labour government that Britain intended to leave South Arabia within two years.(21) But meanwhile, and perhaps due to this inter-Arab war against each other, the Israeli invasion of the United Arab Republic in June 1967 took place. Perhaps also the Egyptian position in the Yemeni conflict "was one of the principal casualities of the Arab-Israeli war," as Dana Adams Schmidt puts it.(22) But the peace and survival of the Yemeni Arab Republic in Arabia was guaranteed by that action. For in August 1967 conference of Arab Heads of States at Khartoum, Sudan, which was convened due to the Israeli aggression, both King Faisal and Nasser finally agreed to actual disengagement from Yemen. And by late 1967 this was carried out. The Yemen Arab Republic stayed intact, and a new set of modern political conditions were established irrevocably in the Arabian Peninsula. But here again the United States failed not only in "finding and supporting" progressive leaders in the Arab world, as Professor Fairbanks exhorted, but eventually failed in its attempts at reversing the clock of progress in the Arab world.

THE UNITED STATES AND THE ALGERIAN REVOLUTION, 1954-1962(23)

The American failure to fulfill the challenge of rising expectations in the Third World was no less evident in America's policy toward Algeria. Dulles, as mentioned earlier, was in feverish pursuit of the creation of Anti-Soviet pacts throughout the 1950s. In this pursuit the United States became--whether consciously or otherwise--a partner to French and British imperial wars of suppression against their subjects throughout the world.

Algeria was a special case in Arab national estimation. Like Israel, Creameans wrote, it has

> presented a more theoretical issue
> but one similar to its power to

---

21 See Lawrence Mosher, "Nasser's Drive for South Arabia," The Reporter, February 9, 1967, pp. 24-27.
22 New York Times, October 20, 1967.
23 For the full story of the Algerian War see a major article by the author entitled, "The Algerian War of Independence in World Politics," published in the International Journal of Economic and Social History, Geneva, 1972, pp. 87-125.

> evoke Arab solidarity. Agreement
> on the righteousness of the rebel
> struggle for independent Algeria
> . . .(has) tended to unify the
> Arab states in their dealings with
> the West and in their conduct in
> the United Nations.(24)

The French conquest of Algeria began in 1830. France's rule there, like its rule in other parts of the world, was characterized by a recurrent pattern of violence and counter-violence. Perhaps this was due to French lack of flexibility to move with the age of nationalism. Thus France experienced bloodshed in Syria, Lebanon, Tunis, Morocco, Indo-China as well as in Algeria. In Algeria France's rigidity was supplemented by the over one million French colons that settled there, and also by a set of myths that France spun about Algeria in which it eventually believed. One of these was the repetition since 1870 that Algeria "is part of France." The Cremieux Decree of 1870 supposedly stamped officiality on this myth. Algeria was then divided into three departments and these were called departments of "metropolitan France." Another myth was that the Cremieux law was a vehicle of "assimilation" in Algeria. In fact the decree served only to make everybody else who came on the heels of French occupation to become French citizens (colons), and to keep the Algerian natives of the country in "citizenship-limbo." A subsequent inherent myth was that the Algerians would accept the habitat of limbo forever. Of course it was due to that thick layer of myths that France reacted most viciously and unreasonably to the Algerian quest for independence. Throughout the 1920s and until the Second World War, French administrators closed their ears to any Algerian nationalist call for reform--mild as most of those requests were. Rather, such would be jailed, house-arrested or banished from the country. French repression reached monstrous proportions when on May 8, 1945 some 45,000 Algerian Arabs were massacred. These massacres were partially due to Free French and Allied promises to the Algerians during the war. From then on, Algerian nationalists began organizing secretly for future revolt. The revolt came in November 1954, and lasted until 1962 with the full independence of Algeria from France. It cost the Algerians, though, an estimated three and a half million casualties out of an estimated population in 1954 of nine million.(25)

24
Charles Creameans, The Arabs and the World, (New York, 1963) p. 19.
25
See R.M. Brace, Morocco, Algeria, Tunisia, (New Jersey, 1964).

The Algerian cause became a cause celebre not only for the Arab world but for all Third World countries. Year after year the Arabs brought the issue to the United Nations in the hope of putting pressure on France to grant Algeria independence. The Algerian case split France along lines of hardliners and liberals, and brought about the collapse of one cabinet after another in the Fourth Republic. It finally brought down the Fourth Republic and the return of DeGaulle to power.

How did the United States act and react in the Algerian case? Regardless of wartime promises mentioned above, the United States after 1945 seemingly accommodated itself easily to the return of French colonial rule throughout North Africa. Not only did the United States acquiesce to this but soon also became a partner--albeit perhaps an unwilling one--in the French suppression of the Algerian people. This is so because American arms given to France after the Second World War (supposedly to forestall a Soviet attack on Europe) were being freely used against the Algerians.

There was no mention of theAlgerian rebellion when it broke out in November 1954 by either the American press or government officials. This silence went on for the rest of the year and a good part of the year after. At the beginning of 1955, French metropolitan troops were sent to help put down the rebellion. In May 1955, France began to withdraw American-equipped NATO troops from Germany and to send them to Algeria. This withdrawal which was announced by France on May 24, 1955 was acceded to by the NATO Council on June 3, 1955. Thus the NATO members including the United States became partners to Algerian suppression. On June 12, 1955 the New York Times reported that France announced the withdrawal of "another NATO division" from Germany. Twelve days later, France stated publicly that the United States was selling her much needed helicopters for use against the Algerian rebels in the Aures Mountains. These developments brought an outcry in the Arab world, charging U.S. collusion with French colonialism. On August 22, 1955 a delegation of Arab League states made representation to the United States State Department protesting the use of American NATO arms in Algeria. Three days later the New York Times reported that the U.S. protested that use to France. That protest could not have been either strong or convincing in light of the extremely poor relations Dulles was having with Nasser and other Arabs (except for the Iraqi leaders) at that time. France, of course, did not heed the American "protest," assuming such was truly issued. For only a day later, the New York Times again reported a French announcement of another army division withdrawn from Germany. In it the paper reported that France stated that "no U.S. material was being used in North Africa." This statement did not convince the American Labor Leader, Walter Reuther, let alone the Arab world. For in the same issue of the New York Times, and in an open letter to Secretary of State Dulles, Reuther denounced the use of American materials and helicopters against the Algerian people. Perhaps to avoid further complaints by other Americans, France (perhaps with State Department and Zionist coaching) began to use the then most handy tactic of the "communist wolf." On October 7, 1955, the French Minister to NATO, Billote, reported to the NATO Council that France was fighting in Algeria "in the interest of the whole Western world." France, he stated, was "resisting communist-inspired" general offensive in the Arab East and he expected France's allies in NATO to back her in that endeavor.(26) Three days later France announced an accord with NATO's American General Gruenther in which he gave France a free hand to withdraw her troops from NATO. Perhaps to complete the scenario of "crusading against communism," France outlawed its own Communist party. Nasser--by then the incarnation of all evil in Paris, was also used to rally France's allies behind her. On this last score France had a major ally in the Zionist-dominated press in the United States. The New York Times (perhaps the most influential newspaper in the United States) was conducting its own private crusade against Nasser and the Arabs. One could comfortably state that no other "culprit" in world affairs got so much negative attention by the New York Times as did Nasser-not even Mao Tse Tung. The Algerians seemingly had to suffer further for being Arab. And whenever the New York Times editorialized about Algeria and the vicious massacres that were going on there, it was in the context of how France could "still maintain her hold" there. This was done not in anger but in sympathy to France's "predicament."(27) And if the brutality in Algeria had to be mentioned, equal guilt was usually assigned to both France and the Algerian National Liberation Front (N.L.F.).

The first official American utterence regarding Algeria came in March 1956. On March 20, the American Ambassador to France Douglas Dillon pledged, in a statement, American support of a "liberal" solution of North African problems that "would ensure continued French presence there."(28) In a news conference the next day, President Eisenhower fully backed the Dillon statement. In answer to a question, he innocuously advocated that the parties

---

26New York Times, October 8, 1955.
27See for instance, C.L. Sulzberger, in New York Times, August 1, 1955.
28See text of statement in Ibid, March 21, 1956.

should seek "mediation rather than conflict," and that they should find a way to not "completely disrupt" their relationships. The President though could not fight the temptation of infusing the "communist menace" at the end of his answer. He then said:

> Now, I recognize, this is an easy
> speech to make. It is a hard thing
> to bring about, because you have
> age-old antagonisms; you have all
> sorts of fanatical thought brought
> to these problems that has no place
> really in it. . .; and you have,
> of course, the Communists interfering
> when they can.(29)

Innocuous or not, that was the type of moral leadership the Asian-African world was getting from the United States. France continued receiving American moral and material help to sustain her repression of the Algerians. In February 1957, American support of France was reiterated to the French Premier Mollet during his visit to Washington. In a news conference on March 5, 1958 Mr. Eisenhower was asked by a reporter whether there was "any thought within your administration of denying economic and military aid to France" unless there was some sort of truce reached there. The President answered:

> No. . .We have a very, very diffi-
> cult problem to solve. . . . We
> do have France as a NATO ally and
> we also are great friends of the
> North African area, so it is a
> very hard problem and one that
> takes the attention of the adminis-
> tration each day.

Perhaps North Africa could have done better without such "great friends." The United States became even more evasive about the issue of its involvement with France in Algeria after De Gaulle came to power in 1958. And De Gaulle, like other French Premiers before him since 1954, was kept armed with American NATO weapons to muddle through the bloody path of Algerian independence for almost four more years.

29
   Dwight D. Eisenhower, Public Papers of the Presidents of the United States, 1956, Washington, 1958, pp. 331-332.

Perhaps the only act of American statesmanship in regard
to the Algerian war came when Senator John F. Kennedy spoke out
on the issue in 1957. Kennedy was then Chairman of the Senate
Foreign Relations Subcommittee on United Nations Affairs. On
July 2, 1957 he took the Senate floor to denounce French policy in
Algeria and the American "head-in-the-sand" attitude toward that
policy. In a resolution he then introduced, he called on France
to start working for Algerian independence; he called on the United
States to back the discussion of the Algerian question in the
United Nations; he called for an "international effort to derive
for Algeria the basis for an orderly achievement of independence;"
he accused France of alienating the whole of Africa from the West;
he attacked the United States government for following a line of
genial compliance with French imperialism and urged the United
States to abandon that policy that had "weakened United States
leadership, aided the Communist cause and denied this nation's
anti-colonial legacy." And reviewing the French claims and American justifications for backing France as a NATO ally and viewing
Algeria as a "French colonial issue," Kennedy stated:

> Whatever the original truth of
> these cliches may have been, the
> blunt facts of the matter today
> are that the changing face of
> African nationalism and the
> ever-widening by-products of the
> growing crisis have made Algeria
> a matter of international, and
> consequently American concern.

He went on to elaborate that the American refusals even to
allow for the discussion of the issue in the United Nations "have
damaged our leadership and prestige."

> It has affected our standing in
> the eyes of the free world, our
> leadership in the fight to keep
> that world free, our prestige
> and security. It has furnished
> powerful ammunition to anti-
> Western propagandists throughout
> Asia and the Middle East.
>
> Finally, the war in Algeria has
> steadily drained the manpower, the
> resources and the spirit of our
> oldest and most consistent allies

> ...which led (it) to stifle
> free journalism, and to release
> the anger and frustration of its
> people in perpetual governmental
> instability and in a precipitous
> attack on Suez.
>
> No, Algeria is no longer a problem
> for the French alone, nor will it
> ever be again.
>
> The problem is no longer to save
> a myth of French empire. The
> problem is to save the French
> nation as well as free Africa
> . . . . The United States. . .
> cannot be tied any longer to the
> French. . . .

One cannot in all truth ascribe purely political motives for
this Kennedy statement. It was made on July 2, 1957, that is,
after Eisenhower had already won his second term in office. It
was also too early for the 1960 Presidential election campaign.
Even then, such a position was not necessarily a popular position
to take in America. Nor were there Arab-Americans in America
powerful enough to influence Kennedy. Apparently, it was a
sheer act of statesmanship.

The Arab world reacted jubilantly to the Kennedy statement.
On the other hand, France and the American State Department were
somber. On the same day (July 2, 1957) and on the same page of
the New York Times the Senator was strongly rebuked by Secretary
of State Dulles. Algeria was primarily a French problem, Dulles
doggedly insisted, "I would be very sorry to see it made ours."
If Senator Kennedy wants to denounce colonialism, the New York
Times approvingly reported Dulles as saying, "he ought to concentrate on the Communist variety rather than the French." Thus
the voice of reason and statemanship was again smothered in
America. And Algeria, and also France went on to suffer for five
more years.

CHAPTER VIII

The Tel Aviv-Washington Alliance After 1967

The Eisenhower attempt at "impartiality" in dealing with Israel and the Arabs, and Dulles' policies in the area were viewed by the Arabs generally as a failure. When Kennedy came to the Presidency in 1960 it seemed more convincing to the Arabs that he was truly going to follow an even-handed policy in the Arab-Israeli issues. He had built a reservoir of goodwill among the Arabs while he was a Senator due to his above-mentioned stand on the Algerian War, and due to his meetings with various Arab leaders before he entered the White House. In internal politicking, though, in 1960 he also competed with Nixon in the usual American politicians' outspoken support for the state of Israel. As he became President, Kennedy wrote a number of letters to major Arab leaders. In these he reiterated support for past U.N. resolutions on Palestine, and promised to use American influence in bringing about a just and peaceful solution to the Arab-Israel dispute. Of course, Kennedy did not live long enough to accomplish these things. His assassination incidentally was linked in the minds of many Arabs "to a nefarious Zionist plot to remove him because of his even-handedness. . . ."(1) With the advent of Johnson to the Presidency, any Arab hope for American-evenhandedness vanished. Johnson was far more vocal in his pro-Zionist statements, and his problems in the Far East made him relegate the Palestine issues to the background.

Whether the United States under Johnson encouraged the Israeli invasion of the Arab states in 1967 or not is hard to ascertain. Nevertheless it fits the American (and generally Western) pattern of dealing with the Arabs before and after the Second World War. In fact the creation of the state of Israel itself is viewed by many Arabs as part of the Western strategy of keeping the Arabs "off-balance," in the words of American strategists. It is perhaps part of that old Palmerston thinking of the 1820s that a "strong Egypt is not in the interest of Great Britain."(2)

1
Don Peretz, "The United States, the Arabs, and Israel: Peace Efforts of Kennedy, Johnson, and Nixon," The Annals. May 1972, pp. 116-125.
2For a detailed exposition of the confluence of Zionist interests and imperial designs, see Rita Freed, "The Middle East Conflict-An Anti-Imperialist View," The Arab World, July-August, 1970. pp. 26-32.

From the Arab view, it would stand to reason that the Western powers would not favour Arab unity. For Arab unity would mean Arab strength. And strength would make the Arabs more"demanding." And in a Middle East that is and has been subject to Western economic and political hegemony, Arab demands would naturally be at the "expense of the Western world." If strong, and if united, the Arabs would ask more for their oil, for instance; would demand and get more Arab rights in Palestine; and would demand more respect and more real independence from Western control. This would seem tolerable if the Western world had learned not to think imperially. But this apparently was not yet the case. And Israel, heavily armed with Western weapons, became a willing instrument to keep the Arabs at bay.

After 1956, Israel went back to her methods of keeping the Arabs off balance. This was done by periodically attacking a Syrian or a Jordanian village, or by conducting menacing troop movements near the borders of her neighboring Arab states. In fact the immediate causes for the outbreak of the 1967 war were just such Israeli actions. On November 3, 1966 the Jordanian village of As-Samu'u was practically wiped out by a massive Israeli invasion. A large number of civilians and Jordanian soldiers were killed then. The usual excuse was given as "retaliation for Arab marauding." The Security Council also issued the usual resolution condemning Israel. In April 7, 1967, a major action was taken against the Syrian border in which Israeli jets attacked within a few miles of the Syrian capital of Damascus. In early May, 1967 their were . . powerful indications and intelligence reports that Israel was planning further massive "retaliation" against Syria. Large Israeli troop depolyments were reported by Lebanese, Syrian and Soviet sources. Egypt was then informed by Syria that Israel was preparing an invasion of Damascus itself with the intent of overthrowing the Ba'th regime there.(3)

This Israeli intent was also stated by Israel's Premier Eshkel after the Israeli air strikes took place.(4) Israel had also been further preparing the spade-work in the United States for the invasion of Syria since January 1967 by warning that Syria was becoming"the next Cuba."(5) And due to the overwhelming evidence that Israel was the perpetrator of aggressive events against its Arab neighbors in May and June 1967, it is amazing how successful Zionist propaganda in the United States was later in portraying

---

3
See Hisham Sharabi, "Prelude to War: The Crisis of May-June, 1967,"
The Arab World, November 1968, pp. 23-29.
4
Jewish Chronicle, May 19, 1967.
5
Freed, "The Middle East Conflict," p. 29.

Israel as the "victim" of Arab aggression. The line of the Zionist-dominated press in America was that Israel was "saved from annihilation" by the bell, and her gallantry. This line was repeated time and again in America even though many military and political leaders of Israel itself have since confessed openly that the existence of Israel had never been threatened by the Arabs since 1948. In fact Dayan and other Israeli military leaders have protested since that such inference was "an insult" to Israel.

Nasser's reaction to Israeli harrassment of Syria was definitely defensive. His movement of troops into Sinai was "to counter-balance the massing of Israeli troops along the Syrian borders."(6) The fact is, Nasser then was not prepared to go to war. This was due to his heavy military commitment in Yemen. His symbolic troop movement, along with his closure of the straits of Tiran gave Israel the excuse to invade Egypt, Syria and Jordan on June 5, 1967.

Ever since 1956, many Israeli leaders as well as Zionist Americans have charged Eisenhower with robbing Israel of the fruits of her 1956 victory by insisting then on Israeli withdrawal from Arab lands. The 1967 conquests in their view was a simple rectification of that Eisenhower "mistake." Israel, as was well and elatedly publicized in America, won in six days. According to Kamel Abu-Jaber,

> the fantastic effusions of pleasure
> and hallelujahs at the success of
> Israel from all walks of life in the
> United States gave further evidence
> of the estrangement of Americans from
> the most basic requirements of justice
> and fair play. The display was the
> more offensive to the Arabs who were
> aware of the strong current of anti-
> semetism and racial bigotry in
> America.(7)

American Vietnam "doves" as well as "hawks" became equally hawkish in backing Israel before and after its stunning blitzkreig. "The gallant little democracy of Israel" was adulated by one Senator after the other. Soon also, after the outbreak of the war,

---

6
  See Kamel Abu-Jaber, "The U.S. Policy and the Arab-Israeli Conflict," Arab Journal, Vol., VI, 1969, pp. 19-30. For further study of the deterrent character of Nasser's moves see Sharabi, op. cit.
7
Op. cit. p. 28.

the neutrality of the United States was seriously in doubt through-out the Arab world. Early on June 5, 1967, the morning of the Israeli attacks on Arab air forces, a Jordanian radar station at Ajlun (some 20 miles north of the capital of Amman) picked up waves of aircraft over the Mediterranean moving toward the coast of the United Arab Republic (UAR). These were assumed by the Jordanians to be carrier-based and therefore of British and/or U.S. orgin. This was confirmed, according to Cairo Radio by a telephone conversation between King Hussain of Jordan and President Nasser.(8) By the end of the first day, whether the United States protested neutrality or not, the whole Arab world seemed to have rather believed in American and British intervention on behalf of Israel.

The immediate American official reaction to hostilities was a declaration of "neutrality." Robert J. McCloskey, then spokes-man for the State Department, stated that the United States was "neutral in thought, word and deed." Later, a qualifying state-ment was issued by White House Press Secretary George Christian reaffirming the May 23, 1967 statement by President Johnson that "the United States was firmly committed to the support of the po-litical independence and territorial integrity of all nations of the area." Despite these statements, violent demonstrations against the United States were taking place throughout the Arab world the very same day of the Israeli attack. Notwithstanding these protes-tations of neutrality,United States action was not convincing to the Arabs. For instance in the U.N. Security Council emergency session that was taking place the very same day of the attack, the United States---perhaps already realizing the extent of the Israeli vic-tory---rejected an Indian proposal for a ceasefire and a return to the positions held before the fighting broke out. U.S. Representa-tive Arthur Goldberg (a known Zionist) suggested a simple appeal for a ceasefire.(9)

The United States involvement was widely accepted in the Arab world. The very next day Egypt closed the Suez Canal. Cairo Radio then gave as the reason that "Anglo-American air intervention on

---

[8]For an excellent day-by-day and hour-by-hour report on the war and the fast-breaking developments, see Menahem Mansoor, Political and Diplomatic History of the Arab World 1900-1967: A Chronologi-cal Study, Vol. 5, 1965-1967.
[9]Perhaps for the same reason India was then punished by Israel. For on June 5, Israeli craft strafed an Indian U.N. peace contingent that was stationed in Palestine, killing 3 Indians. The next day another 14 Indian soldiers were killed and 25 wounded. India then charged Israel of "wanton murder" in the Security Council debates.

the side of Israel had been categorically established, and because
the Israeli forces had been given protective air cover by British
and American carrier-based planes." Violent demonstrations again
took place the next day against the U.S., and for many more days
in Libya, Syria, Algeria, Tunis, Egypt, Jordan, Lebanon and Iraq.
The same day(June 6) Sudan, Syria, Iraq, Algeria, Egypt and Yemen
broke off diplomatic relations with America. The reason again
was American "collusion" with Israel. The same day Arab oil-
producing states -- Kuwait, Algeria, Iraq, Libya, Saudi Arabia and
the Gulf Sheikdoms, placed an embargo on exports of oil and natural gas to Britain and the United States. Algeria and Egypt were
also charging that American planes stationed in Wheelus Airbase
in Libya were used in the attack. Attacks on American embassies
and consulates took place in Syria, Iraq, Egypt and Jordan. These
Arab charges were strongly denied daily by Dean Rusk from the first
day of the war. Denied or not, it soon became apparent to the Arabs
what President Johnson meant by the American "firm commitment to
the support of the political independence and territorial integrity
of all nations of the area." His word "all" apparently meant only
Israel. And as soon as it became clear who the victor was, the
United States began to back down from even that early commitment.
For by October 1973, the "territorial integrity" of Jordan, Egypt
and Syria meant to America further loss of more Arab land to Israel. Nevertheless the United States still protested its "even-
handedness" in Arab-Israeli affairs, come hell or high water. And
since such protestation was the object of only derision in the Arab
world, one must assume it was made only for American public consumption.

　　　　Incidentally, that Johnson "firm commitment" to the territorial integrity of all Mid-East states was repeated verbally a
number of times in the heat of the war period. Later even this verbal commitment was watered down to the vague language that was incorporated in the November 22, 1967 Security Council Resolution
No. 242. On June 9, for instance, and even though the Israeli victory was well known, George Christian, the White House Press Secretary, stated that President Johnson's "commitment to support the
territorial integrity of all Middle East states" remained, in
spite of the Israeli military victories. On June 13, and in answer
to a question in his press conference, President Johnson reaffirmed
his May 23 statement supporting the territorial integrity of all
Middle East states. Yet the rest of his answer indicated that he
was already wavering on his earlier "firm commitment." For he
added that "also a good deal depended on the nations themselves,
what they had to say and what their proposals were." By then
Israeli leaders had made it very clear (as shall be discussed below) that they were going to keep at least some of the occupied
territories, and Johnson's hedging must have been a reaction to

that Israeli position. Of course the United States position in the United Nations debates was also reflecting the Israeli point of view, i.e., no total withdrawal even if that condition might finally lead to a peace settlement in the area. On June 6, only one day after the start of hostilities, Ebba Eban of Israel stated that the "fighting had destroyed the status quo existing in the area since the 1947-1948 Israeli Arab war." Naturally if Eban was not sure of victory even in that early stage of the war he would not have made such a statement. For if there was any faint chance of Israeli defeat, the status quo would be something Israel might have wanted to keep. But regardless, the American representative Arthur Goldberg (himself a Zionist) was also repeating the Israeli line. He was adamant against Soviet, Indian and Yugoslav demands that there must be a ceasefire and immediate withdrawal of Israeli troops from what they had already occupied of Arab territories. He was also repeating the age-old Israeli line that the Arabs and Israel must sit down face-to-face and settle the Palestine question. This the Arabs (as discussed in detail earlier) refused to do. For in their estimation, Israel had made clear often enough that she wanted peace on her own terms, that is, a diktat and not peace. Therefore to ask the Arabs then after their disastrous defeat to sit down with Israel, was definitely asking them to capitulate. Goldberg's call for just such a thing in the U.N. debates of June 7, 8 and later was to the Arabs tantamount to "repeating the Israeli line." Goldberg then asked for "all warring parties to sit down with each other to provide for movement toward the final settlement of all outstanding questions between the parties." The Arabs naturally refused to sit down with Israel while Israel was in actual occupation of three Arab states.

Goldberg repeated Eban's line (or vice versa) a day later on June 8. "The major responsibility for developing a stable peace," he declared, "fell to the governments in the area. These should establish direct bilateral contacts." It could not have slipped Goldberg's attention or the United States Government's, that Israel was daily repeating her intent to keep either all or a good part of the fruits of her victory. On June 7, for instance, and while the war was only in its second day, the Israeli Jerusalem City Council jubilantly declared that Jerusalem "is now united." It decided to expand its "Master Plan" to include the whole of the Old City. On June 9, Ben Gurion suggested "quick settlement of Jews" in Arab occupied territories. The same day Moshe Dayan emphasized Israeli "determination to hold on to the land Israel conquered." The so called "dove" Eban was also repeating the same determination. On June 12, Ben Gurion stated the same position again to foreign correspondents. And by June 14, any suggestion by the Soviet Union or Yugoslavia that Israel should withdraw was

nothing but a "subscription for renewed hostility," according to
Goldberg. The U.N., he insisted, just as Eban was also then insisting, must develop a "new foundation for peace," in the area
"rather than run the film backward." In other words as late as
June 13, the Johnson "firm commitment" to the territorial integrity of all the states of the area was nothing but "running the film
backward" on June 14, in the words of the American Ambassador to
the U.N., Goldberg.

A day later the United States refused a Soviet call for a
special session of the General Assembly to hear demands that Israel should evacuate occupied Arab territories. Eventually, and
after months of negotiations and consultations, the Security Council finally adopted on November 22, 1967, a resolution submitted
by British Representative Caradon. This became celebrated as
Resolution 242. In it the Council:

a. emphasized the inadmissability
   of the acquisition of territory
   by war.
b. reaffirmed that a lasting peace
   required the withdrawal of Israeli
   forces from territories occupied in
   the war, and the termination of all
   conditions and claims of belligerency
   with the acknowledgment of sovereignty,
   territorial integrity and political
   independence within secure and recognized boundaries for all.
c. guaranteed freedom of navigation through
   international waters in the area.
d. called for a just settlement of the
   Palestinian refugee problem.
e. it requested the Secretary General
   to designate a Special Representative
   to proceed to the Middle East to establish and maintain contacts with the
   states concerned in order to promote
   agreement and assist efforts to achieve
   a peaceful and accepted settlement in
   accordance with the provisions and
   principles in the resolution.

The next day the Secretary General designated Gunnar Jarring,
Ambassador from Sweden to the Soviet Union as his special envoy.
Jarring travelled between Cairo, Tel Aviv, Amman and Damascus in
the following months. Jordan and Egypt accepted his proposals for
peace on the condition that Israel declare her agreement to with-

draw from her latest conquests. Israel, as is well known, refused. Evasive and equivocal and finally charging Jarring with
overstepping his mission, Israel insisted that the resolution did
not in the final analysis mean withdrawing from all Arab territories.
And if Israel had since 1948 convinced any one that she was truly
for peace and not for expansion, it would seem clear that her refusal to withdraw after 1967 would set that record straight. Somehow, though, the vast majority of American leaders were finally
brought about to again repeat the new Israeli line—not peace, but
"secure boundaries!"

   One of the primary objectives of the Johnson Administration
when the war began was to "neutralize" the Soviet Union. This, of
course, was done also for the satisfaction of Israel. Naturally
Israel would not want the Soviet Union involved on the side of the
Arabs. Apparently, the United States succeeded thoroughly in that
respect. American actions in that regard were also viewed with
great suspicion in the Arab world. The same day Israel attacked,
the American Sixth Fleet flagship and aircraft carrier America and
her sistership Saratoga were reported sailing closer toward the
scene of battle. Both carried over 200 fighters and bombers. This
was a clear warning (not to Israel) but to the Soviet Union not
to interfere. These ships also reinforced the Arab suspicion that
America was involved on the side of Israel. It seemed clear from
the tame Soviet reaction (notwithstanding their verbal blustering
in the U.N.) that the Soviets got the message fast. For instance,
they ignored the Arab charges that America and Britain gave Israel
air cover. A day later the Soviet Union was reported as "assuring"
the United States that she would not be involved militarily in the
fighting. This brought a Chinese charge the same day that the Soviets were plotting with the United States against the Arab people,
and acquiescing with the Israeli conquest. The next day even the
Cuban government charged the Soviet Union with "scandalous capitulation" to America and its imperialist agent, Israel. The Arabs
by then were also suspicious of Soviet "reasonableness." On June 8,
for instance, Algeria withdrew its trainees from East European
academies in what was described by Algerian communist sources as
"a warning to the Soviet Union about its attitude in the crisis."
Peking went on the next day to denounce again and again the "Russian
betrayal" of the Arab cause, and reported Chou En-Lai messages of
support to Arab leaders. It is interesting to note that the Soviet Union did not sever its diplomatic relations with Israel until
June 10, 1967. On June 10, Algerian President Boumedienne was demanding that the Soviet Union take a firmer stand in support of the
Arabs. To be neutral, he declared, "means to avoid taking a position." Perhaps it was partially due to this disappointing Soviet
attitude that Nasser declared his resignation on June 9, 1967.
Nasser had practically mortagaged his career on Soviet friendship.

He was the one who was charged in the West with inviting the Soviets to the Middle East after some 200 years of Soviet and earlier
Tzarist attempts at entering the area. To be rewarded with such
lukewarm Soviet, and from the Arab view "capitulative" stance, was
too much to bear.(10)

The final Soviet capitulation, from the Arab view, was after
the Glassboro, New Jersey meeting between Johnson and Kosygin,
June 23, 1967. This was later described by American papers as
"very good and very useful." The Arabs though were in a somber
mood.

To the Arabs, American protection of Israel and total identification with that alien state reached a number of preposterous
points after the Six Day war. It reached the point where not only
Arab interests were being freely sacrificed but also America's.
One of these occasions is the case of the USS Liberty.

On June 8, 1967, Israeli planes and torpedo boats attacked
the lightly armed U.S. electronic reconnaissance ship, Liberty.
The Liberty was in international waters, some fifteen miles north
of the Sinai Peninsula. Thirty-four American crewmen were killed,
and seventy five wounded. The U.S. Defense Department, though,
announced that only ten were killed. The Department spokesman
immediately added, and in obvious attempt at minimizing the affair,
that "Israel said the attack was made in error and apologized."
Later in the day, U.S. Assistant Defense Secretary Phil Goulding
explained to the press why the Liberty was there. He said that
the Liberty had left Spain on June 2 to "assure communications
between the U.S. Government posts in the area and to assist in re-
laying information concerning the evacuation of American dependents
and other American citizens" out of the Middle East. The same day
it was reported that President Johnson had written a letter to
Senate Majority Leader Mike Mansfield in effect explaining away
the "incident." Almost apologizing for Israel, he wrote Mansfield
that the "United States had found it necessary to make a prompt
and firm protest to the Israel government which to its credit had
already acknowledged its responsibility and apologized."

The actual number of American crewmen dead trickled down only
as time went by. Whether the incident was a mistake or not, apparently there was never a serious, sincere American effort to find
out.

10
  After announcing his resignation, demonstrations broke out throughout Egypt asking him to reconsider, which he did the next day.

On June 19 Newsweek wrote that some Washington officials believed "the Israeli attack was intentional" and that the Liberty
had been ordered sunk by Israeli military who were "afraid it had
intercepted messages proving that Israel started the war with the
Arabs." The fact is that the latter point did not have to be pro-
ven. For earlier on June 7, the Israeli Ambassador to London made
a public statement to the effect that Israel "had fired the first
shot in the Middle East."

One of the first reactions by the Arab states to the Israeli
attack was the general suspension of all oil pumping and shipment
to the United States (and the United Kingdom). On June 6, 1967
(the next day after the attack) Saudi Arabia suspended all oil
shipment to both countries. The same day Iraq, Bahrein, Qatar,
Abu- Dhabi, Kuwait and Algeria followed the Saudi suit. At that
time the United States was far less dependent on Arab oil than it
became by 1973. Britain though was in a less favourable situation.
This explains why British Prime Minister Herald Wilson assailed,
on June 6, the Arab suspension of oil shipment as "blackmail."
The United States had to carry the tap of supplying Britain with
oil for a number of months after June. The British charge of
"blackmail" would seem preposterous in light of the fact that
British Representative Caradon, like his American counter-part
Goldberg, were both defending the Israeli position in the U.N.
from the first day on, and both were obstructing any Soviet or
Arab call for Israeli withdrawal. For instance on June 14, and
repeating the Washington-Tel Aviv line, Caradon argued in the Security Council that the withdrawal of Israel "could not be secured
in fact and in practice" without discussion of the parties concerned on the spot. One must remember that Israeli withdrawal
(as well as British and French withdrawal) was secured "in fact
and in practice" by Eisenhower in 1956.

Arab retraction of their oil embargo on Britain and the
United States, led by Saudi Arabia started soon after June 6. On
June 14, ARAMCO (Arabian American Oil Co.) of Saudi Arabia which
is also the largest in the Middle East began pumping oil again
to the Lebanese ports. The Saudi government then stated that
"steps had been taken to ensure that oil did not reach either Britain or the United States." The Gulf oil states followed the Saudi
lead. The fact is that these states had no sure proof that oil
sent to Europe would not find its way to Britain or America. On
June 29, and perhaps having this embarrassing resumption in mind
(vis-a-vis the rest of the Arabs), the Saudi Oil Minister Ahmad
Yamani warned that "oil is a double edged weapon." Algeria then
criticized the Saudi position. On July 4, the Jedda (Saudi Arabia)
newspaper Okaz called on the Arabs to "reconsider" the decision to
stop oil shipment to the U.S. and Britain. On July 7, Saudi Arabia

hinted that she might resume oil shipment. There was such a hint
again on July 10. Eventually in the September 1967 Arab Summit at
Khartoum, Saudi Arabia finally convinced the thirteen Arab states
assembled that oil shipment must be resumed. This would be to raise
money to rebuild Arab economies and compensate Egypt for the closure of the Suez Canal. Part of that money would also be used to
subsidize Jordan, Egypt and Syria for the war of attrition that
was going on with Israel practically since the June 1967 war. It
was agreed though that the Arab oil states would become far more
demanding on U.S. oil companies than they had been before. In
this regard, and by January 1968, the OPEC organization (Oil Producing and Exporting Countries), composed mostly of Arab states,
became active in demanding better deals with the American oil
firms. One could safely state that the United States and Western
consumers "lost" many billions of dollars in direct response to
Arab demands since 1967, due mainly to the June 1967 war. In
other words, the June 1967 war was in that respect a windfall for
the Arabs, but not necessarily for the United States or for Europe.
And from the Arab view, and having in mind the energy crisis that
was looming large on America, "the worst was yet to come."(11)
Incidentally, the closure of the Suez Canal was also viewed by
the Arabs since the Khartoum Conference as part of that war of
attrition against the West. For it is estimated by Arab Economist
Rajai Mallakh that it cost Western shipping over four billion
dollars in 1972 alone to go around the Cape of Africa.(12) Also
related to the oil question and the 1967 aggression was the Libyan revolution of September 1, 1969. Military officers led by
Muammar Qaddafi overthrew the "pro-Western" King Idris. Qaddafi
proved to be one of the most ardent Arab nationalists since the
rise of Nasser. He has taken a very militant stand against Israel and the West generally; and due mainly to his leadership since
1970, the OPEC organization has become most vocal and successful
in its oil demands. And between 1970 and 1973 for instance, the
oil income of the Arab world has literally more than tripled.

The Arab Khartoum Conference of September 1967 arrived at
the following agreements also. It was agreed that American and
British military bases throughout the Arab world would be closed,
and Arab pressure would be applied to that effect. Arab leaders
also agreed to seek a peaceful settlement with Israel if possible.

---

[11] The Arabs have a saying: "Do not set a trap for someone lest
you fall in it yourself." In many ways the creation of the state
of Israel by the West in Arab Palestine, proved to be such a trap.
[12] By contrast, Egypt was making less than three hundred million
dollars annually by 1967 from the Suez Canal that was mainly
used by Western Europe and America.

Their main three conditions were non-recognition of Israel; Israeli withdrawal before negotiations take place; and only indirect
negotiations with Israel on the 1948-1949 style in Rhodes. Arab
non-recognition and insistence on indirect negotiations was prompted by the fear that such would enable Israel to gain legal status
prior to her withdrawal from Arab lands.

Based on the above agreement, and with the advent of the
Libyan revolution, Col. Qaddafi almost immediately demanded American evacuation of the huge American Wheelus airbase. This brought
about an American-Libyan announcement in December 23, 1969 - only
three months after Qaddafi came to power - that all American forces
and equipment would be withdrawn from Wheelus by June 30, 1970,
six months hence. This dateline was honored. British bases in
Libya were also closed.

AMERICAN "PEACE PROPOSALS"

After June 1967, the United States adopted a do-nothing attitude in regard to true "peace with justice" in the Middle East. To
the Arabs this was interpreted not as an American lack of interest
or neutrality, but rather as part of an American acquiescence to
Israeli aggression. The only exceptions though-and it is hard to
excape this conclusion-were when American proposals either repeated
the Israeli positions or were timed to serve Israeli purposes. In
retrospect, the main American peace initiative, the so-called
Rogers plan of June 1970, was a prime illustration of that. American arms policy after 1967 also points to that effect.

Immediate American reaction to the hostilities on June 5 was
a declaration of "neutrality." This was later changed to a declaration of "supporting the territorial integrity" of all Middle
East states. In the Security Council debates, the American delegation proved neither neutral, nor supporting the integrity of those
who lost. Rather, the U.S. was very partisan to the Israeli cause.
It stood again and again against a simple call for Israeli withdrawal. It insisted on the Israeli line of "partial withdrawal"
and only after the Arabs would sit down face to face with their
occupier. The U.S. seemingly, like Israel, was hopeful for a fast
diktat. When the Arabs did not oblige, the United States stood
somehow helpless to stop Israel from various immediate moves to
annex and settle occupied Arab cities and territories. Any American talk of supporting the "territorial integrity of all Middle
East states" became simply meaningless. Perhaps it was part of
the idea that talk is cheap. Or it may be part of the American attitude that you can fool all the Arabs all the time. It may also be
an example of the Washington--Tel-Aviv technique since 1948.

That is, make any statement, but do what you want. This could have been done in cahoots with Israel. The idea was to give the Arabs the feeling of American impartiality and action, while America was in reality doing nothing. Rather, American statements and "initiatives" gave Israel time to consolidate its control of more Arab lands. This in fact is what has happened since 1948, except for the Eisenhower anti-Israel action in 1956. In retrospect, one can see how the Arabs were lulled again and again by U.S. and also U.N. resolution after resolution, while Israel was creating "facts," in the words of Moshe Dayan. If all the above assumptions were true, or even partially true, then America and the United Nations again served the same Israeli purpose after the 1967 war. And the Soviet Union also seemed to be in on the game, again. To repeat, the pattern is identical to events after 1948.

Johnson was speaking of "territorial integrity" daily after June 1967. And daily Israel was creating facts. On June 28 Israel proclaimed Old Jerusalem annexed. The same day Johnson "expressed opposition" to that. So did the State Department. On July 6 Dean Rusk, in a speech in Chicago, protested that "the U.S. could not impose a blueprint for peace." He somehow came to the conclusion that "to order Israel to withdraw. . .would be a prescription not for peace but for renewed hostilities." One wonders if Rusk would have applied the same logic on earlier Japanese or German occupations and aggressions. Even his use of words was shockingly akin to the famous Chamberlain statement of appeasement to Hitler after Munich.

As mentioned earlier, the Arabs refused to capitulate after their initial defeat on June 5 to the apparent frustration of the United States and Israel. As soon as the ceasefire was accepted a war of attrition began between Israel and the Arabs. Egyptian, Syrian, Jordanian and Palestinian guerilla (Fateh) attacks were answered by heavy and most successful Israeli attacks. Thus a semi-war was going on in the Middle East after June 11, 1967. Israeli bombardment of civilian targets and towns in Egypt, Syria and Jordan added another one million refugees to the Arab refugee population of 1948. The cities of Suez, Ismailia and Port Said were practically levelled by Israeli guns from across the Suez Canal. Deep Israeli air penetrations into these three Arab countries were also designed to break the back of Arab resistance to aggression. All this proved time and again (as if the June war did not prove it sufficiently) that Israel was far superior in weapons and military capability than all the Arabs combined. And while Johnson and Rusk were protesting their support of the "territorial integrity of all states of the Middle East"; and while Israel was occupying three Arab states; it was announced on October 24, 1967 that the

United States would resume military deliveries to Israel, supplying
Israel with jet bombers. In contrast, six days later the American
House of Representatives voted to cut off all cotton imports from
the UAR. In the summer of 1968 the United States moved to supply
Israel with the most sophisticated military equipment the United
States arsenal had. On July 6, 1968 the U.S. Defense Department
announced it had reached an agreement with Israel to supply the
latter with Hawk anti-aircraft missiles.

The Israeli Zionist lobby though was clamouring for Phantom
Jets. Part of the pressure on Johnson was a vote in the House
of Representatives on July 18, "directing" the President to "sell"
Israel 50 F-4 Pahntom jet fighters. On October 9, President Johnson
directed the State Department to begin negotiations with Israel
for the sale of such. After the Nixon election in November, 1968,
Israel wanted to be sure that the one-sided policies of Johnson
in favour of Israel would be continued. On December 14, 1968 and
after a meeting with President-elect Nixon, Israel Defense Minister
Dayan stated that the U.S. "would not change its Mid-East policy"
and said that Israel was hoping for "further support" and an increase in U.S. military aid. On December 27, 1968 it was announced
in Washington that the U.S. had reached agreement on the sale of
50 Phantom jets to Israel. After that, and to come to the point,
the Nixon Administration opened its faucet of Phantom jets and
other military equipment to Israel. And by the end of the first
four years of the Nixon presidency, it was often repeated in American papers that Nixon gave Israel far more aid in his first
term of office than all the American aid to Israel since the birth
of that state in 1948. This, while Israel was sitting pat on her
occupation of further Arab territory after 1967. In effect the
United States was enabling Israel to consolidate her military hold
on Arab territories. The United States, though, continued talking
of "continuing the search for peace." On September 25, 1968, and
as the Jarring Mission had evidently failed, the Soviet Union proposed a peace plan. This included an Israeli withdrawal to pre-
1967 lines;a revived U.N. presence in the Middle East; an end to
the state of belligerency and a Four power guarantee by U.S.,
U.S.S.R., United Kingdom and France of a future peace. The American
reply to this finally came on January 19, 1969. In it the United
States stated it "would continue working through the Jarring Mission."
The Jarring Mission was already dead.(13) Meanwhile, William
Scranton published his report on the Middle East.

13
It was finally proclaimed so by U. Thant,May 1, 1969.

On December 9, 1968, Scranton had been sent by Nixon as Special Envoy to study Middle East problems at close range. In his report, he stated that the United States policy in the area "should be more evenhanded than in the past." He explained that it was important for the United States to "take into consideration the feelings of all persons and all countries in the Middle East." The Scranton report was sensible in terms of fair play and American interests in the Middle East. But these were the very things that brought about its immediate demise by the Zionist-dominated White House.

On January 17, 1969 France proposed a Four power meeting to "establish a just and lasting peace." Nixon agreed to this on February 1, 1969. A few days later (Feb. 10) Newsweek published an interview with President Nasser. In it he stated that if Israel withdrew, Egypt would offer a declaration of non-belligerency; the recognition of each country to live in peace; honor the territorial integrity of all states in the area—including Israel; accept freedom of navigation for all in international waters—as long as there was a just solution to the Palestinian people.

Now that the Arabs were openly proclaiming that they were ready for a peaceful solution based on Resolution 242 of November 1967, Israel began to create side-issues to avoid abiding by that resolution. First Israel complained bitterly at Jarring's initiative in asking whether Israel was ready to withdraw in principle from Arab territories. Israel called this "overstepping his mandate." As the Jarring Mission collapsed and the Arabs (armies and guerillas) were fighting a war of attrition, it became Israel's intention first to gain a ceasefire before (supposedly) Israel was "ready to sit down and discuss peace"; and second, to bring about the destruction of the newly emerging Palestinian guerilla movement. The Fateh was gaining a great deal of prestige throughout the Arab world-rank and file and governments. The Fateh movement reached the zenith of its prestige after it scored a number of victories against Israel beginning with the battle of Karamah of March 21, 1968. Thousands of hitherto "Palestinian refugees" were joining the movement after 1967. It gained a great deal of momentum in 1968 and 1969. Israel was fearful that if Fateh was unchecked, it could become a truly revolutionary movement in the Arab world which would be the first true challenge to Israel (and other Arab conservative governments) in the area. Knowing also that conservative Arab leaders might be perhaps the best method of checking such a revolutionary movement, Israel began to play up the line that if only Fateh were checked, Israel would be ready for peace. Thus, for instance, as Egypt and Jordan publicly declared that they would accept final peace based on 242, Israel began to play up the Fateh side-issue. Fateh of course was a reflection of Arab

209

frustration over many decades of getting a semblance of justice
in Palestine through their governments and armies. If Israel were
ready in 1968, 1969, and 1970 to truly make an honorable and just
peace in Palestine, one is inclined to wonder about Israel's over-
concern with Fateh! But regardless, the Israeli reaction to the
above-mentioned Nasser declaration (that he was ready for peace)
and similar statements by King Hussain, was for Israel to bring
up the side-issue of Arab commandoes. The United States followed
the Israeli lead.

Two days later (Feb. 12, and perhaps answering Nasser's published report) Tekoah of Israel charged in the U.N. that Egypt was
"directing" the Fateh "terrorists" and was "openly in full support"
of such. Catching the Israeli bait, Egypt's al-Zayyat protested the
next day that Egypt had "no authority or responsibility" for directing Arab guerillas either in Sinai or on other fronts.

King Hussain began to catch the bait also. Thus on March 1,
1969, and in an interview in al-Nahar he promised that "once Israel
had withdrawn from occupied territory" he would halt Fateh attacks
from Jordan. If the Jarring Mission, though, failed, he stated,
"there is no alternative but to take up arms." Needless to say,
any such public talk by Hussain was bound to split the Arab ranks
and alienate Fateh from Jordan. That was perhaps the only goal
Israel was after. But the Arab leaders, Nasser and Hussain, in
their infinite capacity for trust, finally acquiesced to check
Fateh on the strength of Rogers' promises of 1970.

In March 1969, Israel was frantically working against the
French effort to bring about peace through the efforts of the
Four Great powers. Such was called "forced settlement." On
March 14, Eban warned against the "complexity and peril of such
concepts." On March 30, the Israeli cabinet issued a statement
specifically rejecting "any settlement and any procedure that is
not agreed upon by the governments concerned."

On April 3, representatives of Britain, France, the Soviet
Union and the United States met, regardless. In their joint communique they declared that they "have started defining areas of
agreement. There is common concern to make urgent progress."
This, though, was not to the Israeli liking. Three days later
Dayan declared flatly that Israel did not intend to withdraw and
"should create new facts" in the occupied areas. Deputy Premier
Allon urged Israel the same day to establish settlements (in
occupied Arab land) "to insure safe borders," before peace broke
out. Four days later, King Hussain (April 10), speaking in America, offered "with the personal authority of Nasser" a peace
proposal that would include "an end to all belligerency." Jordan

and Egypt, he declared, completely accepted Security Council Resolution 242. Two days later Golda Meir insisted that "peace in the area must come from direct negotiations" and not from Four Power talks. Somehow she came to the skeptical conclusion that she "doubted that Hussain truly carried peace in his baggage."

Israel again killed these Arab initiatives toward peace as well as the Four Power initiative. Even retired Ben Gurion--not a known dove when it came to Arab affairs--stated a few days after Golda Meir's statement (April 19, 1969) that "it would be worthwhile to return all areas occupied in the June war to achieve peace."

The beginning of May also brought official death to the Jarring Mission. U Thant then announced after a meeting with Ambassador Jarring that the latter felt there was nothing he could do for peace in the Middle East. Before and after the failure of Jarring and other peace efforts, the war of attrition between Jordan, Fateh, Syria and Egypt on one side and Israel on the other became more intense. It could be partially for this reason that the United States came up with various peace plans, culminating with the "Rogers' initiative for peace," in June 1970.

In retrospect it seems that the United States first suggested some peace proposals to the U.S.S.R. regarding the Middle East on March 26, 1969. On June 27, Al-Ahram published the main items of these proposals. And even though nothing finally came out of this particular initiative, it is interesting to note that one of the items asked for by the United States was the "end of official assistance" to the commando groups by Arab governments.

To repeat, nothing came out of that initiative. On July 1, 1969 the Four Powers announced an indefinite recess of their meetings. Nine days later Gromyko, in a Tass report, summed up the results of the Four Power talks: "Israel rejects any proposals aimed at settlement." On July 22, Mrs. Meir announced a visit to President Nixon. She came September 25 and 26. Perhaps heading

---

[14]Other points published by Al-Ahram were:
   a. end of state of belligerency.
   b. demilitarization of Israeli-held Egyptian territory and stationing of peace-keeping forces in these areas.
   c. Israeli withdrawal to pre-June 1967 boundaries.
   d. the reopening of the Suez Canal and Gulf of Aqaba to all international traffic.
      U.S. State Department spokesman Robert McCloskey described the Al-Ahram plan as "not correct." This, though, did not deny the main gist of the proposals.

off his own total capitulation as he faced the strong-willed Israeli, Nixon, in a speech to the United Nations Assembly on September 18 (seven days before she arrived) stated that the United
States sought peace based on respect for the sovereign right of
each nation to exist within "secure and recognized boundaries."
He then added in a veiled warning to Israel that "peace cannot be
achieved on the basis of substantial alterations in the map of
the Middle East." Golda came seven days later. After her meeting
with the President she declared that Israel "had been under no
pressure whatsoever" from the United States to withdraw. And
since there was no American refutation offered, one has no reason
to doubt her.

The final split between governments and the commandoes (that
came after June 1970) was of course a major victory for Israel.
It has been part of a pattern of Israeli attempts since 1948 of
trying to make separate peace with the various Arab states concerned. This was discussed earlier. After 1967 Israel and the
United States were again pursuing the same goal. Rumors to this
effect were heard time and again in American papers and from Israel, that one Arab state or the other was on the verge of making
a separate peace. This brought about the desired results. It
sowed the seeds of suspicion between Arab governments, and between
those governments and the Palestine commando movement. It eventually led to open warfare between Hussain and Fateh in Jordan in
September 1970 and intermitent fighting between Fateh and the Lebanese authorities after 1970. It also brought about occasional
polemics between Hussain of Jordan and other more "militant" Arab
governments, the latter charging Hussain with being "soft on Israel." The final success of American-Israeli machinations was
achieved by the so-called "Rogers peace initiative" of June, 1970.

After the Meir visit to the United States in September, 1969
the war of attrition in the Middle East was intensified. A war of
polemics was also going on between the Arab states concerned and
the United States. For instance, on October 18, 1969 the UAR protested in a note to U.N. Secretary General U Thant that the United
States was "encouraging American citizens to take up arms under
the Israeli flag against the Arab people.' Two days later, Assistant Secretary of State, Joseph Sisco, speaking to diplomats of
ten Arab countries, denied that there were U.S. military personnel
aiding Israel. Nevertheless he admitted obliquely that there might
be some American citizens fighting along-side the Israelis. He
then explained that there might be "some few Israelis" who held dual
citizenship (American) who serve and added that the United States
"strongly prefers" that U.S. citizens do not serve in the armed
services of any foreign nation. Of course the question is not
purely academic in measuring the balance of power in the Middle

East. For if these "few Israelis" who are also "Americans" are trained Phantom pilots, they would practically suffice to destroy the air defences of four Arab states within a few hours, as proved by the Six Day War.

On November 6, 1969 Nasser attacked the United States as being the "enemy" of the Arab People. A day later, Rogers righteously protested that Nasser's speech was a"setback to peace efforts." He then added "President Nasser is mistaken in describing the United States as an enemy of Egypt. . . ." The United States, he doggedly insisted, was "genuinely" interested in contributing to a just and lasting peace in the Middle East. Rogers perhaps forgot that his State Department had confirmed only on September 6 that the first consignment of Phantom jets was delivered to Israel! These Phantoms were used, as is well known, for deep penetration of Arab air space hitting civilian and military installations at will. He must also have been aware that this was already official Israeli policy since it was announced by Golda Meir on June 30, 1969.

In his November 6, 1969 speech, Nasser declared his despair of Resolution 242. The Arab-Israeli war of attrition progressed in ferocity, with Israel apparently inflicting far more harm on the Arabs. In retrospect, one might judge that Israel was hurting badly too. For in the opinion of many Arab and neutral observers of the Middle East, and looking back at events, the Rogers so-called cease-fire initiative of June 1970 could be interpreted in that light. That is, it was designed to give Israel a breathing spell from attrition. For it came, suspiciously,only after the Arabs acquired Soviet missiles that proved effective against American Phantoms.

On September 1, 1969 a nationalist revolution took place in Libya. It proved to be part of that Arab nationalist momentum that the United States and the Zionists have refused to recognize since the First World War. Libya's new leadership demonstrated that it was even more nationalist (and from the American view, radical) than Nasser and his colleagues before it. Soon it was to put the full weight of Libya's considerable oil revenues behind the Arab national cause. And since the United States-under heavy Zionist influence since 1917-had chosen to fight Arab nationalism, Libya's revolution was another defeat for the United States. Soon, its new leader, Muammar Qaddafi, began demanding the exit of the significant United States military installation in Libya. This was accomplished on June 30, 1970 when the huge American Wheelus base was evacuated. Soon also the new Libyans were taking the lead in Arab demands for better payments for their oil. It is well understood that it was Libya more than any other oil-producing state that has brought about fantastic new revenues to the Arabs since

1970. Libya became a vocal voice in the Organization of Petroleum Exporting Countries (OPEC) since 1970. The success of OPEC since then could only be viewed with chagrin in Zionist and American exploitive circles. And so it was.

To return to rumors of individual Arab states making unilateral peace with Israel: this, as was explained earlier, could only be listed in Arab estimation as in the category of Zionist "dirty tricks." For the Arab states have made it clear since 1948, and repeated it time and again, that no such thing is forthcoming. Nevertheless after the 1967 war, Zionist propoganda in and outside Israel was back to rumor-mongering. For instance, in June and early July 1968, there were many "rumors" and "speculations" that King Hussain of Jordan was negotiating unilaterally with Israel. This eventually brought about the desired effect. On July 9, Egyptian diplomatic circles were charging that Hussain "either started or is ready to start" a separate peace with Israel. Hussain denied this the same day. Rather, he asked for an Arab summit to discuss joint Arab issues. A day later Hussain denied it again. On October 16, 1968 the International Herald Tribune reported that peace negotiations between Israel and Jordan "were in the process of starting through Jarring." This was emphatically denied by King Hussain on October 30. Hussain then stated that there was "no direct or indirect" negotiations going on with Israel. The fact that Arab leaders were answering the charges indicated that they were catching the "rumors" bait. The fact that the Arab press was then quoting the Zionist-dominated Western press indicated also that it too was catching the Zionist bait.

On March 24, 1969 the New York Times published "reports" of "at least two secret meetings between Eban and Hussain in recent months." One wonders that if they were secret,how did the New York Times know about them? And since the publication of such is detrimental to the cause of peace on Israeli terms, one may readily deduce that the New York Times would not have published such "reports" if there were any truth to their reality.

On December 1970 the United States government and the New York Times were at it again. The Times published on the 22nd what it called a "summary of an American proposal for a Jordanian-Israeli peace settlement." A few days later (January 1, 1970) Nasser charged that the U.S. proposals aim to divide the Arabs. A few days later (January 21) King Hussain himself restated the age-old Arab stand, that "if there is a solution, it has to be a general solution, not a piece-meal one."

With this apparent failure to breach Arab solidarity, the New York Times rumors and Israeli-American "piecemeal" peace initiatives abated. They were exhumed though, whenever a breach in

214

the Arab ranks was apparent. This came after the Nasser-Hussain acceptance of the so-called Rogers "peace initiative" of June 1970. This acceptance split the whole Arab world again between those who advised against it and those who were for it. Its acceptance finally brought about Civil War in September 1970 between the Jordan government and its people and Fateh. And as soon as that civil war broke out, Israel tried another "piecemeal" initiative with Jordan. For on November 16, 1970 and while the Jordan Civil War was raging, King Hussain stated that he had turned down a proposal for bilateral talks with Israel made by Israel to Ambassador Jarring. The same day Time Magazine (November 16) published a "report" that Deputy Premier of Israel, Yigal Allon and King Hussain had met in September of 1968 to discuss peace. It must be remembered that civil war in Jordan was then going on. The question arises: what purpose was there behind publishing in November 1970, a 1968 encounter between Hussain and Allon if such a meeting ever took place? One hardly escapes the obvious conclusion. Needless to say, Hussain again denied the encounter. It was doubtful though, that Fateh then believed him.

Another aspect of the American and/or Israeli relations with the Arabs after 1967 is the art of creating side-issues to avoid the central theme. The central theme of Arab demands (governments and Palestinians) since 1948 is the rights of the Palestinian people dispossessed by Israel. To them, these are based on the fundamental realities of history. In 1917, Palestine was Arab. In 1948 much of Palestine was usurped. Aside from history, these rights are based also on United Nation resolutions since 1947. Since 1948, Israel and the United States have chosen to ignore history, simple justice and the United Nations. "Facts" were created by Israel on the basis of might. Thus, the creation of an enlarged Israel in 1948 became one of these "facts," whether the Arabs liked it or not. The usurpation of Palestinian heritage is another Israeli "fact." Taking the waters of the Jordan River, whether the Arabs concerned, agreed to it or not is another. Their attack on Egypt in 1956 was another attempt to create new "facts." The 1967 invasion of Syria, Jordan and Egypt succeeded in creating further new "facts." Israel got away with these "facts" sheerly because the Arabs were too divided and too weak to stop it.

Needless to say, Arab frustration escalated with every new "fact" Israel forced on the Arabs. The United States stood either actively arming Israel to dictate new "facts" to the Arabs and passively when there was any attempt by the world community to stop Israel. In effect, the United States became a partner to Israeli aggression in the Levant. But regardless of the escalating Arab frustrations, the Arab world consistently kept hammering at the central issue of the Palestinian people. Perhaps it was an Israeli-American hope that if Arab losses escalated beyond Palestine, the

Arab states would be amenable to forgetting about Palestine and its people. This never developed.

Despairing of any solution on the basis of Resolution 242, by the end of 1969, mainly because of open U.S. partiality towards and refusal to put pressure on Israel, Nasser attempted to acquire more military aid from the Soviet Union to intensify his war of attrition. He flew to the U.S.S.R. on January 30, 1970. On March 19, the New York Times reported that a large number of Soviet anti-aircraft missiles and personnel were dispatched to Egypt. Some of these missiles were of the SAM 3 type. The usual Zionist hue and cry took place in the United States over this development. It prompted Rogers to state on March 23, 1970 that if the Soviet shipments of weapons to Egypt "upset the current balance," the President "would not hesitate to act." Of course the "balance" in American estimation has always been an "overbalance" in favour of Israel. One by-product of this persistent American policy is the feeling in much of the Arab world that the United States was going to give Israel more defensive and offensive weapons, whether there was a "balance" or an "overbalance." This could have been designed as part of the Israeli-American psychological warfare against the Arabs. On the other hand this realization could have been counter-productive. For, any further "threats" by the United States to give more arms to Israel would be brushed aside by the Arabs as inevitable anyhow.

The war of attrition was hurting Egypt more than Israel. Nevertheless Israel was getting exasperated with it. Zionist clamour in America against the Soviet Union and its missiles was intensified. American Zionists working in concert with the Israelis apparently were ready to see a great power confrontation in order to have things always their way. At times their game reached the level of recklessness. For instance, on April 29, 1970 Israel charged that in her war of attrition with Egypt "it has become clear beyond any doubt" that Soviet pilots "are flying operational missions" for Cairo. In his announcement of this Israeli charge, Nixon's Press Secretary Zeigler stated that "this Israeli report is a matter of serious concern to the United States." Nixon, he added, ordered immediate evaluation of intelligence reports. A day later, Eban stated that Soviet "operational activity in Egypt" is not only defensive but also offensive. In effect he was asking, as much as inviting the United States to fight the Soviet Union. A day later (May 1) Nasser warned that U.S.-Arab relations were reaching a crucial point. The United States, he said, must order Israel to get out of occupied Arab territories if it hoped for peace. And if that were not possible, America must refrain from arming Israel to the teeth. He went on to remind America that the Soviet Union "is not helping us to launch aggression, but to liberate our occupied lands." Of course, if there were any American policy-maker since 1967 who wanted to listen to Nasser (and later Sadat) he would have heard his anguished cry. Apparently there was none.

216

Israeli charges against the Soviets were part of that Israeli tactic of creating side-issues to divert attention from the central theme. If Israel was truly interested in peace she could have had it since the passage of Resolution 242 on November 22, 1967. She then would not have to worry about Soviet missiles and Soviet pilots allegedly helping Egypt to defend the rest of Egyptian territory. The fact was definitely obvious, if it was ever not, that Israel wanted expansion at the expense of, and not peace with her Arab neighbors. And neither Rustow, Johnson, Rogers, Nixon or Kissinger could have been so obtuse as not to recognize this. But while the United States was apparently oblivious to these facts and incurring Arab wrath, the Soviet Union was basking in the resultant by-products.

The true motives behind the so-called Rogers Peace Initiative of June 1970 are hard to ascertain. Rogers then asked for a cease-fire so as to start the process of negotiations.

A number of questions arise as one looks back a few years later: Was Rogers truly interested in peace when he undertook his initiative? Was he an innocent tool of Israel and the Zionists to exert his prestige to bring about an Israeli-wanted cease-fire? Was he used to give Israel a breathing spell while Israel consolidated her hold on newly conquered Arab territories? Did Rogers promise Nasser ironclad guarantees for some results as to Israeli withdrawal from Arab lands? Did Nasser accept a cease-fire because he too was exhausted from attrition? Was this initiative forthcoming only because Egypt was then doing well in downing Israeli Phantom jets? Was his initiative designed to stall the momentum of the fighting-spirit that was developing in Egypt? Was it designed to split the Arab world as to those who accept it and those who oppose it? Was the proposal designed to finish off the Palestine guerrillas and have other Arabs do the job which Israel could not do? The final question that comes to mind is simple: Was Nasser fooled? Answers though, are hard to find. But these questions become very relevant in light of the fact that that initiative was amazingly successful in bringing about all kinds of bad results to the Arabs and no resultant Israeli withdrawal.

Rogers stated publicly on June 25, 1970 that the United States "has undertaken a political initiative. . .the objective of which is to encourage the parties to stop shooting and start talking" under the auspices of Jarring and in accordance with Security Council resolutions. A day later the New York Times published the provisions reportedly provided for in the United States initiative. These included a 90 day cease-fire; beginning of negotiations under Jarring; Israeli acceptance of all parts of the 1967 Security Council Resolution 242 in return for a commitment by Jordan and Egypt to the principles of peace with Israel. This was acceptable to

217

Egypt and Jordan, and apparently at first by Israel. Soon, though, Israel began her usual attempts at creating diversionary side-issues. For instance, as soon as the "initiative" was reported, Israel raised the "issue" of "temporary cease-fire." Golda Meir on June 29 complained about such since "it would give Egypt time to install missile sites!" The fact was, Egyptian missiles were already taking a toll of Israeli jets, cease-fire or not. For on June 30, Egypt claimed to have shot down four Israeli jets including two Phantoms. On July 2 Egypt claimed another Phantom. A day later Egypt claimed another two jets. A day later Egypt claimed a Skyhawk jet and a Phantom. A day later Egypt claimed another two Phantoms. On July 7 another Skyhawk was claimed. July 9 Egypt claimed to have shot down an American reconnaissance aircraft. A day later two more Israeli jets were claimed. The same day Is-raeli Air Force Commander had stated tellingly that "Egyptian missiles still do not deny us freedom of action over the canal." He went on to state that the Egyptian action was "part of a plan to cross the canal." Now due to the fact that Egyptian missiles were already inflicting a heavy toll on Israel, the Golda protes-tations that a temporary cease-fire would help Egypt become meaning-less. It was the heavy toll of jets that finally made Eban de-clare the Israeli acceptance of the Rogers initiative on July 13, 1970. Perhaps it was that same heavy toll that brought about the Rogers initiative in the first place. Nasser on the other hand was in no hurry to accept it. He was doing well militarily against Israel, perhaps for the first time in his career. He did finally accept it on July 23 and then stated that "the Arabs would de-mand nothing short of full evacuation by Israel." This was coupled with the standard Arab demand that there must be a just solution to the case of the Palestinian Arabs. The next day be-gan the split in the Arab world over Nasser's acceptance. The New York Times then reported strong Palestinian (Fateh) and Iraqi opposition to the Rogers initiative and Nasser's acceptance of it. A day later the Fateh radio stated that the Palestinian commandoes "will foil the American conspiracy." A day later Hussain accepted the Rogers initiative. By that time Algeria was also bitterly de-nouncing its acceptance. On July 30, Pravda denounced Arab critics of Nasser and Hussain for their acceptance of the Rogers plan. Apparently, Fateh opposition to Rogers plan was anticipated by the United States, Israel, Nasser and Hussain. It soon became apparent what contingency plan was prepared for "taking care of the Palestinians." For on July 27, American officials were stating that under the American peace proposals, Hussain "would be com-mitted to controlling the guerillas," as part of the cease-fire. It would seem obvious and without the benefit of hindsight, that Fateh would oppose the stoppage of commando operations against Israel. If this were the case, then Hussain and Nasser were either duped into a confrontation with Fateh or willingly accepted the

218

job of wiping them out. One is inclined to suspect the first.
For the Arabs still have a naive capacity for trust in Western
promises. But if the Jordan government willingly committed fratricide against its Palestinian subjects, in the hope of forthcoming peace from Rogers, the massacre of thousands of well-trained
Fateh fighters in the autumn of 1970 was all in vain.

On August 7, 1970 the cease-fire between Egypt and Israel
finally went into effect. The Central Committee of the Palestine
commandoes immediately announced that Fateh would not abide by it.
Rather, Fateh promised to escalate its attacks inside Israel. Six
days later (August 13) Saudi Arabia, Egypt and Libya announced the
stoppage of financing Fateh movement. Iraq, Algeria and Syria on
the other hand declared their backing of it. The Arabs were on
their way to kill each other. Meanwhile Israeli spokesmen were
creating another side-issue to torpedo the Rogers plan. On August
13, Dayan charged that Egypt had installed new missiles in the
cease-fire zone, "only four hours after the cease-fire began."
One is inclined to ask that if that were the case, why did Dayan
wait six days to complain about it? Nevertheless, he demanded that
the United States should "rectify the situation." Immediately,
State Department spokesmen declared that they had "reached no
conclusion about the Israeli charges." Two days later they were
still "daring" to state that "evidence is still inconclusive."
This statement went on meekly to urge Israel that "the main thing
now is to concentrate all efforts on getting the discussion going."
Two days later, Pravda as well as Al-Ahram of Cairo were both
charging Israel with attempts at evading peace by creating side-
issues.

Israel's clamour, though, continued. For this reason the
United States announced that American planes were conducting reconnaissance flights over Egypt to satisfy Israel. These were of
course unilateral flights, unaccepted and un-authorized by Egypt.
Egypt lodged a complaint against such on August 21, 1970. Objections or not, the State Department declared the same day that such
flights would continue. On August 22, Senator J. William Fulbright
made his famous proposition in regard to the "security of Israel."
He then proposed that the United States sign a security treaty with
Israel pledging to defend her security within the borders which
existed prior to the June 1967 war. Perhaps this was timed by the
Chairman of the Senate Foreign Relations Committee to add pressure
on Israel to come to the Jarring peace table. Things seemed close
to a break-through towards the beginning of discussions between
Egypt, Jordan, and Israel when the Israeli U.N. Ambassador, Tekoah
again raised the "violations" issue. The next day Tekoah did not
show up for his scheduled meeting with Jarring. Jarring met with
the two Arab ambassadors alone. It was explained later that Tekoah

219

left for Jerusalem "for consultations." Discussions were never held, and this initiative was torpedoed. In the meanwhile, though, Israel was rewarded with more American arms. On August 13 the United States announced its delivery of arms to Israel "so the arms balance does not tip against Israel," in the words of the announcement. And by September 4 the U.S. State Department itself began to parrot the Israeli allegations that there was violation of the standstill cease-fire of August 7.

With the death of this Jarring initiative Israel went back to its habit of hammering at its neighbors. This was in response to Fateh attacks from Jordan, Syria and Lebanon. These attacks were in direct proportion to Palestinian and other Arab frustrations vis-a-vis Israel. To the Arabs Israel was obviously in no mood or hurry to make peace. The United States also was apparently in no hurry to force peace on Israel. And both seemed to the Arabs in cahoots to get away with more Arab land. The fact is, such a conclusion was hard to escape. Israel was then bragging daily about its new settlements, "nahals" and "kibutzim" erected in recently conquered Arab lands. Meanwhile the United States was further arming Israel. The incredulous explanation invariably given in Washington was that, that was the way to have influence over Israel. Another warped American logic usually forwarded was that if Israel were not armed enough it would attack the Arabs presumably in an act of desperation.

On September 6, 1970 a Palestinian commando operation took place that had profound repercussions on the whole Middle East. That day Arab commandoes hijacked three passenger jets over Europe. A Swissair and a TWA jet were taken to a desert strip in Jordan. A Pan American jet was taken to Cairo and was blown up after landing. The commandoes later stated that the Pan American was blown up in "retaliation for U.S. support of Israel." They added that next would follow the U.S. oil interests in the Arab world. On September 9 a British Overseas Airway was also hijacked and brought to the same desert strip in Jordan. The commandoes demanded release of hundreds of their comrades that were languishing in Israeli jails. The same day there was an American announcement that Israel would receive 18 more Phantoms. And while Egypt was protesting against the American Phantoms to Israel; and U Thant was still charging Israel with sabotaging the Jarring peace talks; the United States Government and press were waging war against "Fateh terrorism" and "Arab atrocities." The Phantoms and Israeli refusal to make peace notwithstanding, another incident was also forgotten by the State Department and the Zionist-dominated press. That was the hijacking on August 14 (less than one month earlier) by the Israeli government of two Algerian diplomats. Both were in transit on a British BOAC Airliner when it landed in Israel. They were hijacked from the plane. And neither the protests of the British

220

Government, nor the protests of Secretary General of the U.N.
U Thant were to any avail. Both were still in Israeli custody
when Fateh hijacked the three airliners. Neither did the American
government nor the press raise much fuss also when on September 13
Israeli forces "arrested" more than 450 Palestinians in the occupied
territories. This was done, ostensibly, "for the purpose of inter-
rogation." In fact they were taken as hostages, and their number
was approximately the same as that of the European passengers on the
three hijacked airliners in Jordan. In other words Israel as a
government was practicing hijacking. Yet the U.S. government and
press chose to condone these Israeli activities, while they directed
their verbal guns against Fateh "terrorism." This double standard
in American official and press behavior truly reached the point of
racism on many occasions, as it pertained to Arab and Israeli
affairs. A comment by Robert Pierpoint on CBS, March, 1973 well
illustrates this double standard.(15). One might add though that
it was not simply a matter of double standard. A double standard
might indicate that all American policy-makers are either clever
racists or obtuse sinners. All indications point to an American
Zionist and Israeli imperial alliance against the Arabs.

The three planes were blown up by Arab commandoes on September
12. Rumors were then circulated in the American press that the
United States Sixth Fleet might intervene to rescue the airline
hostages. American pundits were condemning "terrorists" violation

---

15
  White House correspondent Pierpoint wrote in part: "During this
period of its emotion over a series of tragedies in the troubled
Middle East the United States appears to have lost its sense of
fair play and justice and seems to be operating on a double standard. When the Israelis a few weeks ago carried out a commando-
type raid deep into Lebanon. . .and snuffing out 30 or 40 lives
in the process, there was next to no outcry in this country.
That event. . .was quickly overshadowed by the Israeli shooting
down of the Libyan airliner. That did cause some official re-
grets although not expressed publicly at the level of the White
House. Nor did any U.S. official ever indicate that the U.S.
might think twice before it dispatched more. . .Phantom jets to
Israel of the type that had shot the Libyan airliner. Indeed, the
very next week President Nixon let it be known, that more such
Phantoms would soon be on their way.
  Contrast these events with what happened after the Arab. . .
massacre of Israeli athletes at Munich. The U.S. from President
Nixon on down, expressed outrage. . .President Nixon expressed
shock and a deep sense of grief. . ".Monitor, March 9, 1973.

of "international law." Naturally the leadership of the Palestinian national movement were repeating to all those who might be
listening, as they did in a statement on September 15, 1970, that
"international law was the same law under which our people were
forced out of the homeland."

The U.S. Sixth Fleet did not intervene. Intervention was left
to another Arab. That, naturally, would have been more productive
to the over-all plan of Zionist imperialism. To have King Hussain
commit fratricide would kill for Israel at least three big birds
with one stone. It would split the whole Arab world asunder which
is part of the overall plan of keeping the Arabs "off-balance."
It would wipe out the effectiveness of the Fateh movement. This
would give Israel more time to create "new facts" in the occupied
territories. And all this would ease the pressure on Israel if there
were ever any pressure on Israel to agree to a just peace in the
Middle East. This master-stroke was accomplished. It was accomplished by playing on King Hussain's fear of losing his sovereignty
in Jordan. It was accomplished also by commando recklessness and
mistakes. It was also accomplished by a large measure of Israeli-
American dirty tricks. Perhaps the Rogers initiative was the major
one. Another major trick was for Israel to finance bogus commandoes
for the purpose of making "the right mistakes" inside Jordan.

Wittingly or unwittingly, King Hussain and Fateh committed
fratricide in September 1970 and later. Jordan's army took the
field against Fateh, and not against Israel. All this, naturally,
was part of the Rogers initiative bargain. And while Nasser closed
the Fateh radio in Egypt, Hussain wiped out the movement in Jordan.
All this might have been justified if the so-called Rogers peace
initiative came to any fruitation. It all might have been justified if the Rogers peace plan was truly a peace plan in the first
place. But since Israel has never been truly interested in peace
since 1948, one could easily deduce that the more the Arabs killed
each other, the less Israel was inclined to make a just peace except perhaps on her own full terms.

Another repercussion of the civil war in Jordan was the death
of Nasser on September 28. He was ailing from a heart condition,
and no doubt the strain of events in Jordan and the whole area
helped bring about his early demise. His death also added to the
Israeli-American peace procrastinations. From then on one would
hear in America and in Israel of the "vacuum" in Cairo. One would
read how "there was no strong man in the Arab world to make peace
with." And with the demise of President Nasser; and the demise
of Fateh; and the demise of any semblance of Arab unity after
September and october of 1970; the Rogers peace plan was also buried
in America. For the next three years Sadat of Egypt tried to re-
suscitate it time and again, but to no avail. The fiction of its

222

being alive was kept up for a while by Rogers and his Assistant, Joseph Sisco. But in the words of one observer, Lawrence Mosher:(16)

> All the travelling and talking by
> Secretary of State William Rogers
> and Assistant Secretary Joseph Sisco,
> could not outweigh the results of
> one brief meeting between Israel's
> Golda Meir and Mr. Nixon in Washing-
> ton in late 1971. Mr. Nixon, it
> seems, did not think a Mideast peace
> agreement was important enough to
> make it necessary to force down
> Israel's throat the American idea
> of how Resolution 242 ought to be
> implemented.

Sadat's pleas for a peaceful and honorable solution went unheeded. With his assumption of leadership on the death of Nasser he first reaffirmed the Egyptian pledge to abide by the cease fire accepted by his predecessor. Then he reaffirmed Egyptian acceptance of the Security Council call for an end to belligerency and for recognition of Israeli sovereignty, territorial integrity and right to use the Suez Canal after peace was achieved. Israel, though, remained adamant in her refusal to return to her 1967 borders. In February 1971 Sadat even offered to sign a formal peace treaty with Israel, but to no avail. Up till then no Arab leader had ever dared to make such an offer without committing political suicide. In May 1971 he even accepted United States mediation between the Arabs and Israel. He then also offered to accept a partial pull-back of Israeli troops from Suez so as to open the canal for international traffic. This was to be a first step in a later overall Israeli withdrawal from Arab territories and the signing of a peace settlement. This offer also never got off the ground. In July 1972 Sadat asked all Soviet military advisors to leave Egypt. This move, he must have thought, would refute the American and Israeli charges that Egypt was becoming a base for Soviet dominance of the Middle East. The move would therefore bring about for him a more sympathetic American position, and in turn would bring more American pressure on Israel to accept peace, and the implementation of Security Council 242. This gesture proved to be even more futile. For after his fallout with the Soviets, Israel and her Zionist allies in America were even less inclined to listen to Sadat or to take him seriously.

---

[16]"Washington: A Vacuum at the Center," Middle East International August, 1973. (The article was originally published in the National Observer).

223

Sadat and the Arabs then resorted to a diplomatic offensive
to isolate Israel and the United States from the rest of the world.
This effort brought signal successes in Africa through the Arab influence within the Organization of African States. Particularly
after the Algiers conference of the non-aligned states that took
place in August 1973, many African states broke diplomatic relations with Israel. Many European countries, and particularly
France also became more even-handed, if not openly impatient with
Israeli intransigence. No doubt many West European countries were
also keeping an eye on the energy situation and their increasing
reliance on Arab oil. Egypt also used the United Nations forum
to expose the American-Israeli isolation. The United States was
forced twice in 1973 and before the October 6, 1973 war to use
the veto to protect Israel. The last veto came in July, 1973 when
Egypt tried to get a resolution passed in the Security Council
condemning Israel for her continued occupation of Arab territory.
This had the positive votes of fourteen Council members as opposed
to the American veto. Perhaps as a last resort, the Arab states
including Saudi Arabia began to give broad hints and pointed warnings that the Arabs were given no option but to use their oil as a
weapon. The American press then began to call this "Arab blackmail." And until the last day before the fourth Arab-Israeli war
broke out, most American reporters as well as politicians were repeating to each other the notion that the Arabs would never use
oil as a weapon against America and Israel. The underlying assumption was that the Arabs would never get together. It could have
also been a form of psychological warfare. This kind of talk was
also coupled with ominous noises about the possibility of the use
of American troops against the Arabs if they dared shut off the
oil from America. On August 27, 1973, for instance, U.S. News
& World Report wrote a major article with photographs of Marines
training for desert warfare. The caption was definitely intended
for the benefit of Arab readers. Its title was "Why Marines Are
Training in Desert." It started like this:

> As general unease builds up
> in the Middle East, the U.S.
> has handed its Marines a new
> assignment - be prepared, if
> ever needed to fight in the desert.

It went on to state flatly that that might be intended for
use against a "desert force, presumably in North Africa or the
Eastern Mediterranean." Aside from these ominous noises, American
politicians including the President himself indulged themselves,
as well as the American people in a fanciful world of delusions.
One such delusion was forwarded by President Nixon himself when he

stated in a news conference in September 1973 that the Arabs "cannot drink their oil." And while practically every layman by then had grasped the fact that much of the world was reliant on Arab oil for energy, President Nixon went on to tell the American people that the Arabs "might lose their markets" if they attempted to use their oil as a weapon. In his estimation, the Arabs would lose just as Premier Mohammad Mossadegh of Iran lost in the early 1950s.

"The reaction in the Arab world was not fear or anger," according to Ian Seymour who wrote in the New York Times,(17) "but simply incredulity," Seymour went on to write:

> Could it really be that the
> President of the United States
> had not yet grasped the predominant
> fact of life in the energy picture
> over the coming decade, that the
> problem is not whether oil will
> find markets, but whether markets
> will find oil?

When pressed later, one of the Presidential advisors stated that the President must have had "stupid advice." More true to the point was that he had Zionist advice. The fact is that most of the so-called energy experts in America are Zionists. Of course the nomination and eventual confirmation of Henry Kissinger as Secretary of State only a few weeks before the 1973 war was also viewed with apprehension in the Arab world. This was due to his Jewish background. After his confirmation by the Senate, Kissinger met various Arab diplomats. And his repetition to them of the vague statement that Middle East problems would take "many months and years" to solve could not have been consoling or helpful to the Arabs. Realizing this, perhaps, the Arabs concluded that there was no hope whatsoever that the United States would ever be impartial in matters concerning the state of Israel. Their only alternative was war, and war it was.

War came on October 6, 1973. Again the big loser from the outset was the United States. Again it was a measure of the failure of American diplomacy in the Arab East since 1917. This failure had reached only the point of a crisis of confidence between the Arabs and America after the creation of the state of Israel in 1948. By 1973 it verged on confrontation.

---

[17]New York Times, October 7, 1973 (Section 3).

CHAPTER IX

Kissinger and the Arabs, 1973-1976: An Epilogue

The impasse in the Middle East after the 1973 war accorded
Kissinger a good testing ground for his Machiavellian tactics and
his romantic wishes that his name be associated with such German
leaders as Metternich and Bismark.

To assess his dealings with the Arabs as Secretary of State
between 1973 and 1976, one must keep in mind that Kissinger is
Jewish and probably a Zionist. His go-slow policies then, and disengagement tactics were perhaps his way of extracting the maximum
benefits possible from the Arabs for Israel. Naturally there is no
sure way of judging his motives. One way though of attempting to
understand his actions, however, is to review the attributes of his
personality and the image he himself actively tried to portray of
himself to many of his image-makers. One may then see a pattern
in his behaviour, whether it fits his aspired-for image, and then
make sense out of his apparently enigmatic actions in the Middle
East between 1973 and 1976.

Some of these attributes revealed then by the media may be
listed and either accepted or rejected. One such was that "he is
one of the most successful negotiators of the post-war period."
Another was that "he has an exquisite sense of timing." Still
another is that "he is brilliant." Another one that became obvious without planned publicity-one that might have been embarrassing as well as harmful-is that he spoke too flippantly about
world leaders. Calling President Sadat names and/or making harsh
remarks about ex-President Nixon might even pass for clever by some
of his media admirors, as it did.(1) The fact is that a Secretary
of State must exercise the utmost discretion whether dealing with
the leader of a smaller power like Egypt, or with an ex-presidential
benefactor. It would seem that if any Secretary of State but Kissinger had then made so many faux pas, the press alone would be
vocal in demanding his resignation. Yet nothing of sort was demanded. Perhaps this was because we were also told by his press
that"Kissinger is almost indispensable."Another publicist then
told us that "the American people have come almost to take his
skills for granted."(2)

1
He was reported at one time as referring to Nixon as "unpleasant,"
and referring to Sadat as a "buffoon."
2
See an article by Simon Head on Kissinger in the New York Times
Magazine, October 26, 1975.

These Kissinger attributes, real or imagined, become insig-
nificant when compared with his grandiose visions and global designs.
But here one discovers in Kissinger the epitome of America's norm-
lessness. Even the historical characters he chose to ape were definitely inconsistent with the expressed norms of American society
and its professed behaviour either on the domestic or the international sphere.

Before discussing his grand scheme politics and the historical names he likes to imitate, one might also mention his cyclical
views. As a student of history, and concerned with the processes of
the rise and decline of civilizations, Kissinger, we were told, was
intrigued with what brings about such a decline. He views "disenchantment" as a heavy contributor to the decline of societies. This
may be so. Yet he somehow failed to detect that his political tactics and international intrigues were in good measure a major contributor to that "disenchantment." In other words, he and other norm-
less policy-makers in America were much to blame for the general mood
of disenchantment that then prevailed in America. Seemingly it was
much easier for Kissinger the academic to pass intellectual judgment
on historical processes, while failing to see the connection between
his role in shaping history and his sophist conclusions.

THE METTERNICH COMPLEX

Kissinger seemed to have been enamored with the Metternich
system of "legitimacy." Legitimacy in 1815 meant the re-imposition of
the conservative ancient regimes on Europe after the defeat of Napoleon. We were told, though, that unlike Metternich, Kissinger
"made the important political distinction between revolutionary and
legitimate international order."(3) A legitimate international order
to him is a world where the superpowers respect each other's vital
interests, thus maintaining an equilibrium which Kissinger choose to
call peace. Simply translated, this might be nothing more or less
than a division of the spoils of the earth among the superpowers.
All the great powers would then naturally agree to maintain the
status quo as that would be of course in their national interests.

Translated in the Middle East, Kissinger's legitimacy must have
meant an American hegemony over a poor and an acquiescent Arab world.
For we are told, and the facts of energy life confirm this, that
the Middle East is designated high on the American list as an area of

---

[3] Robert Isaak, Individuals and World Politics, Duxbury Press, 1975.

"vital interest." The Soviets then would respect this and refrain from "meddling" in the area. This would naturally appease not only the United States but also Western Europe and of course Israel. Meanwhile, the Arabs, one assumes, must find their salvation not in heaven, but presumably in Washington.

If this is the case, then the Helsinki conference and Agreements in the summer of 1975 become explainable: Helsinki legitimized Soviet hegemony in Eastern Europe, in exchange for American hegemony in the Middle East. This would all explain Kissinger's drive toward detente with the Soviet Union between 1973 and 1976. This might also explain why the Soviets slowed down the flow of arms to Egypt--the leading power in the Arab world. It would even explain why Kissinger was intent on selling wheat to the Soviets then, come what may. It would be part of the bargain, so to speak. Otherwise it seemed bewildering and even criminal to the uninitiated American that the United States would be selling wheat to the Soviets, and giving so much as to accept the legitimization of a Soviet hegemony in central Europe only a few short months after the Soviets crushed the very foundations of American diplomacy in Indo-China by proxy. It is in the Middle East that one might find the key to Kissinger's drive then for a Soviet detente.

BISMARK AND THE DYNAMIC EQUILIBRIUM

Like another German Bismark, Kissinger made it clear that he would like to see a dynamic equilibrium through which the "stabilization" of the world could be achieved. According to Nora Belloff, Kissinger also accepted the Bismarkian view that such an equilibrium may be manipulated by amoral diplomats who were also practitioners of secrecy and ambiguity.(4) Such diplomats are amoral in the sense that they have no qualms about using one neighbor against another in maintaining the equilibrium.

One can easily detect this Bismarkian behavior in Kissinger's diplomacy in various regions in the world. His opening to China was his way of encouraging China to harass the Soviet Union and vice-versa. Until the fall of Saigon, one would assume that this was done to divert Soviet attention from the area of Indo-China, and make it easier for the United States to subdue Hanoi. Vietnam or not, though, he persisted in his opening to China and the Soviet Union. He even moved to appease the Soviets in Helsinki. It would make sense that once the Vietnam War was settled in the humiliating

---

[4]"Prof. Bismark Goes to Washington: Kissinger on the Job," Atlantic Monthly (December 1969)

way it was for America, that the United States would be less prone to appease the Soviet Union in Helsinki. This was particularly so when China was also vociferous in its objections to what it called "Soviet hegemonism" in Europe and the Far East. But regardless of China's objections, Kissinger did go to Helsinki and did fulfill a cherished Soviet dream. Questions then arise: a) was Kissinger mainly interested in a general peaceful coexistence with the Soviets? or, b) was he interested primarily in diverting Soviet attention to the Chinese borders? In other words, was China his main target? The latter does not make much sense at a time when he was ostensibly trying to cultivate some kind of detente with China. Nevertheless it might have been in part Kissinger's Bismarkian way of manipulating the Sino-Soviet equilibrium. What makes far more sense, though, is that Kissinger was ready to partially sacrifice China's budding detente with the United States in return for a Soviet hands-off policy in the Middle East. Again, it is the Middle East that gives the key to understanding Kissinger's global moves in that period. The Middle East had become his fixation after 1973. Needless to say, his moves had to be done in utmost secrecy. And Helsinki became a worrisome secret, not only for many Americans, but for those who were even more concerned with it, namely the Chinese and the Arabs. Perhaps Kissinger's trip to Peking in October 1975 was taken to explain the Arab connection with Helsinki. Even then the Chinese leadership was reported to have been unsatisfied. Either he did not completely tip his hand in that regard and his ambiguity left the Chinese uneasy, or their apparent dissatisfaction might have been part of the act. For a seemingly understanding China might well alarm the Soviet Union or more importantly, alert the Arabs.

Soviet cooperativeness would also explain why Kissinger's estimation of the Soviet leadership then became highly complimentary. According to an article by Simon Head in the New York Times magazine, October 26, 1974, Kissinger then thought Brezhnev and Kosygin "dynamic," "alert," "inventive," "flexible" and "daring."

The Bismarkian use of one neighbor to pull the other's teeth was also evident in the Middle East. Kissinger, like many Western and American leaders before, had used Israel to remain at the Arab throat. In his old C.I.A. habits, one was also sure that he was using the Arabs to keep Israel down to manageable size.(5)   Thus while billions in American arms were going to Israel, other billions

---

5
Miles Copeland, an ex-CIA agent, tells us in his book The Game of Nations that the CIA was also involved in this activity throughout the 1950s and after. There is a theory floating among Arabs that Sadat's preparations for war and attack on Israel in Oct. 1973 was done with American knowledge and/or agreement.

were also going to conservative Arab states. We were also told by
Robert Isaak(6) that while the 1973 war was going on, it was Kissinger and not Schlesinger who delayed rushing arms to the battle-
shocked Israel in the first few days of the war. Isaak seems to believe that Kissinger was worried about Arab "pride and sensitivities."
More like it, he was more concerned with an even more overgrown Israel if Israel defeated the Arabs in the usual manner. While arms
were sent to the conservative Arab states, Kissinger also hoped to
keep the Arab "radical nationalists" at bay in the inter-Arab equilibrium. Thus, one of the main lessons of the 1973 war was missed
by Kissinger: That was, whether Arab nationalism rested on Nasserism,
radicalism or conservatism, it remained equally vocal in demanding
Arab rights in Palestine. It was most obvious to the whole world
that Saudi Arabia and Kuwait were more adamant about Arab rights
in Palestine and in Jerusalem than Nasser's Egypt ever was. Yet
Kissinger, in the usual American policy-makers' head-in-the-sand
Zionist attitude, still wished Arab nationalism away. One is sure
after 1973 that Kissinger felt most successful in prodding Sadat
toward "conservatism." It is incredible to believe that he also
forgot that this "conservative" Sadat is the same Sadat who was the
first Arab leader to decide to attack Israel first, rather than be
the recipient of Israeli first blows. The fact is, Nasser was perhaps more conservative and less militant than Sadat. Their biogra-
phies attest to this. But Kissinger dogmatically insisted on his
hopes and wishful thinking. One of his most cherished hopes was
how to re-divide the Arab world. For Kissinger, as well as Israel,
knew well that the Arabs won what they won after the 1973 war--which
was considerable--with mere ad hoc Arab unity. Therefore, it was
imperative for him--and perhaps the Israelis were slow to grasp
his grand scheme--that even an ad hoc Arab unity must not become
a habit. It had to be thwarted, and fast. For success begets
success. Therefore, if he could persuade Israel to pacify Egypt,
at least temporarily, and keep the Syrians and their type unsati-
ated, this would do the trick. For some reason, Sadat went along
with this scheme. Whether he was secretly intimidated by Kissinger
or truly accepted his promises at face value is hard to ascertain.
It would also make sense that the Saudis might have encouraged
Sadat to try the American option first. But once Sadat went along,
Kissinger and his cult took glorious credit for the "conservatiza-
tion" of Egypt, and the re-division of the Arab world.

Naturally, it is not too early to tell that Kissinger was not
true to his promises to Sadat, that is, if he ever promised Sadat
anything. More true to Kissinger's nature, and his love for

---

[6]Individuals and World Politics, p. 239.

ambiguity, secrecy, manipulations and schemomania; and perhaps strongly influenced by a natural Zionism, Kissinger was neither able nor even willing to deliver the Israeli goods. His so-called step-by-step procrastinations were a clear indication of that.

Needless to say, it did pass Kissinger's mind, one is sure, that oil is what has given the Arabs effective muscle since 1973. Arab oil producers happen to be the majority of OPEC (Oil Producing and Exporting Countries). They also happen to produce the maximum amount of oil needed by the West. It was their oil embargo that gave meaning to the 1973 war. For even if some insist that Israel finally won more than it lost militarily, the Arab oil weapon did play havoc with the economies of the Western World. Some observers even go so far as saying that the Arabs emerged as a great power after 1973. This result was very cutting to Kissinger. For, having his total lack of sympathy for the Third World and particularly the Arab world, the Arabs' newly discovered power was nothing short of a personal insult to him. His lack of sympathy was naturally part of his imperial grand designs and innate sentiments. For to him the Arab Third World is but an object of great power "vital interest" and not to be morally or humanly considered. Thus, ever since the basically Arab OPEC asserted itself, Kissinger went about frantically to discover a way to break it. It did not occur to him that he might have been able to deal fairly with it. And in his fixation to break OPEC he had to bring into play all his accumen of secrecy, balance of power acts and legitimacy acrobatics.

Commenting with a straight face about Kissinger's need for secrecy, Robert Isaak (7) candidly wrote that,

> If it came out, most of the nations
> of the world would protest that, in
> effect, the plan (that is, Kissinger's
> grand scheme, ed.) was designated
> to promote and preserve the interest
> of the rich Western capitalist coun-
> tries of the globe, particularly
> the United States. Such a protest
> would hit the nail on the head, put
> people on their guard, and block his
> future actions.

Between 1973 and 1976 Kissinger went into constant secret huddles with various nations of Western Europe (and perhaps with the Soviets) on how to thwart the Arabs and OPEC. Immediately after the 1973 war, most Western powers were apparently ready to concede to legitimate Arab rights in Palestine. Not so, Kissinger. He refused for over two years to agree to a conference proposed by OPEC

7
 op. cit.

over the general subject of world natural resources. Naturally to him what was America's was America's, and what was the Third World's was also America's. This again fits his Matternichian image and his imperial nature. Many of his major Western allies were practically demanding such a conference. But Kissinger resisted and prevailed. Meanwhile, he was exploring ways to break up OPEC. He tried to goad the Shah of Iran to do so by playing on Iran's so-called traditional rivalries with the Arabs, and by selling Iran arms. But once the Iraqi-Iranian border dispute was then settled, the American arms to Iran only helped to strengthen OPEC. Kissinger then resorted to intimidation by openly threatening to invade the Persian Gulf. This helped only to alert the Arabs and the Iranians and made them perhaps stick closer together. Kissinger finally had to do something about Israel. Yet his Zionist fear that Israel might lose its Arab empire stopped him from pushing for a then possible peace and solution of the Palestine question. This explains his stone-walling step-by-step diplomacy in those years.

The step-by-step technique did have some signal successes. Sadat somehow accepted the Kissinger go-slow policies. Not only that, but the Egyptian leader went about parroting Kissinger's admonitions that an over-all Geneva peace conference was bad for the Arabs. Sadat's conversion was not only bewildering but also alarming to the rest of the Arabs. And as Arab criticism of Sadat snowballed, Kissinger must have been pleased. For his manipulations were working on the Arabs. And once the Arabs were back snarling at each other again, that would give him and Israel time to figure a way out of the Arab energy noose. If all ultimately worked out as planned, as it did, one must admire Kissinger for his cleverness. In brief, he felt: give him more time, and he would completely isolate the Arabs by satiating the Soviets. And that he did.

Once that was done, he would, if necessary, go as far as occupying the Arab oil fields and get done with the Arabs. This would, in his estimation, satisfy Western Europe since the sources of their energy would be in good hands. And naturally Israel would remain in what she further occupied in the Arab world after 1967--that is, if the Arabs were lucky.

It may be asked why Sadat collaborated with Kissinger in his own isolation and possible eventual destruction? Two possible explanations come to mind. First, he might have been simply innocent of Kissinger's grand designs and global strategies. He might not have been aware of Kissinger's "linkage" mentality. After all, many Arabs have been similarly baffled for over thirty years as to how a simple regional issue like Palestine became the unbelievable political football it did become in cold war rivalries!! To them it is an obvious case of Zionist settler imperialism. It is a case that has nothing to do with either Hitler, Stalin or Ho Chi Minh. Needless to say, the Zionists insisted on making it a cold war issue. Eventually, they succeeded in making it a case of the forces of Good vs. the forces of Evil. The role of Ahrumazda was naturally given to Israel backed by the good democracies. The role of Ahriman was played by the Arabs backed by the bad communists. Perhaps Sadat was then still trying to bring back to the American people the Palestine drama in its original cast. Perhaps he was hoping that Kissinger will finally see it that way. After all, Kissinger fancies himself an historian. He must know the true story of Palestine. He must know that the act of the so-called forces of virtue versus the forces of sin is nothing but what Senator J. William Fulbright once described as Israeli "communist-baiting humbuggery."

A second explanation for Sadat opting to cooperate then with Kissinger might well have been Sadat's bad connection with the Soviets. There was then ample evidence that that connection had been deteriorating for at least one year before the 1973 war. Sadat had loudly complained after 1972 that the Soviets were becoming heavy-handed in Egypt. He also complained that they were not giving him offensive weapons. Seemingly they were also putting the squeeze on him economically. Sadat was also beginning to complain about the obvious Soviet satisfactin with the no-war no-peace situation in the Middle East since 1967. For ever since the Glassboro meeting between Premier Kosygin and President Johnson immediately after the 1967 war, the Arabs generally suspected that either the Soviets were then cowed by Johnson, or that they had quietly made a deal with America over the heads of the Arabs. Sadat's disenchantment with the Soviets led to his expulsion of the Soviet advisors in 1972. It was later reported that Sadat finally went to war in 1973 either against Soviet advice or even without their knowledge. It was also publicized by Sadat after and during the 1973 war that the Soviets refused to replenish his heavy battle losses so as to enable him to keep fighting. At least that was how he explained his final reverses in the war. Naturally once the war was over and a better showing against Israel escaped Sadat, he was further embittered against his so-called Soviet allies. Of course the more he showed it, the more the Soviets resented him. As mentioned earlier, perhaps the Soviets had already made a deal with America since Glassboro in 1967. After all, all indications pointed to Soviet satisfaction. One must also wonder why the Soviets chose to give Kissinger a free hand in the Middle East after 1973. For regardless of their protestations--and perhaps mainly for Arab public consumption-- that they resented Kissinger's step-by-step diplomacy, their protests then seemed amazingly mute. Then one might speculate that perhaps Helsinki was the pay-off for their vanishing act from the Middle East after 1973. All this naturally left Sadat on a limb with no choice but to take the Kissinger option. For even the so-called radical Arabs were relatively subdued in attacking Sadat for picking up the Kissinger option. Perhaps they already knew what Sadat knew, that the Soviets had sold out the Arabs to America.

Kissinger's famous insistence on what he called "linkage" in the solution of world problems seemed to have finally led him to Helsinki. There in Helsinki, Eastern Europe was accepted as a Soviet "vital interest" area. Naturally there is no way of being absolutely sure of such a deal. But other things did remain sure. One was that the Soviets seemed to have lost interest in the Middle East. Another was that there was no Israeli withdrawal from Arab land,or peace in the Middle East by 1978. A third was that Amer-ican-Arab relations, thanks to the Zionist connection, remained mainly a dialogue with the deaf.

- - -

Some two years went by between the departure of Kissinger from making American foreign policy and the submission of this study to the press in September 1978. In those interceding years Lebanon became involved in a vicious civil war. How that civil war began has many elements of mystery and suspicion as being the work of foreign unfriendly hands. By 1978 it cost Lebanon over 60,000 dead, and untold destructions of that once prosperous Arab country.

The Lebanese civil war was another fruit of the no-war-no-peace condition which Kissinger, for one reason or the other, wished for the Middle East again after the 1973 war. In it Israel was again obviously involved in dividing the Arabs against each other. Israel then succeeded in enlisting elements of the Christian Mar-onites, who historically refused to share their feudal power with the majority Lebanese, in resisting any change in that feudal set-up. Eventually Israel invaded and occupied southern Lebanon ostensibly to help those collaborating factions against their own people. Naturally the pro-Zionist American press portrayed the Israeli ac-tion as an Israeli Crusade "to save the Lebanese Christians." Meanwhile a possible President Carter pressure on Israel to accept a final just peace with the Palestinians abated.

On his part, President Carter was showing signs of genuine interest in the plight of the Palestinians and how to solve it. Naturally the energy crisis, and further American dependence on Arab oil, one is sure, was never far from his mind. At times he even mentioned the "legitimate rights of the Palestinian people."

He even ventured at times to mention favourably the Palestine Liberation organization. As expected, there was the usual Zionist hue and cry protesting his statements. Yet there was still no sustained American pressure on Israel to comply with many, many, U.N. resolutions passed since 1947. Rather Israel was even further armed by the Carter administration, even though Israeli air attacks on so-called Palestinian guerrilla camps in Lebanon were taking a heavy toll of Lebanese and Palestinian civilian lives. The Israeli invasion of southern Lebanon alone took over 2,000 Arab lives.

In those interceding two years Sadat made his historic trip to Jerusalem. That action alone infuriated much of the Arab world. In it he in effect recognized the state of Israel. Sadat's hope of Israeli reciprocation never came. His hope then was that Israel would readily agree to a final peace with the Arabs on the basis of the 1967 242 U.N. Resolution. Rather, Israeli Prime Minister Begin proceeded to build further Jewish settlements in Sinai, the West Bank and the Golan Heights. Nine months went by after the so-called Sadat Peace initiative, when finally President Carter succeeded in bringing Sadat and Begin to the September 1978 Camp David Conference.

The results of the Camp David conference are still fresh in the headlines. So far they are tooted as a great success for both President Carter and the Middle East as a whole. The fact is that the agreements there have in them further elements of disaster to the region involved. Seemingly Israel finally succeeded in breaching the age-old Arab solidarity vis-a-vis their opposition to making separate peace agreements with Israel. Egypt, no less, among the Arab states began this breaching process. This very act is enough to set the Arab world, and particularly Syria and the Palestine Liberation Organization, against Egypt. Also, these Camp David Agreements, so far as is apparent, did not stipulate complete and final Israel withdrawal either from the West Bank of Palestine or Palestine Gaza. Nor did the Camp David accords mention specifically Israeli withdrawal from the Syrian Golan Heights. Palestinian right to sovereignty was also glossed over. There was also no mention of the historic demands of the Arabs; like raparations for lost Palestinian properties or repatriation of Palestinian refugees, as stipulated in numerous U.N. resolutions since the creation of Israel in 1948 in Arab Palestine.

To conclude, it is naturally too early to tell what will develop in the Middle East after Camp David. Meanwhile, a true, comprehensive and a just peace still remains illusive in that area.

Selected Bibliography

Abdel Nasser, Gamal. Egypt's Liberation: The Philosophy of the
    Revolution. Washington: Public Affairs Press, 1955.
--------------------. Where I Stand and Why. Washington: Embassy
    of the United Arab Republic, n.d.
Abu-Diab, Fawzi. Immigration to Israel. New York: Arab Information
    Center, 1960.
Abu-Jaber, Faiz S. Middle East Issues. Washington: University
    Press of America, 1975.
Abu-Jaber, Kamel S. The Arab Ba'th Socialist Party: History, Ideol-
    ogy and Organization. Syracuse: Syracuse U. Press, 1966.
Abu-Lughod, Ibrahim, ed. The Arab Israeli Confrontation of June
    1967: An Arab Perspective. Evanston, Ill.: Northwestern
    U. Press, 1970.
Adams, Michael. Suez and After: Year of Crisis. Boston: Beacon
    Press, 1958.
Ahmad, Maqbul. Indo-Arab Relations. New Delhi: Indian Council for
    Cultural Relations, 1969.
Alami, Musa. Palestine Is My Country. New York: Praeger, 1969.
Alleg, Henri. The Question. London: John Calder, 1958.
Antonius, George. The Arab Awakening: The Story of the Arab
    National Movement. Philadelphia: Lippincott, 1939.
Avnery, Uri. Israel Without Zionists. New York: Macmillan, 1968.
Barbour, Nevill. Nisi Dominus, A Survey of the Palestine Controversy.
    London: Harrap Press, 1946.
Barker, A.J. Suez: The Seven Day War. New York: Frederick A.
    Praeger, 1964.
Beal, John Robinson. John Foster Dulles. New York: Harper and
    Brothers, 1957.
Bentwich, Norman and Helen. Mandate Memories, 1918-1948. London:
    Hogarth Press, 1963.
Berger, Rabbi Elmer. Who Knows Better Must Say So! New York:
    American Council for Judaism, 1955.
Brockelmann, Carl. History of the Islamic Peoples. New York:
    Capricorn Books, 1960.
Bustani, Emile. March Arabesque. London: Robert Hale Limited,
    1961.
Childers, Erskine B. Common Sense About the Arab World. New York:
    The Macmillan Co., 1960.
--------------------. The Road to Suez. London: MacGibbon and
    Kee, 1962.
Churchill, Randolph S. The Rise and Fall of Sir Anthony Eden.
    New York: G.P. Putnam's Sons, 1959.
Coon, Carleton S. Caravan: The Story of the Middle East. New York:
    Holt, Rinehart and Winston, 1961.
Cremeans, Charles D. The Arabs and the World. New York: Frederick
    A. Praeger, 1963.
Crum, Bartley. Behind the Silken Curtain. New York: Simon and
    Schuster, 1947.

237

Davis, John H. Evasive Peace. New York: New World Press, 1969.
Dallin, David J. Soviet Foreign Policy After Stalin. Philadelphia:
    Lippincott, 1961.
Denovo, John A. American Interests and Politics in the Middle East
    1900-1939. Minneapolis: The University of Minnesota Press,
    1963.
Doherty, Kathryn B. Jordan Waters Conflict. New York: Carnegie
    Endowment for International Peace, 1965.
Dunlop, D.M. The History of the Jewish Khazars. Princeton:
    Princeton University Press, 1954.
Eden, Anthony. Memoirs: Full Circle. Boston: Houghton Mifflin
    Co., 1960.
El-Farra, Muhammad H. Arab Nationalism and the United Nations.
    New York: Arab States Delegations Office, 1958.
Epp, Frank H. The Palestinians. Scotdale, Pa: Herald Press, 1976.
Erskine, B. Strong. Palestine of the Arabs. London: Harrap, 1935.
Eudin, Z.K. and North, Robert. Soviet Russia and the East 1920-
    1927, a Documentary Survey. Stanford: Stanford University
    Press, 1957.
Finer, Herman. Dulles Over Suez. Chicago: Quadrangle Books, 1964.
Fischer, Louis. The Soviets in World Affairs. Princeton: Prince-
    ton University Press, 1952.
Fisher, Eugene M. & Bassionni, M.C. Storm Over the Arab World.
    Chicago: Follett, 1972.
Fisher, Syndey N. The Middle East, A History. New York: Alfred
    A. Knopf, 1960.
Forrest, A.C. The Unholy Land. Old Greenwich, Conn.: Devin Adair
    Co., 1974.
Gabrieli, Francesco. The Arabs. New York: Hawthorn Books, 1963.
Glubb, John Bagot. Britain and the Arabs. London: Hodder and
    Stoughton, 1959.
------------------. A Soldier with the Arabs. New York: Harper and
    Brothers, 1958.
------------------. The Middle East Crisis: A Personal Interpreta-
    tion. London: Hodder and Stoughton, 1967.
Hadawi, Sami. Palestine Partitioned 1947-1958. New York: Arab
    Information Center, 1959.
------------. Bitter Harvest. New York: New World Press, 1967.
Howard, Harry N. The King-Crane Commission: An American Inquiry
    in the Middle East. Beirut: Khayats, 1963.
Hutchison, Elmo H. Violent Truce. New York: Devin-Adair, 1956.
Ionides, Michael. Divide and Lose: The Arab Revolt of 1955-1958.
    London: Geoffrey Bles, 1960.
Issawi, Charles. Egypt at Mid-Century. New York: Oxford Univer-
    sity Press for the R.I.I.A., 1954.
Izzeddin, Nejla. The Arab World. Past, Present and Future.
    Chicago: Henry Regnery, 1953.

Jansen, Godfrey H. Nonalignment and the Afro-Asian States. New
York: Praeger, 1966.
Koestler, Arthur. The Thirteenth Tribe. New York: Random House,
1976.
Laqueur, Walter Z. Communism and Nationalism in the Middle East.
New York: Frederick A. Praeger, 1956.
----------------. (ed.) The Middle East in Transition. New
York: Frederick A. Praeger, 1958.
----------------. The Soviet Union and the Middle East. New
York: Frederick A. Praeger, 1959.
----------------. The Struggle for the Middle East: The Soviet
Union and the Middle East, 1958-1968. New York: MacMillan,
1969.
Lasky, Moses. Between Truth and Repose. New York: American Coun-
cil for Judaisim, 1956.
Lenczowski, George. The Middle East in World Affairs. Ithaca:
Cornell University Press, 1958.
------------------. Oil and State in the Middle East. Ithaca:
Cornell University Press, 1958.
Lewis, Bernard. The Middle East and the West New York: Harper &
Row, 1964.
Lilienthal, Alfred M. The Other Side of the Coin. New York:
Devin-Adair, 1965.
--------------------. The Zionist Connection. New York: Dodd,
Mead & Co., 1978.
--------------------. There Goes the Middle East. New York:
Devin-Adair, 1957.
--------------------. What Price Israel. Chicago: Henry Regnery,
1953.
Little, Tom. Egypt. New York: Frederick A. Praeger, 1958.
Marlowe, John. Arab Nationalism and British Imperialism: A
Study in Power Politics. New York: Frederick A. Praeger, 1961.
Naguib, Mohammad. Egypt's Destiny. New York: Doubleday & Co.,
1955.
Nuseibeh, Hazem Zaki. The Ideas of Arab Nationalism. Ithaca:
Cornell University Press, 1956.
Nutting, Anthony. The Arabs. London: Hollis and Carter, 1964.
----------------. No End of a Lesson. London: Constable, 1967.
Philby, St. John M. Saudi Arabia. New York: Frederick A. Praeger,
1955.
The Political History of Palestine Under British Administration.
New York: British Information Services, 1947.
Robertson, Terence. Crisis: The Inside Story of the Suez Con-
spiracy. New York: Atheneum, 1965.
Sanger, Richard. The Arabian Peninsula. Ithaca: Cornell Univer-
sity Press, 1954.
Sayegh, Fayez A. Arab Unity: Hope and Fulfillment. New York:
Devin-Adair, 1958.
----------------. The Record of Israel at the United Nations.
New York: Arab Information Center, 1957.

Spector, Ivar. The Soviet Union and the Muslim World 1917–1956.
Seattle: University of Washington Press, 1959.
Stein, Leonard. The Balfour Declaration. London: Vallentine
Mitchell, 1961.
Stetler, Russell. Palestine: The Arab-Israeli Conflict.
San Francisco: Rampart Press, 1972.
Stevens, Richard P. American Zionism and United States Foreign
Policy. New York: Pageant Press, 1962.
Tannous, Izzat. The Policy That Invited Soviet Russia to the
Middle East. New York: The Palestine Arab Refugee Office,
1958.
Tibawi, Abdul Latif. A Modern History of Syria Including Lebanon
and Palestine. New York: St. Martins, 1969.
Toynbee, Arnold. The West and the Arabs. London: Britannica
Book of the Year, 1959.
Utley, Freda. Will the Middle East Go West? Chicago: Henry
Regnery, 1957.
Wheelock, Keith. Nasser's New Egypt. New York: Frederick A.
Praeger, 1960.
Williams, William A. America and the Middle East. New York:
Rinehart and Co., 1958.
Wynn, Wilton. Nasser of Egypt: The Search for Dignity. Cambridge:
Arlington Books, 1959.
Yale, William. The Near East: A Modern History. Ann Arbor:
University of Michigan Press, 1958.
Yost, Charles. The Conduct and Misconduct of Foreign Affairs.
New York: Random House, 1972.

242

243

U

Umari,A.,152
United Arab States Federation,
    181
United Nations,11,17ff,24,29,31,
    63,69,72,75,93,100ff,106,118,
    128,167,176,185ff,212,215ff,224
U.N.Security Council,32,33,34,
    35,36,41,42,93,100,111,159
U.N. Truce Commission (Palestine),
    29,141f,185
U.N. Special Commission on
    Palestine,19
U.S. aid,61,78f,103,107
U.S. cotton and Egypt,103f
U. Thant,185,212,220f

V

Versailles Peace Conference,4ff
Versailles Treaty,6,87
Voice of the Arabs (radio),35,
    82
Von Horn, General,185
Vyshinsky,A.,36,93,111,119

W

Wafd party,92,114
Ward,B.,117n
Wazir,A.,180
Weizman,14
West German reparations to
    Israel,69
Wheelus air base,199,206,213
White,Lincoln,142
Wild, J.D.,153
Wilson, H.,204
Wilson, W.,2ff,917
Wise, S., Rabbi,4

Y

Yahya,Imam,9.91,180

Yale, W.,3,17
Yalta Conference,8,16
Yamani,A.,204
Yarmuk River,43
Yemen Revolution,180ff

Z

Zahidi, General,80
Zaidi Imamate,180
Zayyat,210
Zeigler,216
Zinoviev,G.,89
Zionism and Soviet attitude,
    93ff
Zionist Wrecker-doctors,96
Zughlul,S.,6,92